Somewhere
Under the Rainbow

A Christian Look
at Same–Sex "Marriage"

Geisler and Van Gordon have done both Christians and non-Christians a great service by writing Somewhere under the Rainbow: A Christian Look at Same-sex "Marriage." They furnish concise yet comprehensive answers to the objections and alternate "interpretations" of God's Word employed by same-sex apologists to justify their lifestyle. Importantly, they also compose a compelling narrative of how Jesus is the answer to same-sex attraction and how the Church can witness and minister to those mired in such a life style. Van Gordon's compelling personal testimony of how Jesus liberated him from a homosexual lifestyle provides a personal dimension that will have a powerful impact on readers.

I cannot think of a better volume to place in the hands of all those desiring to be the ambassadors of reconciliation and redemption that our Savior has called all of us to be.

–**Dr. Richard Land**
President, Southern Evangelical Seminary

This work addresses one of the most controversial and sensitive ethical topics in our culture today with clarity, thoroughness, and grace from a Christian perspective. Geisler and Van Gordon leave no stone unturned as they address with incisive logic the historical and biblical matters that have a direct bearing on understanding same-sex marriage. What is often missing in many other books that provide only academic answers is offered here with Van Gordon's testimony and an appeal to healing and hope for those who choose change. This is a must-read book for all those who seek a broader understanding of the issue and desire to be an agent for change and clarity when interacting with those who are confused with same-sex marriage.

–**Dr. Joseph M. Holden**,
President, Veritas Evangelical Seminary

Geisler and Van Gordon offer a clear, insightful look at both the biblical information regarding the same-sex marriage issue and the hope Jesus offers. They address the modern history of the topic, Scripture's teachings, answer objections, and suggest ways God's people can offer help through the work of Christ and the power of the Holy Spirit.

–**Dr. John Ankerberg**,
President and host of The John Ankerberg Show

Are homosexuals "born this way" through a pre-determined genetic orientation or is homosexuality the product of "desires run astray" from God's design? This book offers a refreshingly fair and helpful summary with astute analysis of the most important assumptions and arguments of both views while offering an objective, logical and biblical conclusion–and don't miss the compassionate preface.

–**Karl Elkins**, LPC-S, ThM, MA,
Psychotherapist

Geisler and Van Gordon take you on an enlightening ride through the last several decades to show you how sex has become, in effect, the new religion in America. Along the way, they blow several myths, and offer some very practical advice that will help you minister to loved ones who may be same sex attracted or think the Scriptures support same-sex marriage. This is the much needed reasoned response to a position often defended by emotional appeals.

–**Dr. Frank Turek**,
Author, *Correct, Not Politically Correct*

Somewhere Under the Rainbow

A Christian Look
at Same–Sex "Marriage"

Norman L. Geisler
Doug Van Gordon

Bastion Books

Somewhere Under The Rainbow: A Christian Look at Same–Sex "Marriage"
Norman L. Geisler & Doug Van Gordon

Published by Bastion Books | P.O. Box 1033 | Matthews, NC 28106 | USA
www.bastionbooks.com

Printed in the United States of America

ISBN–13: 978-1978111035
ISBN–10: 1978111037

Contents

Dedication

To my mother (now with the Lord) who always said I should write and teach and to my wife Michelle who's steadfast support and encouragement enabled me to keep going.
Doug Van Gordon

Acknowledgements

Special thanks to Douglas Potter and Christina Woodside for the many dedicated hours spent in editing this manuscript. Their work significantly improved the final product and is greatly appreciated.

Preface

There is more than just good theology.
A personal note from Douglas Van Gordon

We try in this book to put forth some good theology and reasons as to why same–sex "marriage" is wrong and how it is outside of what God intended for human sexuality. Laying a good foundation is important, but the fact remains that we don't live in the foundation; we live in the house built upon it. In that house where daily life is lived, things are not always as they should be.

I was blessed to be born into a Christian home with one older sister, two younger sisters, a younger brother, and two loving parents who took us to church most every Sunday. My parents did not have much money but saw to it we had everything we really needed. I was a typical kid with several friends but was a little overweight, which did bother me at times. In those days during summer break I could stay out late and no one really worried too much about it. I had a good relationship with my parents. My dad worked mostly as a salesman, which meant we moved about every two years. My mother was easy going and had a wonderful sense of humor. By age 12 like most boys that age I began to have a definite interest in sex, but that interest was not directed specifically towards girls or boys at that time.

At the age of 14 an event occurred that would impact my life forever. An older male relative (early twenties) came to live with our family. He played upon my natural curiosity about sex and was seduced and molested me. Even though I was a willing participant, it was nonetheless molestation. The relationship grew stronger over time, and I felt accepted and loved by this older adult. We were able to keep the sexual part of our relationship, which lasted for about 10 years hidden from family members. There were some suspicions, but I believe they did not *want* to believe it and dismissed the suspicions as being "paranoid" or "reading things into" the relationship.

At the age of 19, I joined the military, and the male relative followed me to where I was stationed. We rented a one–bedroom apartment near the base and began to widen our involvement with the homosexuals in the area.

I did not attend church on a regular basis like I used to when I lived at home. The excitement of being on my own away from home and in the military had a kind of intoxicating effect on me, as I was able to do what I wished with whomever I wished. I began to walk away from God. After I reenlisted, I was sent to a duty station thousands of miles away, and even though the male relative followed me there, I no longer felt the same towards him. Shortly thereafter he returned to where we had lived, and we never had intimate relations again.

I befriended some fellow service members who were homosexual and began to visit a local gay bar where I could hook–up with someone for a brief sexual encounter. It was during this time period that I met a young man who was also in the military that I fell in love with. He had a wonderfully accepting family, and I basically moved in with him at their house. I began to desire to attend church again, so we went where we would feel comfortable, which meant attending the local Metropolitan Community Church. The Methodist church allowed MCC to use its facilities on Sunday afternoons and most services were well attended.

As the relationship with my lover grew, we both felt the urge to make a public commitment, so we decided to have what MCC called a "holy union" ceremony. Even though it was not at that time recognized as official by the state, it had all the outward appearance of a wedding complete with tuxes (mine was black and his was white), cake, and the giving of rings. We were a model gay couple to many in that church. We were a symbol of what a loving same–sex relationship could be. Once, a group of young men asked us how long we had been together, and we replied, "Two years" to which they said, "Two years, and you are still lovey dovey. How incredible that is." But even our close relationship began to wane not long after the ceremony, as

I began to have some doubts about the reinterpretations of Scripture that I heard at the Sunday services.

I believe the Lord used one of those services to wake me up. The minister was preaching on one of the Apostle Paul's letters when he made a kind of off the cuff remark and said, "This is one place where I disagree with Paul." That statement hit me like a slap across the face because it implied that you could disagree with Paul like you could disagree with the guy at the grocery store or the gas station attendant. Paul was the divinely appointed ambassador to the Gentiles, and Christ was continuing His ministry through Paul, which meant that to disagree with Paul was to disagree with Christ (Galatians 1).

I soon stop going to the MCC church and started to attend a local Baptist church but kept to myself about my recent involvement with homosexuality out of fear for the reactions it might cause. But my fears were unfounded, as I became acquainted with people who loved me in a Christ–like manner even after I let my guard down and opened up to a few about my former life. A couple of months after I left MCC, I had the chance to ask the pastor of my former church a question. I wanted to find out the level of commitment he had to the Scripture and to his homosexuality. I asked how he would react if God appeared directly to him the same way He did to Moses in the burning bush and said to him, "John, this is not the way of my righteousness; turn from your sexual sin and follow me." His reply was very revealing: "I would be in total confusion, I wouldn't know what to do, and I wouldn't know why God would ask this of me." I realized then that it would take more than theological argumentation to persuade him of the wrongness of his homosexual practice.

Nonetheless, it was a firm conviction that the Bible was the inerrant Word of God, and that my life–style was contrary to it that served as the basis of my decision to leave my old life–style for a new one in Christ. God used a couple of friends to help me see that this was the clear teaching of Scripture.

The months and years that followed were a time of healing and growth with some failures along the way. The old ways did not fade so easily and quickly for me. But each time I failed, I remembered the promise of that He would never leave or forsake us even as I prayed, "Lord please don't give up on me." I am always so moved by the par-able of the prodigal son in Luke 15: 11–32 and the words of Paul in 1 Corinthians 6:11: "And such were some of you. But you were washed, you were sanctified, you were justified in the name of the Lord Jesus Christ and by the Spirit of our God" (RSV). I am moved not just because of the theological truth but because I have seen and felt that truth in my own life. I also had the prayers of many faithful friends, especially those of my mother and father.

Our Lord has blessed me more than I could imagine, not by an instant *zap* or the flicking of a switch but like a tree planted by the water, growing deeper in His Word, listening to the counsel of those farther along the walk of faith than I and trusting in Christ each and every day even when I fail to do that which I know I should do. This is not to say that I have not had some bumps along the way, including a divorce (which had nothing to do with my past life). I have never returned to a gay life style or activity.

God has blessed me with a wife, three children (and as of now 4 grandchildren), but this should not be taken to mean that marriage and children are for everyone dealing with same–sex attraction. Marriage is part of the result of healing not the means of healing. There are many places for celibate, single, same–sex attracted people to serve the body of Christ, and they should be honored for that service.

If you are a person struggling with same–sex attraction and you feel God is calling you to a closer walk with Him, please don't believe the propaganda that you cannot truly stop your homosexual practice. In this book we present scientific evidence that people can and do change their sexual orientation. There is also the testimony of many people whom Christ has changed and with the help and support of a loving church family are living lives that honor Him. Christ forgave me of going through a ceremony that mocked marriage, and He forgave me of attempting to become "one flesh" with someone of the same sex, of presenting it to others as just another individual choice, of encouraging others to follow my example. For these and many other things, this is what Christ did for me, and He will do the same for you. May you experience the love Christ offers to each of us.

Doug Van Gordon
September 2017

Introduction

Singer Bob Dylan wrote in 1964, "The times they are a–changing." These words are just as true about the present day as they were when he wrote them, especially for the traditional understanding of marriage. Throughout its history, the Church has faced many challenges to its fundamental and core beliefs, from Gnosticism and cults that deny the divinity of Christ, to modern philosophers and skeptics. But the current issue of same–sex marriage that would redefine marriage is unique to our time. Many Christians are asking, "How did this happen?" How did something so self–evidentially wrong just twenty years before becoming not only a topic of serious debate, but of actual law?

In the first part of this book we will look at the events and forces that over the course of decades have undermined the traditional view of marriage to such an extent, as to allow the idea of same–sex "marriage" to become the law of the land, so that, many of us agree with Dorothy from "The Wizard of Oz" when she exclaimed, "Well, Toto, I guess we're not in Kansas anymore." In part 2 we will examine the biblical view of marriage since that view has been the assumption of most of western civilization for the last 2,000 years. We will also look at the early Church Fathers to see what their view on marriage was. We will also look at ancient Greece and Rome to see if the idea of same–sex "marriage" entered their thinking. The last chapter of part 2 will look at the arguments used by same–sex marriage advocates to see if in fact Christians need to rethink the issue of homosexuality and marriage and adopt a more "inclusive" interpretation of Scripture.

In part 3, we will look at how the church can help those struggling with homosexuals who desire to lead godly lives in accordance with His Word--the hope we have in Christ and the power of the Spirit to overcome the sins that so easily beset us ALL. We will also look at the difference between healing and "cure" and ask if the idea of a cure is really the best approach that has been held out to many wanting to live a life more in line with God's Word. Let's be clear about the authors' assumptions and starting point; we are conservative evangelicals who believe in the inerrancy of Scripture and that it is sufficient for faith and practice. We believe that the issue of same-sex "marriage" goes to the heart of who we are as human beings and challenges the biblical teaching that the church has held for over 2,000 years. The goal is not to win arguments but to win souls, to give clarity to those confused by the claims of same-sex "marriage" advocates, and to help the church reach out anew to those dealing with homosexuality in their lives.

PART 1

*HOW DID WE GET HERE AND
WHAT DID WE LOSE ALONG THE WAY?*

1

But the H–bomb was here to stay; movies went to cinema wide, and television brought it inside; the law would end segregation. . . .

The 1950s

Kinsey Makes the Sexual Revolution Shake, Rattle, and Roll

New discoveries were being made as science took the center stage: DNA was discovered, and the Rosenbergs were uncovered; MacArthur was fired, and Eisenhower "hired"; Sputnik round the world did go, and Elvis put on quite a show; Einstein passed away, but the H–bomb was here to stay; movies went to cinema wide, and television brought it inside; the law would end segregation, but many hearts moved with hesitation; denominations heard the liberal call, and one by one grew very small while conservative watchmen on the wall grew tired of yelling to one and all; "it's not that bad," came the reply; they were just too focused on the sweet bye and bye.

Have you ever been traveling and then suddenly realized you were on the wrong road and asked, "How did we get here?" In the next 4 chapters we want to look at some of the events and forces that changed our culture over the forty years from 1950 to the end of the 1980s. It might be asked, why stop at the 80s? Haven't many things happened since then that are worth noting? The reason we stop there is because after a certain "tipping point" in a cultural shift when enough minds and attitudes have been changed, some issues like same–sex "marriage" become almost inevitable so that by the end of the 1980s "that train had left the station." As we will see in the coming chapters, the forces that go into changing a culture are many, and this is not meant to be an exhaustive list, but the two most important factors for the following chapters will be the slow decay of traditional or natural marriage and the strengthening and visibility of the homosexual movement.

The 1950s were a time of great expectation and hope. The "greatest generation" had defeated the enemies of freedom and liberty, the future looked bright, and we felt we could accomplish anything we put our minds to. There were of course new fears such as the threat of communism and the dread of the atomic bomb, but for the most part Americans were optimistic about the future. Church attendance was at an all–time high, and even for the secular part of society, there was a generally agreed to morality that ran parallel to much of Judeo–Christian teaching on sex and marriage. This is not to claim that it was some kind of "golden age"; after all, there was still racial inequality, and women were moving into the work force into areas that were not considered to be "woman's work."

Even though there was sexual immorality, the people involved in it knew it was wrong because of this "shared morality" and the societal pressure that helped restrain it. In other words, the laws and customs did not, as they do so often today, bend to the desires of the individual, but held people to a higher standard even if that standard was not practiced. But this understanding of marriage and morals was about to have a "Hiroshima" moment. The "bomb" that was dropped was a book, and even though it did not destroy any buildings, it did begin to crack the foundations of America's moral landscape, and its effects, like that war ending bomb, would be lingering for decades.

The book was *Sexual Behavior in the Human Male*, published in 1948 by Alfred C. Kinsey. The second and even more controversial "bomb" was the publication of Kinsey's *Sexual Behavior in the Human Female* in 1953. The impact and influence that these two books had on both layman and professionals would be difficult to overstate. *Sexual Behavior in the Human Male* was published in January 1948 and by March of that year was a bestseller, selling over 200,000 copies, which is remarkable when you consider that it was just over 800 pages and filled with enough charts, graphs, and statistics to warm the heart of a federal accountant. *Sexuality in the Human Female* sold about 250,000 copies and was on the *New York Times* bestseller list. Who was Alfred C. Kinsey, and what did his books say?

Alfred C. Kinsey, considered by many the founding father of the sexual revolution, was born in Hoboken, New Jersey on June 23, 1894. According to author James H. Jones, whose 900+ page biography titled *Alfred C. Kinsey: A Life* tells of the impact religion had on Kinsey, says, "The Kinseys belonged to the Methodist Church, and as evangelical Protestants, they practiced a brand of Methodism that was heartfelt and fiery. Their God was no benign patriarch; neither was He a disinterested deity who had created a world that operated according to natural laws and could be left to its own devices. In spirit if not in name, He was the God of the Old Testament––a jealous and vengeful God, a God who knew a person's every thought and deed and punished those who broke His commandments."[1] Jones says of Kinsey's father, "Alfred Seguine Kinsey would not allow family members to ride to church; they had to walk. Nor would he let the milkman make Sunday deliveries. . . . Religion had a profound influence on Kinsey. One could say he was reared in the 'nurture and admonition of the Lord', save for one fact–his pious father admonished far better than he nurtured. Alfred Seguine Kinsey commanded dual authority: he acted as the head of the house and as God's spokesman to his family."[2]

Kinsey received his B.S. in biology and psychology from Bowdoin College in Maine and his Sc.D. in biology from Harvard in 1919. Kinsey joined Indiana University as assistant zoology professor in 1920 and was a noted expert on the Gall Wasp. He was the founder of the Kinsey Institute for sex research at Indiana University, Bloomington, Indiana. The center was renamed the Kinsey Institute for Research in Sex, Gender and Reproduction in 1982. After the publication of his second book *Sexual Behavior in the Human Female*, Kinsey and his "report," as it came to be known, almost reached rock star status.

Kinsey's popularity was such that articles appeared about him and his work in magazines such as *McCall's, Life, Look*, and on the cover of the August 24, 1953 issue of *Time*. He had a guest appearance on the "Jack Benny Show," September 15, 1953. Actress/singer Martha Raye even sold a half–million copies of the song "Ooh, Dr.

---

1. James H. Jones, *Alfred C. Kinsey: A Life* (New York: W. W. Norton and Company, 1997), 13.

2. Ibid., 14.

Kinsey!" Kinsey died in 1956 at the age of 62. In 2012, Kinsey was inducted into The Legacy Project, an organization dedicated to "celebrating lesbian, gay, bisexual and transgendered (LGBT) contributions to history."

What was it that made Kinsey's work at once celebrated by homosexuals and damaging to traditional marriage? Kinsey's "research" appeared to show a real difference between what people proclaimed and what they practiced. For example, in his first book Kinsey states,

> All of these, and still other types of sexual behavior (chapter 8), are illicit activities, each performance of which is punishable as a crime under the law. The persons involved in these activities, taken as a whole, constitute more than 95 per cent of the total male population. Only a relatively small proportion of the males who are sent to penal institutions for sex offenses have been involved in behavior which is materially different from the behavior of most males in the population.

> But it is the total 95 per cent of the male population for which the judge, or board of safety, or church, or civic group demands apprehension, arrest, and conviction, when they call for a clean-up of the sex offenders in a community. It is, in fine, a proposal that 5 percent of the population should support the other 95 per cent in penal institutions. The only possible defense of the proposal is the fact that the judge, the civic leader, and most of the others who make such suggestions, come from that segment of the population which is most restrained on nearly all types of sexual behavior, and they simply do not understand how the rest of the population actually lives.[3]

In other words, those who pass laws restricting sexual behavior do so because they are ignorant of what people are actually doing. So using Kinsey's logic, we should not ticket speeders except when they do something that is "materially different," say destroy property or cause injury, but the rest we should let go, or laws against car theft, since over 1,000,000 cars are stolen in the U.S. each year, as long as it's not "materially different," it should be considered just part of the

---

3. Alfred C. Kinsey, Wardell B. Pomeroy, and Clyde E. Martin, *Sexual Behavior in the Human Male* (Philadelphia: W.B. Saunders Company, 1948), 392.

car owning experience. Kinsey's work was so shocking to the "greatest generation" because it had the look of objective research, scientific methods, and the fact that there was still in the public's mind the idealistic view of the white–coated researcher gathering data and presenting the objective results. Not every professional, however, was "wowed" by Kinsey's work. Lewis M. Terman, (1877–1956), an advocate of eugenics from Stanford University, published a 16 page review of Kinsey's first volume in 1948, in which he makes the following observations: "In almost every comparison the religiously active groups have lower incidences and frequencies than the religiously inactive groups of the same denomination. Unless religion merely attracts persons of low sexual drive (which is doubtful), it would seem that religious attitudes exert a definitely restraining influence. . . . The author attributes the relatively low sexual activity in this group to 'the pervading asceticism of Hebrew philosophy (p. 486), and in other passages he blames this ancient Jewish asceticism for the unrealistic severity with which most of the Christian peoples condemn departures from the Talmudic ideals.'"[4]

"Notwithstanding Kinsey's frequent reiteration that his job is to report facts rather than evaluations, it has been possible to quote numerous passages in which recklessly worded and slanted evaluations are expressed, the slanting being often in the direction of implied preference for uninhibited sexual activity."[5] As we shall see, Kinsey's work was not that "objective." Kinsey was dismissive of the moral aspect of sexual behavior and concentrated on the mechanical aspects of sex with a "just as birds do it, bees do it, so should we do it" approach. Let's take a look at some of the "data" Kinsey published.

"On the basis of these active data, and allowing for the cover–up that has been involved it is probably safe to suggest that about half of all married males have intercourse with women other than their wives, at some time while they are married"[6] So, 50% of all married men commit adultery.

---

4. Lewis M. Terman, "Kinsey's Sexual Behavior in the Human Male: Some Comments and Criticisms," *Psychological Bulletin* 45, no. 5 (September 1948): 455.

5. Ibid., 459.

6. Kinsey, Pomeroy, and Martin, 585.

"We find that about 69 per cent of the total white male population ultimately has some experience with prostitutes."[7] So, according to this, just about 7 out of 10 men have used prostitutes. "10 percent of the males are more or less exclusively homosexual (i.e., rate 5 or 6) for at least three years between the ages of 16 and 55. This is one male in ten in the white male population."[8] This is the birth of the "10%" myth of the number of homosexuals in the population. This myth continued for decades even after most other data indicate that no more than 2–3% are exclusively homosexual.

➥ The myth was helpful in the changing of attitudes, laws, and putting pressure on professional organizations such as the American Psychiatric Association (APA) which removed homosexuality from its list of "disorders" in 1973. "The significance of pre–marital intercourse depends upon the situations under which it is had. If it is had under conditions which are physically uncomfortable and not conductive to a mutually satisfactory relationship, if it is had under conditions which leave the individuals disturbed for fear that they have been or will be detected, the outcome is one thing. If it is had under satisfying circumstances and without fear, the outcome may be very different."[9]

For the Christian, it is not the situation that determines the rightness or wrongness of sex, but whether it is in accordance with how God determined sex to be experienced (Gen. 1:28, 2:24). In later chapters we will discuss the biblical concept of marriage.

In chapter 21, titled "Homosexual Outlet," we read the following:

> Whatever factors are considered, it must not be forgotten that the basic phenomenon to be explained is an individual's preference for a partner of one sex, or for a partner of the other sex, or his acceptance of a partner of either sex. This problem is, after all, part of the broader problem of choices in general: the choice of the road that one takes, of the clothes that one wears, of the food that one eats, of the place in which one sleeps, and of the endless other things that one is

---

7. Ibid., 597.

8. Ibid., 651.

9. Ibid., 561.

constantly choosing. A choice of a partner in a sexual relation becomes more significant only because society demands that there be a particular choice in this matter, and does not so often dictate one's choice of food or of clothing.[10]

So, for Kinsey, if it were not for the demands of society (i.e., morality), choosing a sex partner would be like choosing clothes that you wear or food that you eat. But, roads, clothes, and food are not usually moral choices. For the Christian choosing someone to have sex with has the most profound, permanent implications that touch every aspect of one's life. Kinsey has reduced sex down to pleasure and what each individual can get out of it. As we will soon see, Kinsey had a less than objective motive for his conclusions.

We descend ever deeper into the moral abyss of Kinsey's research in chapter 22, on "animal contacts" in which he reports about rural farm boys and their interactions with animals. "Ultimately, 14 to 16 per cent of the rural males of the grade school level, 20 per cent of the rural males of the high school level, and 26 to 28 per cent of the rural males of the college level have some animal experience to the point of orgasm (Tables 91, 151). In this upper educational level, nearly one rural male in three has such contact to the point of orgasm, and well over half of these upper level males have some kind of sexual contact with animals."[11]

"Anglo–American legal codes rate sexual relations between the human and animals of other species as sodomy, punishable under the same laws which penalize homosexual and mouth–genital contacts. The city–bred judge who hears such a case is likely to be unusually severe in his condemnation, and is likely to give the maximum sentence that is possible. . . .It is only when the farm–bred male migrates to a city community and comes in contact with city–bred reactions to these activities that he becomes upset over the contemplation of what he has done. This is particularly true if he learns through some psychology course or through books that such behavior is considered abnormal."

Finally, Kinsey pulls back the curtain, and we see the man standing behind it:

---

10. Ibid., 661.

11. Ibid., 671.

> To each individual, the significance of any particular type of sexual activity depends very largely upon his previous experience. Ultimately, certain activities may seem to him to be the only things that have value, that are right, that are socially acceptable; and all departures from his own particular pattern may seem to him to be enormous abnormalities. But the scientific data which are accumulating make it appear that, if circumstances had been propitious, most individuals might have become conditioned in any direction, even into activities which they now consider quite unacceptable. There is little evidence of the existence of such a thing as innate perversity, even among those individuals whose sexual activities society has been least inclined to accept. There is an abundance of evidence that most human sexual activities would become comprehensible to most individuals, if they could know the background of each other individual's behavior.[12]

So, for Kinsey, if we could just get to know the background of persons engaged in adultery, pre–marital sex, homosexuality, or sex with animals, we would come to see them as persons who have different sexual needs and not as immoral persons. Kinsey saw rather than sharp distinctions between right and wrong, moral and immoral, that human sexuality should be seen as a rainbow where one color slowly changes into another with no clear boundaries. With this in mind, we will now shine a light on what is the darkest corner of Kinsey's "report." Chapter 5 of the "Male" book is about the sexual development of children. Kinsey was interested in ALL forms human sexual activities including "pre–adolescent experience in orgasm." On page 176 of the Male volume we find in table number 31, a list of 317 young males who range in age from 2 months to 15 years. This chapter and the method by which Kinsey and his team obtained the data seems to have been overlooked by virtually every reviewer of Kinsey's book until 1981 when Dr. Judith Reisman delivered a paper at the Fifth World Congress on Sexology in Jerusalem. She looked at the children (pre–adolescents) Kinsey reported on and not just the adults and how his data was obtained.

At the conference, her paper was received about as well as the news of a poison–ivy patch at a nudist camp. She has tirelessly written on and spoken about Kinsey and the porn industry for which

---

12. Ibid., 678.

she has been called "nut," "whacko," etc. but has never been refuted. Kinsey tells us how this data was obtained:

> Better data on pre–adolescent climax come from the histories of adult males who have had sexual contacts with younger boys and who, with their adult backgrounds, are able to recognize and interpret the boys' experiences. Unfortunately, not all of the subjects with such contacts in their histories were questioned on this point of pre–adolescent reactions; but 9 of our adult male subjects have observed such orgasm. *Some of these adults are technically trained persons who have kept diaries or other records that have been put at our disposal, and from them we have secured information on 317 pre-adolescents who were either observed in self masturbation, or who were observed in contacts with other boys or older adults.*[13] (emphasis added)

Jones puts it this way: "But Kinsey was adamant, insisting that science needed data regardless of their source. As a researcher, it was not his job to pass moral judgment on the sources of his data."[14]

➥ Sarah D. Goode of the University of Winchester, UK, in her 2011 book *Paedophiles in Society,* devotes an entire chapter to Kinsey's "chapter 5" and points out that the Kinsey Institute has never offered a rebuttal or explanation of the charges made by Dr. Reisman:

> To date, Reisman's remains the sustained critique of Kinsey's work. Her work, situated firmly within the intellectual compass of the American political right, is distinctly unappealing to more liberal academics.
>
> This is a pity because Reisman raises serious allegations about the work of Kinsey's team and the Kinsey Institute which in turn require serious refutation. Instead, Reisman has been the target of contemptuous derision while the charges she raises have been ignored and trivialized. . . . The voices on the political left, the voices of lesbian, gay and bisexual academics

---

13. Ibid., 176–177.

14. Jones, *Alfred C. Kinsey: A Life,* 513.

and activists are all surprisingly quiet (or mumbled) on this question.[15]

To be clear, then, what Kinsey is here describing is not a situation where children or adults were asked to remember back to their first sexual experiences. Nor is it a situation where mothers or other carers are asked about when they noticed their child's first genital exploration or masturbation. The data in Table 31 are based on the observations of nine "adult males who have had sexual contacts with younger boys." Kinsey calls some of them "technically trained persons"–this phrase has never been adequately explained by the Kinsey Institute but apparently means that they were taught to use a stopwatch.

In order for this to happen, the Kinsey researchers did not have one–off interviews with these men; they corresponded with them and, told that these men were having sexual contact with small children and babies, they supplied them with stopwatches. There is a name for such behavior in civilized countries, but that name is not "science."[16]

Let us say what Sarah did not: these children were raped, the information was sent to Kinsey, and Kinsey reported this with the same detachment he had when he recorded the various wing sizes of gall wasps. Because the issues raised by Dr. Reisman just would not go away, former Director and now Senior Research Fellow at the Kinsey Institute, Dr. John Bancroft, published a paper attempting to answer Reisman's claims about the source of the data in Tables 31 to 34 in Kinsey's first book.

However, I confirmed beyond any doubt, that all of these data in Tables 31 to 34 had been collected by one man, who from 1917 until Kinsey interviewed him in the mid–1940s, had been documenting his numerous sexual experiences, not only with children but with adults of both sexes. It is also possible that all or some of the other eight men that Kinsey referred to had provided information about boys' orgasms, which he used in other ways. But why Kinsey did not reveal

---

15. Sarah D. Goode, *Paedophiles in Society: Reflecting on Sexuality, Abuse, and Hope* (n.p., UK: Palgrave Macmillian, 2011), 120.

16. Ibid., 105.

that there was only the single source for the four tables we do not know–perhaps because he did not want to draw attention to this one man, or alternatively because he was particularly interested in this evidence and did not want to diminish its possible scientific credibility by revealing its single source.[17]

Notice that Bancroft does not reveal how he has "confirmed beyond any doubt" that only one man was the source contrary to what Kinsey reported, but then speculates as to what is "possible" or "perhaps because" which seems odd for something he said was "confirmed beyond any doubt." Could it not be that the source of the data on children's sexuality is exactly as Kinsey reported and it is only those who in our time do not wish it to be true that motivates them to deny it?

There are two other events in U.S. history that bears some resemblance to the "pre–adolescent data" collecting methods used by Kinsey. The first is the infamous Tuskegee experiment conducted by the U.S. Public Health Service from 1932 to 1972 in which 400 black male sharecroppers who had contracted syphilis were not given any treatment and were never told they had syphilis in order that "data" might be collected on the long term effects of syphilis on black males.[18] The second was the U.S. involvement in the eugenics movement of the early 20th century (1904 to the late 1940s) during which an estimated 60,000 men and women who were deemed "feebleminded" or otherwise "unfit" were sterilized without their knowledge and sometimes against their will in order to help "improve" the race.[19]

The connection between these three events is that "data" was collected from persons who could not resist, did not understand, or were lied to by those they trusted. James H. Jones provides some insight into Kinsey's motivations: "However much he talked about science's need for data, this was not his primary motivation. Again, his research sprang from a private agenda shaped by personal politics. Decades of inner turmoil had transformed Kinsey into a rebel, a man

---

17. John Bancroft, "Alfred C. Kinsey and the Politics of Sex Research," *Annual Review of Sex Research* 15 (2004):16–17.

18. See also James H. Jones, *Bad Blood: The Tuskegee Syphilis Experiment* (New York: The Free Press, 1992).

19. See Edwin Black, *War against the Weak* (Washington DC: Dialog Press, 2003).

who rejected the sexual mores of his age. He meant to change the public's thinking on sexual matters. Convinced that cold, hard facts alone would persuade the public to develop more tolerant sexual attitudes, Kinsey was determined to provide those data. And if that meant trafficking with someone like Mr. X, then so be it. The end justified the means."[20] Mr. X is thought to be the source of much of the "data" on children that Kinsey used. According to Jones, Kinsey felt that

> social factors do a great deal to force an individual into an exclusively heterosexual or homosexual pattern. Most of the social forces encourage the heterosexual, but society's ostracism of the homosexual similarly forces him into the exclusive company of other homosexuals and into an exclusively homosexual pattern.

> Along with Freud, Kinsey believed that human nature was basically bisexual possessing in equal measure the capacity for relating to the same sex or to the opposite sex. In Kinsey's judgment, restrictive sexual mores alone prevented people from acting upon their bisexuality.[21]

Kinsey's interest in homosexuality was more than scientific; it was during his trips to Chicago to interview members of the homosexual community that it became personal. "Chicago's homosexual community would always have a special hold on Kinsey, largely because it was the first he studied in depth. Like a thirsty man in need of water, he traveled there again and again. And the more trips he made the stronger the bond he felt to the men he interviewed. . . . During his many visits to Chicago, Kinsey learned all about this world, both as an observer and as a participant. This was the segment of the Chicago gay community he went to for physical release, as it contained the only group with whom he could enjoy sex with a minimum risk of recognition."[22]

For Kinsey, this must have seemed the perfect situation. He had a wife and family and all the comforts of home, and when his lust be-

---

20. Jones, *Alfred C. Kinsey: A Life,* 513.

21. Ibid., 384.

22. Ibid., 384, 385.

came too strong, he could engage in anonymous sex with men who would never reveal his identity. This then is a brief look at a founding father of the sexual revolution, the wizard behind the curtain who would grant the desires of every depraved, darkened heart, a man who is said to have brought "freedom" and "liberation" to a "repressive society," someone who desired "openness" and "tolerance" to all forms of sexual expression, someone whose influence would extend far beyond the pages of academic journals and into the arts, entertainment, education, law and even the church itself. Jones sums up Kinsey's goal: "Reducing and abolishing rigid controls on human sexual behavior was thus the great cause of Kinsey's life, the quest that put him to bed at night and got him up in the morning. More than any other figure of his day, he set Americans to thinking about how much authority society should exercise over intimate matters."[23]

He gave to the world his scientific sanctification of every sexual practice that fallen human beings do when they turn away from God and suppress the truth in unrighteousness (Romans 1:18). We will see the shadow of Alfred C. Kinsey again and again as we see the destruction of natural marriage and the rise of the homosexual movement.

At this point some Christian readers might be asking, "Why this look about the past; why not just deal with the present situation, give us the biblical verses to deal with it, and be done?" The answer is because if we are to understand an idea or movement, we need to know how and why it came about, who the people were, and why they did what they did. What would we think of an atheist who attacked Christian beliefs and never once picked up the Bible and read it? We would certainly not be impressed with their intellectual honesty, but would feel they should have at least read something of they were attacking.

Too often many Christians do not have even a passing understanding of the cultural issues around them, and this lack of understanding can make it more difficult to clearly present the gospel to the unbelieving world as well as helping other Christians who have become confused by the constant drum of non–biblical views and assumptions all around them.

---

23. Ibid., 773.

With this in mind, we turn to our next person of interest, Donald Webster Cory, whose groundbreaking book *The Homosexual in America, a Subjective Approach* was published in 1951. Cory was inspired by the work of Alfred Kinsey and even asked Kinsey if he would write the foreword to his book, but Kinsey declined.

Cory's book was an inspiration to early homosexual activists and was an intellectual response to the government crackdown on homosexuality in the late 40s and early 50s. Cory was the pseudonym for Edward Sagarin (Sept. 18, 1913 – June 10, 1986) who was a tenured sociologist at John Jay College of Criminal Justice. Cory was conflicted about his homosexuality, and although his book dispelled many myths about homosexuals and their feelings, he was never able to come to terms with his own homosexuality. In the preface to his book he writes, "This book is, in a sense, a spiritual autobiography. In a work of this type the facts of a man's life are of secondary importance; the thoughts he espouses are of primary significance."[24]

Later, on page xv of the preface he writes,

> At the age of twenty–five, after determining that I was capable of consummating a marriage, I was wedded to a girl whom I had known from childhood, a lovely and outgoing person, who brought deep understanding to our union and who shared many interests with me. I resolved that marriage would be the end of my sins, that I would sever my ties with the homosexual circles and with my dear friends therein, and build what appeared to be the only life that might be fruitful for me.

> I was not long in learning that marriage did not reduce the urge for gratification with men and that I could never have the energy and peace of mind to continue a fecund career while I was in constant struggle with something that was living within me. I needed my former companionships, but would not allow myself to admit, even in the silence of the thought process, that I wanted them.[25]

---

24. Donald Webster Cory, *The Homosexual in America, A Subjective Approach* (New York: Greenberg Publisher, 1951), xiv.

25. Ibid., xv.

Cory, like many of that time period, thought that marriage could be a "cure" for homosexual urges only to find that it was not a cure but made it easier to blend in with the heterosexual society around him. Cory became more conservative in his later years and believed that homosexuality was not normal and that he believed homosexuals could be helped with therapy and a kind of Alcoholics Anonymous approach. Cory did not like the activist approach of the late 1960s and 70s and as a result was marginalized by the leaders of the homosexual movement. Cory died of a heart attack in 1986 and is considered both a pioneer and a stumbling block by leaders of the homosexual rights movement.

Mattachine Society

The first modern homosexual organization was begun by members of the Communist Party in Los Angeles in 1950 under the leadership of Harry Hay. Hay (April 7, 1912 – October 24, 2002) was living in Los Angeles in 1932 when he met and befriended Will Geer (the actor who played "Grampa" on the Waltons TV show). In his book *Before Stonewall*, biographer Vern L. Bullough writes about Hay and Geer. "One of his friends was Will Geer who introduced Harry to the left–wing community of Los Angeles and eventually to the Communist Party. Increasingly, Harry became a hard–core activist in the radical community, often joining with Geer in what was known as agitprop, acting out scenes at picket lines to keep spirits of the strikers high, or doing planned demonstrations or scenes at large meetings to keep audience attention focused."[26] Harry had one big problem with the Communist Party: it was hostile to homosexuality. Bullough writes,

> The conflicts between his gayness and his left–wing ideology led him to seek psychiatric help, and out of one such session came a decision to marry and to leave the gay life.

> In 1938 he and Anita Platky, a fellow activist, were married. They set up housekeeping in the Silver Lake district, the first time Harry had ever formally moved out of his parents' house. One of the first actions the couple took was to officially

---

26. Vern Bullough, *Before Stonewall* (New York: Harrington Park Press, 2002), 76–77.

join the Communist Party. Although they never had children
of their own, they eventually adopted two girls.[27]

Hay saw what he felt was the need for homosexuals to organize,
so he adopted the Communist model he had learned from them. In
1951 Hay divorced his wife Anita, and at his request was expelled
from the Communist Party because he could not stand the Party's
anti–homosexual stance.

The Mattachine Society was mostly a secret society, but was effective in giving homosexuals a gathering place to discuss issues and
make connections with others in their community. The Society drew
up a mission statement in order to identify what the purpose of the
society was; it reads: "(1) to unify homosexuals isolated from their
own kind and unable to adjust to the dominant culture, (2) to educate and improve and add to the information about homosexuality
through further research, and (3) to lead those who are regarded as
socially deviant to achieve the goal of unification and education."[28]

During the early 1950s the anti–communist movement intensi-
fied, and many members wanted to rid the society of the so–called
communists in leadership. "The result was the end of what Harry
called the First Mattachine, and the appearance of the Second
Mattachine, a much–sanitized organization which spread throughout
the country over the next two decades. The new Mattachine moved
its headquarters to San Francisco and became what Harry called a
'white glove' assimilationist group."[29] "Harry has continued to push
his vision of a gay community, different than the heterosexual one
with all gays coming together. He planted seeds for gay organizations
far and wide and some grew into trees, although not always in the
way that Harry had expected or anticipated."[30]

There was justifiable fear on the part of homosexuals with regard
to their actions being made public. The loss of jobs and the rejection
of family and friends were all very real fears in those days.

The FBI was monitoring groups like Mattachine mostly because
those in leadership were either members or former members of the

---

27. Ibid., 76.

28. Ibid., 79.

29. Ibid., 80.

30. Ibid., 82.

Communist Party or had very left–wing ideals. Also, not unjustifiably, was the thought that a homosexual could be more easily blackmailed than say someone caught in an adulterous relationship. As far as the FBI was concerned, homosexuality was more of a security issue than a moral one.

There were many other homosexual activists in the 1950s and most were working quietly to try and unite into groups with the goal of being able to associate without fear of prosecution, loss of job, or outright rejection by society. At the beginning of this book we stated that there were two main things that had to occur before same–sex "marriage" could become the issue it is today. One was the growth of homosexual organizations (inspired by the work of Alfred Kinsey) that began to make themselves known to the mainstream through marches, protests, books, plays, movies, and then television. The other was the destruction and devaluing of natural marriage and the sacredness of it. These two events were beginning to take root in this decade and bore fruit in the decades that followed.

– Hugh Hefner and His Playboy World

Nothing changed more in the 50s in America than the attitudes about sex, marriage, and morality. One of the paradoxical things about the changing sexual morality that was going on during the 1950s was the help that *Playboy* magazine provided to the homosexual movement. At first, it might seem odd that the VERY heterosexual world of *Playboy* could be of help, but, when you think about it, the view of sex and morality that *Playboy* put forward is one of an alternative to the traditional "puritanical" Christian understanding of sexual relationships. Biographer Steven Watts, in his book *Mr. Playboy, Hugh Hefner and the American Dream* says about Hefner, "He was no homophobe, and in fact urged toleration for this sexual behavior. But, like even the most progressive figures in the 1950s, he saw homosexuality as an aberration, a sign of maladjustment."[31] So, even though Hefner viewed homosexuality as a "maladjustment, the lifestyle and morality promoted by *Playboy* magazine weakened

---

31. Steven Watts, *Mr. Playboy, Hugh Hefner and the American Dream* (Hoboken, NJ: John Wiley & Sons, 2008), 112.

the biblical view of marriage and faithfulness and by doing so helped pave the way for more acceptance of homosexuality.

Hugh Marston Hefner (April 9, 1926 – September 27, 2017) was born in Chicago, Illinois to Grace and Glenn Hefner. They were a strict Methodist family, and Sunday was set aside just for church and family activities. Biographer Steven Watts writes,

> As Hefner would recall throughout his life, restraint and repression colored the atmosphere of his family as he came of age. Orderly rules and sobriety muffled expressions of emotion. Hugh and Keith had to be at home and in bed earlier than their playmates, and they were not allowed to play with friends on Sunday, which was set aside for church and family activities. Grace and Glenn also shied away from displays of affection to each other and to their children. Little kissing and hugging occurred in this emotional climate of cool reserve. . . . In fact, Grace and Glenn buried emotions so deep that feelings of any kind--anger, affection, disputes-- seldom came to the surface. There was much calmness and kindness among the Hefner's but little passion. 'His parents are very controlled people,' Hefner's first wife reported. "In the three years we lived there, I never heard them raise their voice. Never."[32]

Hefner joined the Army in early 1944 and served most of his time as a clerk in S–1, or personnel, because of his excellent typing skills. He received an honorable discharge from the Army in 1946 and then returned to Chicago. On June 15, 1949, Hugh Hefner married his college sweetheart Millie Williams. Before their marriage Millie had confessed to Hugh of her one time sexual liaison with a coach at the school where she taught. Stunned and shocked, Hefner told her he could forgive her, but, as Steven Watts reports, "Hefner was deeply hurt by Millie's revelation. Later he described it as 'the single most devastating experience of my entire life.' He sat in his room for days afterward playing records, especially the Billy Eckstine song 'Fool That I Am,' over and over. . . . 'Nothing was ever the same between us again'. The affair, it seems clear, encouraged Hefner to distrust women and the notion of commitment to, and from, them."[33] Hefner

---

32. Ibid., 19.
33. Ibid., 48.

was frustrated with what he considered to be the sexual hypocrisy and repression that governed sexual conduct in the laws of the U.S.

Hefner felt that "modern freedoms had not been extended to sexuality. Hefner blamed Christianity, which had denounced carnal urges and idealized celibacy, as the culprit. He offered as a counterpoint the light of reason, which, if allowed to shine on sexuality, would lead to the decriminalization of many activities that hurt no one. 'Man's moral life, as long as it does not harm others, is his own business, and should be left to his own discretion,' he concluded."[34]

In 1948, a book was published that would have a profound impact on the 22 year old Hefner. It was none other than Kinsey's *Sexual Behavior in the Human Male.* "Like nothing else, however, Kinsey's *Sexual Behavior in the Human Male* electrified Hefner. It confirmed his growing sense that sex was central to the human experience and that Americans had enshrouded it in mists of superstition and hypocrisy."[35] Kinsey's influence would be behind Hefner and *Playboy* magazine in the years ahead. Watts shows how important Kinsey was to Hefner,

> But Kinsey also became a catalyst for Hefner's thinking in a larger sense. This scientist, in his view, had demonstrated that more sex was going on than polite American society ever admitted, and that ordinary people flouted rules and conventions. Fascinated by Kinsey's findings, Hefner read everything about the book that he could get his hands on. "Kinsey had a tremendous impact on me," he recalled later. "It supplied the evidence that proved the things that I had been feeling for so many years, which was that what we said about our sexuality was not what we did. That we were hypocrites, and out of that came a good deal of hurt." Kinsey spoke directly to important issues in the young man's life, illustrating that `they` made those laws and `they` wouldn't let me be intimate with my girlfriend.[36]

Another biographer, Thomas Weyr, in his book *Reaching for Paradise–The Playboy Vision of America*, confirms the importance of Kinsey in Hefner's thinking: "The Kinsey Report marked the begin-

---

34. Ibid., 55.

35. Ibid., 46.

36. Ibid., 47.

ning of scientific probing into the sexual process, a probing based on statistical method more than on Freudian intuitive insight. Hefner recognized Kinsey as the incontrovertible word of a new God based on the new holy writ--demonstrable evidence. Kinsey would add a dash of scientific truth to the Playboy mix."[37]

The first issue of *Playboy* magazine was published in December 1953; it was cobbled together on a card table in Hefner's apartment. With about $8,000 raised from family and friends, he was able to obtain the rights to a nude Marilyn Monroe photo from a calendar shoot, and cover printing costs. When the magazine hit the newsstands, it sold 50,000 copies and the rest, as the saying goes, is history. By 1960, Playboy was selling about 1,000,000 magazines a month, and by the early 1970s it was selling 7,000,000 copies per month.

By that time, following *Playboy*'s lead, there was a flood of ever more sexually explicit material coming from books, magazines, art, film, and even television. Steven Watts comments,

> Indeed, *Playboy*'s own survey on sexual behavior underlined the significant shift in American mores since the Kinsey research two decades earlier. Titled "Sexual Behavior in the 1970s," the study was funded by the Playboy Foundation and published in six monthly installments in 1973–1974.
>
> It examined the sexual attitudes and behavior of about two thousand people in a variety of cities and towns and reported that "we are now surrounded by evidence that people are openly doing things that a generation ago were unthinkable, or at least among the most guarded of personal secrets." Investigators found that Americans engaged in sex more frequently and increasingly endorsed premarital sex, oral sex, and the end of the double standard for men and women. Statistics revealed a marked increase in every category of sexual practice since the Kinsey Reports.[38]

Hugh Hefner built *Playboy* magazine into an empire, an empire based on his own view of what the "good life" means. For Hefner, it meant striving for more money, more wine, more cars, more casual

---

37. Thomas Weyr, *Reaching for Paradise–The Playboy Vision of America* (New York: NYT Times Books, 1978), 11.

38. Watts, 304.

hopping from bed to bed, more of everything to satisfy the flesh, but it is an illusion, like biting into a piece of cotton candy that melts away the moment it touches your tongue. Hefner was married (legally) to Mildred Williams (1949–1959), Kimberly Conrad (1989–2010), and Crystal Harris (2012–2017) and had two "partners," Barbi Benton (1969–1976) and Brande Roderick (2000–2001). In the April, 2013 issue of *Esquire* magazine, Hefner was asked how many women he has had sex with. "How could I possibly know?" he says, "Over a thousand, for sure. There were chunks of my life when I was married, and when I was married I never cheated. But I made up for it when I wasn't married. You have to keep your hand in."

Make no mistake, the *Playboy* empire was not built on wonderful articles by famous authors or humorous cartoons. It was built on the photos of, and the exposing of, young women who should have been reserving that sight for the sacredness of marriage. As the old saying goes, however, a picture is worth a thousand words. The most celebrated element in the *Playboy* crusade for sexual liberation, of course was visual. The "Playmate of the Month," whose revealing fold–out portrait graced every issue of the magazine, became an American icon. As Hefner noted years later, "'The Centerfold, in its own way, was as much of a statement in terms of the sexual revolution as the Playboy Philosophy.'"[39] Hefner's version of morality for men 18 to 80 is based on Kinsey's "scientific" view and a very strong individualistic outlook where each man is deciding for himself what is moral or immoral. Hefner should consider the words of Jesus Christ when He asked in Mark 8:36–37, "What good is it for a man to gain the whole world, yet forfeit his soul? Or what can a man give in exchange for his soul?"

Playboy magazine has from its beginning set itself against natural marriage and even helped to change the laws that affect marriage. For example, the Playboy Foundation was "funneling hundreds of thousands of dollars to the Kinsey Institute and Masters and Johnson for sex research, assisting with the *Roe v. Wade* case that established women's abortion rights––the foundation proved that Hefner's philosophy was more than mere rhetoric: it was a heartfelt manifesto

---

39. Ibid., 114.

of social reform."[40] For the man who follows the playboy morality, abortion is the last line of defense against the public consequences of his private actions. In the September 2012 issue of *Playboy*, Hefner wrote an editorial in support of gay marriage, which, when you think about it, would be a logical position for a man who argues against the Christian understanding of marriage and morality and for the "sexual freedom" of all. "Without it, we will turn back the sexual revolution and return to an earlier puritanical time." Nothing would terrify Hefner more.

Much more could be said about Hefner and his destructive influence on morality and marriage, but before we move on, here is one more quote from biographer Steven Watts:

> The Playboy Philosophy had fingered Christianity as the source of most modern emotional and social woes, and many religious spokesmen responded in kind. The resulting debate between Playboy and the preachers provided a glimpse of the cultural ferment beginning to bubble in 1960s America. . . . Indeed, the *Playboy* editor minced few words in identifying Christianity as the bogeyman in the evolution of stultifying moral codes in Western civilization. The Playboy Philosophy blamed both Catholic and Protestantism for nurturing repressive, restrictive, hypocritical attitudes that had denied physical needs and stunted emotional health. Hefner contended that Christianity while sometimes engendering sympathy, understanding, and charity, more often had inspired "bloody wars," kept millions "in abject poverty," and promoted "the tyranny of man over his fellow man." This indictment of Christianity reflected *Playboy's* twin preoccupations–sex and material abundance.[41]

Playboy's influence went far beyond the pages of the magazine or even Hefner's "philosophy." Like a pebble in a pond, its ripple effect touched many areas of the culture making it easier to accept even more degrading images in magazines, movies, and television, slowly, slowly desensitizing us to things that would have shocked and shamed earlier generations. Hefner, now in his 90s, no longer commands the headlines he did in the 60s and 70s, and his magazine

---

40. Ibid. 179–180.
41. Watts, 180.

by comparison to our current moral abyss seems almost quaint. But Playboy did help to move the culture from the traditional view of marriage as a lifetime God ordained covenant between one man and one woman and sex as a sacred blessing, to the view of staying married as long as you are happy, and sex as something for your own personal pleasure and enjoyment.

Derrick Sherwin Bailey and the Beginnings of Homosexual Theology

Not only were sex research and entertainment changing in the area of morals during the 1950s, but in theology as well. Derrick Sherwin Bailey's influential *Homosexuality and the Western Christian Tradition*, published in 1955, is the first serious work that reinterprets the traditional, historic understanding of what the Bible teaches about homosexuality.

Derrick Sherwin Bailey (1910–1984) was an Anglican clergyman and canon residentiary of Wells Cathedral, England. Although Bailey wrote several books on love, sex, and marriage, none had the impact on future theological discussions like *Homosexuality and the Western Christian Tradition*. Bailey's views were influential in the Church of England at a time in the mid–50s when the issue of homosexuality was coming to the attention of lawmakers, educators, and clergy to reexamine the laws governing homosexual activities between consenting adults.

Bailey begins his reexamination, or reinterpretation, of biblical texts on homosexuality with a look at the account of Sodom and Gomorrah in Genesis 19:4–11. He then moves on to definite biblical references, possible references, Roman law, the Church Fathers, Mediaeval opinion and finally English law. In a later chapter we will critique the arguments Bailey puts forward in support of his non–traditional interpretation of the biblical texts, but for now it is important to note how influential Bailey was. In the mid–1950s, England was becoming increasingly aware of the issue between homosexuals and the law. By 1955 there were over 1,000 men imprisoned for various homosexual acts under British law that had been passed a century before. There was a growing concern about the need to address and even re–examine those laws.

Bailey was an influential voice representing the Church of England, which was considered the "moral voice" during the discussion of the relationship between the law and homosexuality. While Bailey felt that the laws were too harsh and that these laws in turn were based on a misunderstanding of the biblical texts, it should not be forgotten that Bailey did not believe that homosexuality was the norm for human relationships. In the *Anglican Theological Review* of April, 1988, Jonathan Sinclair Carey writes, "The biblical, historical, and legal discussion in the book was undergirded by the assumption that the extent of homosexual practices and perversion in a society indicated its general picture. Bailey believed adamantly that the so–called problem of homosexuality was produced by the corruption in society and, equally as important, the abandonment of moral responsibility in the field of heterosexual relationships." Carey continues, "For Bailey, the heterosexual relationship was the standard, homosexuality aberrant. Only in the context of the family can the rightful nature of creation be established, both law and the Church must work for this man–woman balance."[42]

Bailey was also influential in another important document called "Report of the Committee on Homosexual Offences and Prostitution," which came known as "The Wolfenden Report" named after the Chairman of the committee Sir John Wolfenden. It was published in 1957, and based on its recommendations, homosexual acts between consenting adults were decriminalized in England in 1967. Bailey's work influenced later theologians and historians such as John McNeill, Dale Martin, Troy Perry, John Boswell (all of whom were homosexuals), and many others, but in an ironic twist, Bailey also supports one of the central themes of this book, namely, the best way to deal with homosexuality is not with jail, therapy, or drugs but by modeling biblically based man–woman marriages that show, not just tell, how the "one flesh" of man and woman is lived out.

The committee on homosexual offenses and prostitution was appointed on August 24, 1954 and met for 62 days, of which 32 were given to oral examination of the witnesses. D. S. Bailey, being one of the witnesses who submitted arguments to the committee as a rep-

---

42. Jonathan Sinclair Carey, "D. S. Bailey and 'the Name Forbidden among Christians,'" *Anglican Theological Review* 70, no. 2 (April 1988): 108.

resentative of the clergy, argued in favor of decriminalizing homosexual activities between consenting adults.

The committee heard arguments both for and against changing the law and quoted from our old buddy Alfred Kinsey as to how many people might be expected to be involved in homosexual activities in England if Kinsey's figures were applied. The committee felt that Kinsey's data would be about the same for England as the United States. "Dr. Kinsey's findings have aroused opposition and skepticism. But it was noteworthy that some of our medical witnesses expressed the view that something very like these figures would be established in this country if similar inquires were made. The majority, while stating quite frankly that they did not really know, indicated that their impression was that his figures would be on the high side for Great Britain."[43]

The committee summarized its conclusions as follows:

> Further, we feel bound to say this. We have outlined the arguments against a change in the law, and we recognize their weight. We believe, however, that they have been met by the counter-arguments we have already advanced. There remains one additional counter-argument which we believe to be decisive, namely, the importance which society and the law ought to give to individual freedom of choice and action in matters of private morality. Unless a deliberate attempt is to be made by society, acting through the agency of the law, to equate the sphere of crime with that of sin, there must remain a realm of private morality and immorality which is, in brief and crude terms, not the law's business. To say this is not to condone or encourage private immorality. On the contrary, to emphasize the personal and private responsibility of the individual for his own actions, and that is a responsibility which a mature agent can properly be expected to carry for himself without the threat of punishment from the law.[44]

One of the critics of the committee's recommendations was Lord Patrick Devlin (1905–1992), a prominent British jurist who put to-

---

43. Great Britain: Committee on Homosexual Offenses and Prostitution, *The Wolfenden Report: Report of the Committee on Homosexual Offenses and Prostitution*, Authorized American ed. (New York: Stein and Day Publishers, 1963), para. 38, 37.

44. Ibid., para. 61, 48.

gether a book published by Oxford University Press in 1965, based on lectures he had given titled "The Enforcement of Morals." In this book, Devlin points out that the idea of a "private morality" comes right out of the English philosopher John Stuart Mill (1806–1873) in his book "On Liberty." Devlin questions whether a "private morality" exists and how the law would interact with it. The old issue of "you can't legislate morality" has been dealt with in the book by Norman Geisler and Frank S. Turek, *Legislating Morality*, where they argue that *all* laws legislate some morality. The question is not can we legislate morality, but *whose* morality shall we legislate.

Margaret Sanger

Margaret Sanger was one of the most influential and radical women of the early to mid–twentieth century. She was energetic, driven and let nothing stand in the way of her main passion–birth control. We need to take a quick look at this feminist icon and founder of what would become Planned Parenthood.

She was born Margaret Louisa Higgins in Corning, New York on September 14, 1879. She was the middle child of 11 in the home of Michael and Anne Higgins. Margaret was exposed at an early age to her father's heroes such as the "free–thinker" and anti–Christian Robert Ingersoll and Socialist Party organizer Eugene V. Debs. Ellen Chesler, in her biography of Margaret Sanger titled *Woman of Valor,* writes about how the issue of birth control was dealt with as far back as the early 1800s and how the attitudes in America changed over time.

> Until the 1870s, in fact, American birthrates declined steadily, and the commercial trade in contraception prospered, with remarkably little accountability or controversy, and with virtually no resistance from organized religion. The silent complicity of the nation's clergy reflected the ascendance of a liberal theology and utilitarian moral theory in the Protestant churches . . . . This new relativism admitted the possibility of reasonable differences of individual conscience and behavior in such matters as family size, and contraception was tolerated within marriage, because it promoted the desirable ends of smaller families, improved standards of living, and human happiness. . . . American Protestants made no official statements on birth control until into the twentieth century,

and even then, only over the protest of conservative and fundamentalist elements among them.[45]

At White Plains, New York, Margaret entered into training to become a nurse, and it was during this time that she met William Sanger. Margaret Higgins married William Sanger on August 18, 1902 after knowing each other for less than six months. William, who was a socialist and rebel against religious orthodoxy, introduced Margaret to many prominent socialists of the day.

In December 1914, Margaret met Henry Havelock Ellis (1859–1939) in England, and this meeting would have a profound influence on Margaret. Ellis enjoyed popular and intellectual prestige as one who wrote about sexual psychology, especially among the rising revolt against Victorian fear of unlicensed sexual behavior. His multivolume *Studies in the Psychology of Sex* discussed all manner of human sexual activities in a detached non–moral approach.

According to Chesler,

> Margaret was overwhelmed to have conversed with "the one man who has done more than anyone in this century toward giving women and men a clear and sane understanding of their sex lives and of all life." . . . It is virtually impossible to overestimate the impact Ellis would have on Margaret. She met him when he was at the height of his influence, having established an international professional reputation with the completion in 1910 of his path–breaking *Studies*, an iconoclastic, multivolume taxonomy of the range and diversity of human sexual expression.[46]

Chesler continues, observing that

> Ellis viewed sexuality as an inborn drive that could only become repressed or distorted by culture. He argued that more liberal social attitudes would necessarily breed contentment by setting men and women free from inherited taboos and letting them do whatever seemed natural and right.

---

45. Ellen Chesler, *Woman of Valor* (New York: Anchor Books, Doubleday, 1992), 38.
46. Chesler, 112.

This optimism was born of his faith, at least before World War I, in the educability and malleability of the human personality––a viewpoint that rejected both traditional Christian doctrines of man's fall from grace and Freud's secular reformulations on the subject. . . .[47]

Unlike Freud, Ellis did not demand that his patients change their habits, whatever they might be, only that they accept them. His standards for what ought to fit within a reasonable spectrum of normal sexual activity accommodated not only conventional practices, but many that were then commonly labeled perverse, and often still are. . . . His sexual theory was premised on a willingness to understand and tolerate sexual diversity as a dimension of what he simply called 'nature's balance.' He believed in complete sexual freedom, apart from society's interest in protecting innocent individuals from behavior to which they do not consent, though he never spelled out exactly how this enforcement should work.[48]

In 1914 Margaret published her magazine called *The Woman Rebel*, with the banner "No Gods, No Masters," so titled, according to Chesler, "because I believe that woman is enslaved by the world machine, by sex conventions, by motherhood and its present necessary childrearing, by wage–slavery, by middle–class morality, by customs, laws and superstitions. . . In a signed editorial she lamented the criminal sanctions then imposed on contraception, abortion, and illegitimacy and attacked the deeply rooted conventions of marriage and motherhood that governed the behavior of women and limited their opportunity. She called on working women to reject the standards and values of the upper classes . . . ."[49]

Margaret Sanger opened the first birth control clinic in America on October 16, 1916 in the Brownsville district of Brooklyn, New York. Within a few days, Margaret and her staff were arrested and the clinic closed. Margaret, ever the opportunist, made the most of this event and used the publicity to further her birth control cause. Margaret Sanger was a woman of action. While others wrote about or talked about "population control," she acted, and when she acted,

---

47. Ibid., 114.

48. Ibid., 114–115.

49. Ibid., 98.

she put into practice the ideas of her teacher and lover, Havelock Ellis. Ellis, like many famous intellectuals of his day (i.e., Henry Ford, H. G. Wells, Luther Burbank, Supreme Court Justice.

Oliver Wendell Holmes Jr.), believed in the idea of "eugenics." The term coined by Francis Galton (1822–1911) in 1883, means "well born." Galton was a cousin of Charles Darwin, and eugenics has as its basis the idea that men could take control of and breed a superior race while at the same time weeding out what were considered to be inferior races along with those that were thought to be "feeblemind-ed." Eugenics is the attempt by man to create man in his own image.

Edwin Black in his book *War against the Weak* says,

> In a flourish, Galton invented a term that would tantalize his contemporaries, inspire his disciples, obsess his later followers and eventually slash through the twentieth century like a sword. The finest and the fiendish would adopt the new term as their driving mantra. Families would be shattered, generations would be wiped away, whole peoples would be nearly erased––all in the name of Galton's word. The word he wrote on that small piece of paper was eugenics. . . . In theory, the master of any enforced eugenics program could play God––deciding who would be born and who would not. Indeed, the notion of constructing a brave new world by regimented reproduction has never receded.[50]

The eugenics movement did not envision the improvement of all races but only one––the white race––and for Margaret Sanger eugenics and birth control were simply two sides of the same coin. In perhaps her most famous book *The Pivot of Civilization,* published in 1922, she writes,

> The lack of balance between the birth rate of the "unfit" and the "fit," admittedly the greatest present menace to civilization, can never be rectified by the inauguration of a cradle competition between these two classes. The example of the inferior classes, the fertility of the feeble-minded, the mentally defective, the poverty–stricken, should not be held up for emulation to the mentally and physically fit, and therefore less fertile, parents of the educated and well–to–do

---

50. Edwin Black, *War against the Weak* (New York: Four Walls Eight Windows, 2003), 16.

classes. On the contrary, the most urgent problem today is how to limit and discourage the over–fertility of the mentally and physically defective. Possibly drastic and Spartan methods may be forced upon American society if it continues complacently to encourage the chance and chaotic breeding that has resulted from our stupid, cruel sentimentalism.[51]

Margaret hated large families. She wrote and lectured on this topic almost endlessly and placed the blame for most of the evils of war, disease, and poverty on large families. In chapter 5 of her book *Woman and the New Race*, published in 1920 titled "The Wickedness of Creating Large Families," she wrote, "Many, perhaps, will think it idle to go farther in demonstrating the immorality of large families, but since there is still an abundance of proof at hand, it may be offered for the sake of those who find difficulty in adjusting old–fashioned ideas to the facts. The most merciful thing that the large family does to one of its infant members is to kill it."[52]

Margaret surrounded herself with and courted many leaders in the eugenics movement including a man named Lothrop Stoddard. Stoddard (1883–1950) was a Ph.D. from Harvard whose book *The Rising Tide of Color against White World Supremacy*, published in 1920, so impressed Sanger that she asked him to join the board of directors of the American Birth Control League, which she founded. Stoddard retained that position for many years.

Sanger believed in denying reproductive rights to those considered "unfit" or "feeble–minded" who might become a "burden" on society:

> The emergency problem of segregation and sterilization must be faced immediately. Every feeble–minded girl or woman of the hereditary type, especially of the moron class, should be segregated during the reproductive period. Otherwise, she is almost certain to breed other defectives. The male defectives are no less dangerous. Segregation carried out for one or two generations would give us only partial control of the problem.

---

51. Margaret Sanger, *The Pivot of Civilization* (New York: Humanity Books, 2003), 64.

52. Margaret Sanger, *Women and the New Race* (New York: Truth Publishing Company, 1920), 63, 64.

> Moreover, when we realize that each feeble-minded person is a potential source of an endless progeny of defect, we prefer the policy of immediate sterilization, of making sure that parenthood is absolutely prohibited to the feeble-minded.[53]

Margaret was also critical of philanthropy and charity, which she deemed more hurtful than helpful because "it encourages the healthier and more normal sections of the world to shoulder the burden of unthinking and indiscriminate fecundity of others; which brings with it, as I think the reader must agree, a dead weight of human waste. Instead of decreasing and aiming to eliminate the stocks that are most detrimental to the future of the race and the world, it tends to render them to a menacing degree dominant."[54]

We will site just one example of how far the eugenics movement had penetrated society. In a high school biology textbook used throughout the country titled *A Civic Biology* by George William Hunter, published in 1914, said the following about the different races on the earth: "These are the Ethiopian or negro type, originating in Africa; the Malay or brown race from the islands of the Pacific; the American Indian; the Mongolian or yellow race, including the natives of China, Japan, and the Eskimo; and finally, the highest type of all, the Caucasians, represented by the civilized white inhabitants of Europe and America."[55] This was the biology textbook used at the time of the famous "Scopes Trial" in 1925.

You might be asking, why are we taking this trip down the dead-end street of eugenics and what in the world does it have to do with same-sex marriage? It is important to understand a little bit of the background and thinking of one of the most influential people for birth control and feminism of the early to mid-twentieth century and how her thinking helped to undermine natural marriage and values, which in turn helped pave the way for same-sex marriage by tearing down what God had set up. *As the original is effaced, the imitation takes its place.*

---

53. Sanger, *The Pivot of Civilization*, 122.

54. Ibid., 133.

55. George William Hunter, *A Civic Biology: Presented in Problems* (New York: American Book Company, 1914), 196.

Margaret Sanger used words like "bondage" and "slavery" to describe marriage and motherhood. Her dream was not just to help women "burdened" by large families, but to find a safe and effective contraceptive that would give women the same "freedom" from the consequences of casual sex that she felt men had. That dream began to be realized in 1951 when Margaret met biologist and researcher Gregory Pincus and soon after introduced him to Margaret's long time friend Katherine McCormick, whose husband Stanley, the owner of International Harvester Company, had just died, leaving Katherine more than $15 million. Pincus and other researchers made breakthroughs in research on contraceptives and were supported by funds from McCormick to the tune of 2 million dollars over the course of several years.

McCormick supplied the money, and Sanger supplied the propaganda. It can be said that two ageing feminists helped to bring into being a drug that changed the world and was the seed for the next step in the sexual revolution, and that drug, which obtained FDA approval in 1960, came to be known as . . . the Pill. Margaret Sanger died on September 6, 1966, a few days before her eighty–eighth birthday. She remains an important figure in the cultural drift away from natural marriage and is an icon of the feminist movement to this day. We hope that her face and ideas do not find renewed currency in our time since she was one of the twenty finalists in the selection process to replace Jackson on the $20.00 bill.

The Fifties have been called "the quiet decade," but from this short look at it, we can see that it was anything but quiet. There were many more influences on the culture than we have looked at here. As the nation prospered after World War II, more and more wants could be fulfilled in less and less time, and we moved from "I want" to "I deserve."

Traditional marriage was being attacked from several different angles but all headed in the same direction. Just as streams flow to make a river, so the Bible–believing church found itself swimming upstream against an ever stronger current. The seeds that were planted in that decade would grow in ways those living in it could not imagine. The assumptions of the past were challenged and things that were spoken of only in whispers were now talked about in public, and the general feeling began to grow (thanks to Kinsey) that everything people want to do in sexual matters is right and normal as long as no one does harm.

The Church, instead of just preaching AT the culture, needed to talk TO the culture and explain and defend the assumptions of the past to a new generation. The new generation, feeding on Kinsey, Hefner, Sanger and others, even though they did not know where they were headed or what the consequences would be, were sure of one thing; they did not want their father's way of doing things. "The old is mold, and the new is true," or as C. S. Lewis put it, they were guilty of "chronological snobbery," and in the coming decades as the distinction between the "progressive" mainline churches and the secular culture grew less and less and the assumptions of that culture were accepted more and more, it's no wonder that a new generation began to rejected natural marriage and sexual morality as God intended. As homosexual groups organized and moved into a vacated battlefield, they took a page from the civil rights and feminist movement to become a force that would accomplish things even they had never dreamed of.

Historian George M. Marsden sums up the issue facing Christianity in the "quiet decade" of the 1950s:

> Despite the prestige of mainline Protestantism in the 1950s, and despite all the public expressions of a broad piety, some of the most prominent and pervasive ideals of the mainstream culture were in deep conflict with traditionalist sorts of religious faith held by many Americans. To return to a theme mentioned before in other contexts: one of the major implications of the midcentury consensus critiques of conformity and affirmations of scientific outlooks and individual autonomy was that they seemed to promise a new moral order that would help to free individuals from traditional communities and moral strictures.
>
> Much of the religious revival was fostered in a myriad of traditionally religious communities–Catholic, fundamentalist, Pentecostal, holiness, Jewish, Eastern Orthodox, African American, Midwest Lutheran, Southern Baptist, and many more. Yet the message that one would hear most often from the cultural mainstream–as in the national media, public education, and academia–was that one would

be better off as an individual liberated from such community constraints. Individual self–development and self–fulfillment should be one's overriding goals.[56]

---

56. George M. Marsden, *The Twilight of the American Enlightenment* (New York: Basic Books, 2014), 151– 152.

2

The 1960s

A New Generation with a New Explanation

As the 1960s began, the seeds that had been planted in the 50s were starting to take root. Natural marriage continued to be eroded and attacked by those believing in the work of Kinsey, being entertained by the publishings of Hefner, and building on the ideas of Sanger. The 1960s could be called a "bridge" decade because it would lead from the more conformists times before it to the more non–conformists times after it. In 1960, the country would experience a culture shaking event with the FDA approval on May 11th of a drug that would become known as "The Pill." Like most scientific break-throughs, the Pill carried both a blessing and a curse. The blessing was that married couples could more easily space the time between having children or cease having children because of some medical issue. The curse was that one of the main physical consequences of sex outside of marriage, namely, the chance of pregnancy, was removed and the likelihood of discovery greatly reduced. Supreme Court decisions would give more evidence of Christianity's waning influence in the culture by ruling on June 25, 1962 that prayer in public schools was banned, and on June 17, 1963 and that Bible reading was also banned in public schools.

The 1960s opened up with the election of a young President who proclaimed "the torch has been passed to a new generation" and that generation would see changes and assumptions challenged like no other generation had seen before.

The 60s was the beginning of what came to be known as "The Sexual Revolution" with the fuse being lit in the 50s and sending that rocket up in the 60s with the real explosion taking place in the 70s, coming back down to the real world in the 80s. The 60s have often been called the decade of "Sex, Drugs and Rock & Roll," and while everyone was not buying into the "revolution," it cannot be denied that a large part of the culture, especially those between 15 and 25 years old, were being influenced by what they heard and saw in magazines, in newspapers, in movies, in art, in fashion, on radio, and on television. An atmosphere of permissiveness and rebellion was in the wind against all that had been given to this generation from the generation before it, and even though the majority of people still held many of the beliefs of the past, what came into the living rooms of America via television, radio, and other means night after night was that challenges to the "establishment" were everywhere. The Vietnam War like no war before it was brought into our living rooms night after night, dividing the country with no seeming end in sight.

Traditional boundaries were being pushed, taboos broken, and those born at the end of World War II were entering colleges and universities and being told by "learned" professors, "Now that you are away from mommy and daddy, let me tell you how the world really is." Even years later when the sandals were gone, the shower taken, and the hair cut obtained, for most, the permissive attitude would remain. The 60s was a time of fading morality and the coming of the era of "I got my rights." It was the decade of the rise of radical feminism, and in its last year, an event took place that would be a turning point of the homosexual movement.

In addition to radical feminism and a more organized homosexual movement, another influence on the culture and especially the young was music. It has been known for centuries that music has the ability bypass the rational mind and appeal directly to the emotions in ways that are not clearly understood even to this day. The words carried on a catchy tune convey ideas and attitudes of the musician that will give his or her philosophy to the listener without any need of rational argument. The difference between the popular music of the 40s and 50s and music in the 60s and beyond is the difference between mood and message.

On August 15–18, 1969 on a dairy farm in Bethel, New York, a defining event of the counterculture generation took place. Nearly half–a–million people came to listen to many of the most popular artists of the time. The festival would be known as WOODSTOCK, and through the music and the film, it would influence vast numbers of the younger generation. The message that poured forth in the 60s was "freedom of sexual expression," "freedom of the use of drugs," "freedom to openly attack authority," and "freedom to disregard the traditions and morality of society." It was this power to persuade that the Scottish politician Andrew Fletcher (1655–1716) wrote about when he said, "Let me make the songs of a nation, and I care not who makes the laws."

As powerful as music is, there is an even more powerful way to convey a message to millions of people: the movies. When people sit in a darkened room and watch the images on the screen and hear the sound all around them, it can and often does have a definite impact on people, and when you combine that with the impact of popular music, you get a kind of one––two punch for whatever ideas the artists want to impart. It becomes part of the "atmosphere" we breathe and the culture in which we live. Think about it; for an hour and a half or two hours you are receiving whatever message, idea, or philosophy those who make the movie wish to convey.

The church was facing not only pressure from the outside, but also from the inside. Young people were leaving the church in greater numbers as reported by Hugh McLeod in his book *The Religious Crisis of the 1960s*. "The University of Michigan, which asked new students about their religious affiliation, found that the proportion claiming an affiliation had risen from 68 per cent in 1924 to 78 per cent in 1952–5––before dropping very fast to 40 per cent in 1968."[1]

One of the major influences that came about in the 60s was what has been called "second wave" feminism. The start of this "second wave" has most often been attributed to the publication of *The Feminine Mystique,* by Betty Friedan, in 1963.

Born Betty Goldstein on February 4, 1921, in Peoria, Illinois, where she lived for the first seventeen–and–a–half years with her father Harry, her mother Miriam, younger sister Amy, and brother Harry Jr. As early as high school, Betty showed interest in some of the political issues of the day, as biographer Daniel Horowitz says in his

---

1. Hugh McLeod, *The Religious Crisis of the 1960s* (Oxford: Oxford University Press, 2007), 36.

book *Betty Friedan and the Making of the Feminist Mystique.* "There is also some evidence of Betty's awareness during her last years in high school of conflict between workers and capitalists. Betty castigated boys who with a "childish spirit" would "imitate factory workers" by staging " 'sit–down' strikes on girls' front porches. . . . ' Now,' she remarked humorously, 'somebody ought to imitate the militia.' While still in high school, she drafted an outline for a play about a strike at a mill, in which, after the bosses ignored the pickets, scabs and pickets fought, prompting the police to enter the fray."[2]

Betty entered Smith College, which is located in Northampton, Massachusetts in 1938. Her time at Smith transformed her "from a provincial outsider and largely apolitical rebel into an advocate of trade unions as the herald of a progressive social vision, a student exposed to feminist concerns, and a fierce questioner of the social privilege of her wealthy peers."[3]

"At least from 1940 until 1953 she inhabited a world where Communists and their sympathizers held influential positions, where she witnessed redbaiting, and where she encountered the ideology of American Communists, especially in their Popular Front appeals."[4] In 1946, she met Carl Friedman, (who would drop the "m" from his name), and nine months later they would be married in a civil ceremony. Some months later, for the sake of Carl's mother, they had a Jewish ceremony in Boston.

Before publishing *The Feminine Mystique* in 1963, Betty Friedan had an extensive background and exposure to radical thought and teaching, which was not evident in the book itself. However, she did compare the life of the American suburban housewife to living in a "comfortable concentration camp" and that "they have become dependent, passive, childlike; they have given up their adult frame of reference to live at the lower human level of food and things."[5]

---

2. Daniel Horowitz, *Betty Friedan and the Making of the Feminist Mystique* (Amherst: University of Massachusetts Press, 2000), 29.

3. Ibid., 33.

4. Ibid., 133.

5. Betty Friedan, *The Feminist Mystique* (New York: W.W. Norton and Company, 1963), 369.

The book was met with lavish praise from the media and the left. Given the endorsements she received, it is interesting to note that in her discussion of sexuality, "She hinted at the dangers of lesbianism when she discussed the sexual role models she had known in Peoria and at Smith. She was concerned that some mothers' misdirected sexual energies turned boys into homosexuals. She warned that for an increasing number of sons, the consequences of the feminine mystique was that 'parasitical' mothers would cause homosexuality to spread 'like a murky smog over the American scene'"[6]

Betty Friedan was a co-founder and first president of NOW (National Organization for Women) which announced its formation on November 21, 1966. "As an Old Leftist and sometimes new liberal, Friedan felt that sexual matters were private. Wanting a broad-based movement that would appeal to what she called mainstream, she feared that linking feminism and lesbianism would diminish the support of the kind of people she had grown up with in Peoria and then, in writing her book, had come to feel she both understood and spoke for. Consequently, she had insisted on excluding lesbian issues from NOW's agenda."[7]

In her autobiography, *Life so Far,* Friedan states that in 1977 at the National Women's Conference she supported a lesbian rights resolution so as to stop any debate about the issue and move on to what she thought were more important things. Although Betty Friedan grew up in a Jewish home, she was for most of her life an agnostic. In 1973, she signed the Humanist Manifesto II, and in 1975 she was named "Humanist of the Year" by the American Humanist Association. Betty Friedan died on February 4, 2006 at the age of 85 of congestive heart failure.

The Feminine Mystique is, by most accounts a culture shaping book, but in all the praise and fanfare that came with it, and the other feminist books that followed, what must not be forgotten is that the main target of most of them was not men but that of the housewife. Author F. Carolyn Graglia, in her book *Domestic Tranquility,* writes,

---

6. Horowitz, 204.

7. Ibid., 231, 232.

As one feminist baldly put it when discussing social security, the law should not make it psychologically comfortable to be a housewife because this will impede feminist goals. Whatever subsequent apologist might argue to mitigate feminism's excesses, status degradation of the housewife has been the purpose of its attack. Far from being the enemy, it was men that feminists admired––at least in the public sphere. The enemy is the housewife who contentedly lives a different life from the male role–models feminists seek to emulate. Tracking Friedan's path, the women's movement set out to undermine the self–esteem and contentment of a woman at home and to diminish her worth in men's eyes.[8]

Graglia further explains, "Feminist success in reshaping social attitudes has been facilitated by our media's eagerness to adopt and propagate the feminist perspective and by feminism's ability to piggyback on the black civil rights movement by portraying women as victims."[9]

To be sure, there are feminists who are anti–male and question the need for the very existence of men, but they are by and large on the fringe left and do not represent the majority of those in the feminists movement. It is interesting to note, that the "Playboy" attitude towards sex and relationships and feminist attitudes about marriage and home life, attack the same thing, namely, the traditional moral standards upon which sex, relationships, marriage, and home life were built. The culture was shifting as TV, movies, magazines and media diminished, dismissed, and derided the moral standards of past generations.

The homosexual community was becoming more organized, more outspoken, than ever before. The Mattachine Society was growing, but many of the younger homosexuals were increasingly frustrated with the old guard's approach of "play it cool." In the mid–sixties, there were beginning to be picketers, and various protests for homosexual "rights" in cities across the country, which brought a new voice and visibility to what most people never even thought of, namely, a homosexual community. Taking a page from the civil

---

8. F. Carolyn Graglia, *Domestic Tranquility: A Brief against Feminism* (Dallas: Spence Publishing Company, 1998), 121.

9. Ibid., 12.

rights protests of that time, homosexuals were putting a face and name to what had before been spoken of only in whispers just a decade before.

The churches were also facing challenges not only from the outside, but from inside as well. Liberal theologians and professors were teaching new "modern" understandings of the Bible, God, Christ, man and woman, sex, love, and a host of doctrines and teachings against what the church had understood for centuries. Church attendance was on the decline especially among young people as many felt the teachings were irrelevant and not in touch with the changing times or with the explosion of alternatives to Christianity. With the culture changing all around them, believers felt the pressure between what they said on Sunday and what they did Monday to Saturday, between their belief and their practice. In 1968, Troy Perry began the Metropolitan Community Church, which would become the largest church whose main mission was to reach out to the homosexual community. It has grown to more than 46,000 members, with 300 congregations in 22 countries. Troy Perry, was born in Florida on July 27, 1940 into a home with a Baptist background. By the age of fifteen, young Troy was licensed to preach by a local Baptist church. Troy's early life was not pleasant. His father was killed in a car crash following a police chase when Troy was twelve. His mother remarried, but the step–father had a drinking problem and was physically abusive to Troy, his mother, and his four brothers.

Troy became involved with the Cleveland, Tennessee based Church of God, where he met Pearl, the daughter of a Church of God pastor whom he married even though he still had sexual feelings for men. Troy was not faithful to his wife and had multiple encounters with men. When he could no longer stand to live a lie, he went to see the district overseer and told him he was homosexual. The bishop told Troy's wife and told Troy to leave the denomination because he was homosexual. Shortly after this, his wife and two sons left him. Perry has been given various awards and honors such as honorary doctorates and humanitarian awards from activist's organizations and continues to work for homosexual "rights."

Another revolution took place in 1969. It has been called "the silent revolution" because not much was said about it at the time it happened. That silent revolution was another name for No–Fault

Divorce. The first country to use no-fault divorce was communist Russia right after the Russian revolution of 1917. The state took over all marriages, which had been a function of the churches. In the United States, the first state to adopt no-fault divorce was California, with the Family Law Act of 1969, signed on September 4, 1969, and other states soon followed.

The divorce rate did spike up right after the law was passed, then leveled off, and in recent times the rate has been in decline, which makes sense since fewer people are getting married and have opted instead just to live together. The law had an unintended consequence, which was the undermining of marriage by making divorce quick and easy with neither person having to go through the painful process of proving a wrong. It was almost like dating again, only you had more than just a skate board or pompoms.[10]

Stonewall

To say that homosexual political activities only began after Stonewall, would be as wrong as saying that U.S. history began only after the Alamo. But, as we shall see, that activity would never be the same *after* it.

The Stonewall Inn was the name of a bar in the Greenwich Village area of New York City that saw a series of violent protests and demonstrations that began on June 28, 1969 and continued on and off for about six days. The Stonewall Inn was a mob owned bar, which was not unusual since the mob owned many bars in New York City. Greenwich Village or just "the Village" as it was known, had a long history of attracting those with different lifestyles, as David Carter points out in his book *Stonewall, The Riots That Sparked the Gay Revolution,* "It was the Village's reputation for unconventional lifestyles that first attracted gay people to the area around the turn of the century, as they sensed that a place known for wide tolerance might even accept sexual nonconformists."[11] Carter adds, "The club was only a short city block and a half from Greenwich Avenue, the premier cruising ground for gay men in New York City in the 1960s.

10. For more on the impact of no-fault divorce, see Douglas W. Allen, "Economic Assessment of Same-Sex Marriage Laws," *Harvard Journal of Law & Public Policy*, 29, no. 3 (June 22, 2006): 966–971.

11. David Carter, *Stonewall* (New York: St. Martin's Press, 2004), 7.

Moreover, the new bar was located the same distance from what these men called The Corner, the intersection of Greenwich Avenue and Christopher Street, the most popular meeting place for gay men on all of Greenwich Avenue. The bar could not possibly have been more centrally located."[12]

In the early morning hours of June 28, the police made a raid on the bar for "Operating without a liquor license." It was not unusual for a homosexual bar to be raided in those days, but this time the patrons said, NO! "The first hostile act outside the club occurred when a police officer shoved one of the transvestites, who turned and smacked the officer over the head with her purse. The cop clubbed her, and a wave of anger passed through the crowd, which immediately showered the police with boos and catcalls, followed by a cry to turn the paddy wagon over."[13] The result of the riot was to galvanize homosexual groups and to make Stonewall a rallying cry for their cause. Soon after Stonewall, two homosexual action groups were formed, the Gay Liberation Front (GLF) and later the Gay Activists Alliance (GAA). These groups were more militant, energized, and determined to change minds in their quest for homosexual rights with a more bold "in your face" approach. They began to get press coverage like never before.

The "Gay Pride Parades" held in many major cities across the country are a direct result and remembrance of Stonewall. David Carter puts Stonewall into context: "Finally, that the Stonewall Riots occurred during a period of great social change and unrest--the civil rights and antiwar movements in particular--has to be added to the list of factors that caused the riots. The sixties was a time so open that even society's basic beliefs about sex, gender, and sexuality were being questioned on multiple fronts; by the reborn movement for women's rights, the sexual revolution, and androgynous styles in fashion. Challenging bedrock belief's about sex and gender led to questioning assumptions about sexual orientation."[14]

The sixties was a decade like no other, and multiple volumes have been written about it. In that decade we witnessed the violence

---

12. Ibid., 11.

13. Ibid., 148.

14. Ibid., 259.

to the marchers in Selma, Alabama, the assassination of President John Kennedy, and later his brother Robert Kennedy, the killing of Martin Luther King Jr., the construction of the Berlin wall, and ever increasing shopping malls. Men would land upon the moon, and missiles in Cuba might end us all soon. We had massive protest marches against the war in Vietnam, the explosion of drug use, the decline of mainline churches, the introduction of transcendental meditation, the increase of sexually explicit material in magazines and movies. All of these and more were as James T. Patterson notes in his book, *Eve of Destruction*, "Dramatic changes in sexual behavior and family life--more demands for sexual freedom, more premarital sex, more cohabitation, more fatherless children, more divorce--began to shake American society and culture in ways that could scarcely have been imagined before 1965."[15]

Some who were involved in those culture changing times had definite goals in mind. Dr. Timothy Leary, the "guru" of LSD, in one of his more lucid moments wrote in the 80s,

> Everything we did in the 1960s was designed to fission, to weaken faith in and conformity to the 1950s social order. Our precise surgical target was the Judeo–Christian power monolith, which has imposed a guilty, inhibited, grim, anti–body, anti–life repression on Western civilization. Our assignment was to topple this prudish judgmental civilization. And it worked! For the first time in 20 centuries, the good old basic paganism got everybody moving again. White people actually started to move their hips, let the Marine crewcuts grow long, adorn themselves erotically in Dionysian revels, tune into nature. The ancient Celtic–pagan spirit began to sweep through the land of Eisenhower and J. Edgar Hoover. Membership in organized churches began to plummet. Hedonism always the movement of individuals managing their own rewards and pleasures ran rampant. . . . Millions of Americans writing their own Declarations of Independence: My life, my liberty, my pursuit of happiness.[16]

---

15. James T. Patterson, *Eve of Destruction: How 1965 Transformed America* (New York: Basic Books, 2014), 246.

16. McLeod, 131.

By the time men had walked upon the moon, our culture had taken one giant leap away from the moral behavior of the decade before. What was done in secret when Kinsey wrote his books would soon be paraded down the streets of cities all around the country. With these things in place, as we will see in the next decade, the incredible gains made by homosexuals to change the minds, hearts, and laws of the country.

3

The 1970s

Party Like There's No Tomorrow

The 1970s would witness some of the greatest gains of the homosexual rights movement in America. The party was on!! It was a time of shag carpets, bell–bottom pants, pastel leisure suits, platform shoes, and disco. The 70s would also witness a gas embargo, the resignation of a President, and we would be shocked to learn that Elvis had left the planet. Just to give only the bare facts, a short lived fad appeared called "streaking," which involved running in public places or events wearing only a smile (and maybe a pair of tennis shoes). It passed from the scene and was the butt of many jokes. The sexual revolution was at full speed ahead with the porn industry seeing explosive growth and the culture at large becoming more tolerant of all types of sexual expression.

By most accounts, San Francisco is the birthplace of almost the entire porn industry in the United States. What started out as nothing more than amateur home movies done in a garage or vacant house would grow into a multi–billion dollar business affecting the lives of millions of people far beyond the dingy theaters in which they were shown. The Feminist movement became more radical and vocal than just a decade before, and now lesbians were joining the ranks and adding their voices for "equality" and an end to male "domination."

On May 4, 1970 the country witnessed an event that would shake the confidence of many about government and its authority. On the campus of Kent State University, in Kent, Ohio, about 2,000 students were protesting the expansion of the war in Vietnam, when about 77 armed National Guardsmen arrived on campus to disperse the protesters. During the confusion, the Guardsmen opened fire on the un-armed crowd, resulting in the death of 4 students and the wounding of 9 others. An investigation never determined why the Guardsmen fired on the protesters.

The first "Gay Liberation Day March" would be held on June 28, 1970 in New York City. The march involved about two hundred marchers, and was done as a remembrance of the Stonewall riots the year before. On the same day, marches were held in Los Angeles and San Francisco. In 1972, San Francisco became one of the first cities in the country to pass a homosexual rights ordinance. Also in 1972, ABC aired a made–for–TV movie titled "That Certain Summer," which is the story is about a divorced, homosexual father coming out to his fourteen–year–old son. Television was more cautious than movies when it came to dealing with sex and sexual subjects. Television used more suggestion and humor because it could not narrow the audi-ence like movies theaters could and because television had to con-form to what network censors (following the FCC) would allow.

Another even more powerful influence that was moving away from traditional values and standards was . . . the movies. Hollywood, especially since the 1930s, was always pushing the envelope with regard to language, sex, and violence. To be sure, there was some backlash and protests made, but Hollywood and the media in general wrote it off as nothing more than coming from "conservative narrow minded Christians who are sexually repressed and have puritanical views."

In 1973, two monumental events took place that would have a tremendous impact on American society for decades to come. The first was the landmark Supreme Court decision in Roe v. Wade and the second was the removal of homosexuality from the American Psychiatric Association's Diagnostic and Statistical Manual of Psychiatric Disorders, which is the official list of mental diseases. First though, we need to look at two important Supreme Court cases that would pave the way for Roe v. Wade. The first is the Griswold v. Connecticut decision of June 7, 1965. The court ruled 7–2 against a Connecticut law, which said that you could not use any drug or medi-cal device for the purpose of preventing conception (this decision was aimed at married couples).

With this decision, the court cooked up the "right to privacy" even though it was known that no such right was stated in the Bill of Rights. In order to serve up this decision "dish," the court simply flavored it with a little 1st amendment, added a dash of the 5th, a pinch of the 9th, and a tablespoon of the 14th, making sure to drain off the natural law as many have a violent reaction when trying to swallow it. When it is served, it will have the odor of John Stewart Mills' "private morality," but that would soon pass. The next serving of this decision "dish" would come in 1972, where the court ruled 6–1 in the Eisenstadt v. Baird case that contraception must be made available to unmarried people as well, and again, the 9th and 14th amendments were used to flavor this decision.

On January 22, 1973, one of the most important and divisive Supreme Court decisions of the twentieth century, Roe v. Wade, was handed down. The case was filed in 1971 to the Supreme Court by Norma McCorvey (Jane Roe) against Dallas County District Attorney, Henry Wade for enforcing a Texas law that prohibited abortion except to save the mother's life. The 7–2 decision sited the same "reasoning" and language as the Griswold and Eisenstadt cases. When the court handed down its decision, it overturned the abortion laws in some 30 states. But, this time, many people were not going to swallow the "dish" the court served up and silently allow the murder of the unborn for any reason the mother desired. There were large marches and protests and even some law breaking over blocking abortion clinics by those opposed to the decision.

The decision has become a standard question for those seeking political office as to which side of the issue they stand on. In August 1995, Norma McCorvey (Jane Roe) announced that she was now pro–life and would work for the pro–life movement.

In his excellent book, *The Supreme Court and Religion in American Life,* Vol. 2, author James Hitchcock sums up the impact the "Roe decision" made and its implications:

> Perhaps beginning with Roe v. Wade (1973), the decision that announced a constitutional right to abortion, there has occurred a "Third Disestablishment," which is the separation of law from traditional moral principles, a result that perhaps flowed inevitably from the Second Disestablishment, since moral principles once thought of as common to all are now

seen as merely "sectarian." Liberal Protestantism, which in the nineteenth century sought to replace piety by morality, by the 1960s found that there was no longer an accepted moral consensus. Like religion, morality had come to be regarded as essentially irrational. On this basis the social influence of conservative churches can be restricted, in part because there is to be no right to inhibit, on religious grounds, whatever subjective conceptions of the good life individuals might have.

Official government neutrality in practice becomes an "ideology of non–orthodoxy," and churches that advocate absolute moral standards are considered dangerous, religion not considered to have any role in maintaining personal liberty.[1]

American Psychiatry Gets an Offer They Can't Refuse

In December 1973, one of the major milestones in the homosexual rights movement occurred when the American Psychiatric Association voted to remove homosexuality from the list of mental disorders in the Diagnostic and Statistical Manual of Psychiatric Disorders (DSM–II). The story of how and why this came about is an interesting one that involves activism, politics, harassment, and bullying. The homosexual movement after Stonewall adopted a more activist and militant stance after seeing the success of the civil rights and feminist movements. They realized that it would be more difficult to demand tolerance and equality if they were officially labeled as having a mental disorder by the APA.

Ronald Bayer in his 1987 book, *Homosexuality and American Psychiatry*, writes, "Only gradually did those with the audacity to identify themselves as homosexuals begin to challenge the primacy of heterosexual standards. By the late 1960s the tentative thrusts of the early leaders of the movement had become a full–blown attack, with homosexuality presented as an "alternative life style" worthy of

---

1. James Hitchcock, *The Supreme Court and Religion in American Life* (Princeton: Princeton University Press, 2004), 2:137.

social acceptance on par with heterosexuality. Mere tolerance was no longer the goal; the demand was for social legitimation."[2]

Bayer states in the introduction to the book his stand on the issue:

> This book presents a political analysis of the psychiatric battle over homosexuality. Such an analysis is not, however, external to the "real issue" of whether homosexuality represents a psychiatric disorder. To assume that there is an answer to this question that is not ultimately political is to assume that it is possible to determine, with the appropriate scientific methodology, whether homosexuality is a disease given in nature. I do not accept that assumption, seeing in it a mistaken view of the problem. The status of homosexuality is a political question, representing a historically rooted, socially determined choice regarding the ends of human sexuality. It requires a political analysis.[3]

So, we see with Bayer that the purpose of human sexuality is a "socially determined choice." In their decision to remove homosexuality from the DSM–II, the APA relied on the work of sex researchers like Alfred Kinsey, Evelyn Hooker, and others. One of the tricky lines in their research was the reciprocal relationship between those doing the studying and those who were being studied. Bayer explains,

> More important, however, was the new wave of homosexual activism. Between the homophile movement and the critical line of research there developed a complex, reciprocal relationship. The existence of the movement had a subtle but nonetheless crucial impact upon the social context within which such research was undertaken. The findings of the research were, in turn, vitally important to the early leaders of the homophile movement, encouraging them in their early, tentative efforts at organizational and ideological development. Finally, it was the struggle for homosexual rights that ultimately transformed this research from an interesting methodological critique of psychiatric theory

---

2. Ronald Bayer, *Homosexuality and American Psychiatry* (Princeton: Princeton University Press, 1987), 8.

3. Ibid., 4–5.

and practice into a weapon in the assault on the power of psychiatry.[4]

⏤ Evelyn Hooker (September 2, 1907–November 18, 1996) was one of the most influential and important sex researchers of the twentieth century. Like Kinsey, her importance to the homosexual movement is difficult to overstate. Her most noted work was published in 1957. Bayer states, "Hooker denied the centrality of psychodynamic factors. Instead she emphasized the pressures on the homosexual world, pressures that could be traced to heterosexual hostility. With fear of public exposure and humiliation dominating the homosexual's life, it was extraordinarily difficult for relationships to last. What was a source of security for the heterosexual was a source of risk for the homosexual."[5]

Bayer continues, "As important as her findings was her willingness to share them with the ordinary men and women of the homophile movement. Her collaborative relationship with the Mattachine Society went beyond using it as a source of informants. She spoke to its members, published in its Review, attended its meetings, and received its honors. She became not only a source of ideological support, but an active participant in the homosexual struggle."[6] Hooker, even published articles in the homosexual newspaper "The Advocate." She had close associations with homosexuals, many of whom were her friends. The University of Chicago even opened the Evelyn Hooker Center for Gay and Lesbian Studies. To say the least, her objectivity could be called into question on this issue.

The growing militant homosexual groups in the early 70s, looked for opportunities to shut down any presentation or discussion that was not favorable to the homosexual cause. "

Thus the American Psychiatric Association became the target of homosexual attack in 1970, when gay activists in San Francisco saw in the presence of the APA convention in their city yet one more opportunity to challenge the psychiatric profession. That decision was no different from the many others that had preceded earlier challenges to psychiatry. It

---

4. Ibid., 42.

5. Ibid., 52.

6. Ibid., 53.

was the status of the Association that gave the decision its significance. With the APA designated as a target, gay groups throughout the country could direct their wrath against a common organizational foe . . . gay groups in alliance with feminist engaged in the first systematic effort to disrupt the annual meetings of the American Psychiatric Association.[7]

The sedate and professional APA members were unprepared and unable to counter the disruptive, militant, loud, and angry homosexual activists as Bayer makes plain:

> The planned disruption occurred on May 3, when gay and antiwar activists stormed into the prestigious Convocation of Fellows. During the ensuing uproar, Kameny grabbed a microphone and denounced the right of psychiatrists to discuss the question of homosexuality. Borrowing from the language of the antiwar movement, he declared, "Psychiatry is the enemy incarnate. Psychiatry has waged a relentless war of extermination against us. You may take this as a declaration of war against you." Fist–shaking psychiatrists, infuriated by the invaders, compared their tactics to that of Nazi storm troopers.[8]

Their tactic worked; the psychiatrists gave in. "The long–sought–for goal of homosexuals speaking about themselves to psychiatrists in a form that rejected the assumption of psychopathology had been attained. To those who had so boldly challenged the professional authority of psychiatry it was clear that only the threat of disorder or even violence had been able to create the conditions out of which such a dialogue could occur. That lesson would not be forgotten."[9] "Frank Kameny noted with discernible pleasure that for the first time at these meetings the only views on homosexuality heard in public forums were those that could be considered friendly. The impact of the increasing power of gay groups had been revealed in the successful intimidation of old enemies."[10] "And so, eleven months after their first presentation before the Nomenclature Committee, homosexual activists had succeeded in achieving their long–sought goal. If con-

---

7. Ibid., 102.

8. Ibid., 105.

9. Ibid., 104.

10. Ibid., 111.

tinued distrust prevented the perception of psychiatry as a true ally in their struggle, at least it had been neutralized. What Frank Kameny had been referring to for years as the major ideological prop of society's antihomosexual bias had been shattered."[11]

The removal of homosexuality from the DSM–II was not the result of and had nothing to with some new data that had just been discovered, but was the result of good old–fashioned bullying, intimidation, disruption, and shouting down the opposition, you know, the way most new scientific discoveries are made. The removal was aided by sympathetic members of the ADA thich included homosexual psychiatrists.

Ronald Bayer, in the Afterword to the 1987 edition of his book, says, "Though there are exceptions, most notably Judd Marmor, most psychoanalysts viewed the 1973 decision to delete homosexuality from DSM–II as a misguided, even tragic capitulation to extra-scientific pressure."[12] The ripple effects of this were many as Dudley Clendinen and Adam Nagourney note in their book, *Out for Good*, "The APA's decision and the National Gay Task Force's aggressive use of it in its lobbying efforts, would have a sweeping cumulative effect in the next few years as dozens of other national professional and church organizations voted on their own resolutions of nondiscrimination, and as gay people sought to overturn sodomy laws and legal discrimination against homosexuals."[13] After the APA's decision, one by one in domino fashion, the various professional organizations fell into lock–step with the "new understanding" they had received. If anyone should go outside the bounds and question the "new knowledge," you can be sure the whistle will blow, the spot lights turned on, and the attack dogs loosed.

Many churches would find themselves on the receiving end of the same type of tactics. Pro–homosexual groups would picket churches that announced a sermon or lecture on the Bible and homosexuality, or they would have people sitting with duct tape over their mouths, or dressed in ways to try to draw attention to themselves in hopes of

---

11. Ibid., 137, 138.

12. Ibid., 208.

13. Dudley Clendinen and Adam Nagourney, *Out for Good* (New York: Simon and Schuster, 1999), 216.

distracting from the message. Many churches decided to talk around the issue of homosexuality instead of speaking directly to the issue for fear of the possible negative reactions that might follow.

The ERA Almost Takes the Day

Shortly after the ratification of the nineteenth amendment in 1920, which gave women the right to vote, the Equal Rights Amendment was introduced in Congress in 1923. It was felt by some feminists that the right to vote did not give the level of equality that these women felt they needed. Over the next five decades the ERA was in and out of Congress until 1972, when Congress passed and sent to the states for actual ratification the "Equal Rights Amendment." This had been a goal of the feminist movement for years and most commentators felt it would be ratified quickly. In 1972, 22 states voted for ratification; in 1973, 8 states; in 1974, 3 states; in 1975, 1 state; and in 1977, 1 state. The deadline for ratification was 1979, and by then the amendment was 3 states short of the 38 needed for ratification. The 95th Congress passed a resolution to extend the deadline to June 30, 1982.

Five states that voted for ratification rescinded their vote, and no states were added or rescinded after 1977. The amendment died after failing to get the necessary votes. The issues raised by the amendment were on the front pages of newspapers and magazines, to the back porches of homes, from Congress to colleges, and from offices to living rooms all across the country.

The opposition to the ERA was lead by Phyllis Schlafly (1924–2016) ,who started the "stop era" organization. She was a powerful, dynamic speaker who had excellent organizational skills and is credited by many as the single most effective force at stopping the ratification of the amendment. She spoke all over the country and argued that if the amendment passed, women could be subject to being drafted by the military. Her most effective argument was that the ERA would begin the destruction of traditional gender roles.

Keeping Their Eye on the Pies

One of the most dramatic confrontations in the homosexual movement occurred, in January 1977, when Miami–Dade county commissioners passed by a 5–3 vote an ordinance against discrimination in housing and employment based on "sexual orientation." Many residents were outraged and wanted to reverse the decision. One of those residents was Anita Bryant. She was a former Miss Oklahoma (1958) and was second runner–up in the 1959 Miss America pageant.

She was *Good Housekeeping* magazine's "Most Admired Woman in America," as well as the spokesperson for the Florida Citrus Commission. She did numerous commercials for several large companies like Coca Cola, as well as making records. Her campaign in June 1977, to repeal the Miami–Dade ordinance was successful by a margin of 69 to 31 percent. After her victory in Florida, she vowed to take the fight to several other cities across the country and was again successful. This was the first major setback for the homosexual movement since Stonewall, and they were shocked.

Anita Bryant was now in their crosshairs. The homosexual rights group organized a boycott of Florida orange juice and harassed and heckled Anita wherever she went. On October 14, 1977 on a trip to Des Monies, Iowa, an event took place that would change her life.

> When she received keys to the city in Des Moines, Thom Higgins and Patrick Schwartz, members of Jack Baker's pie–throwing guerrilla brigade from Minneapolis, were waiting in ambush. Hit with a strawberry rhubarb pie, Bryant dropped to her knees to pray and to weep. . . . Support came from unlikely sources. "She has been threatened with violence, hit in the face with a pie, and called unprintable names. Her views, we think, are benighted," the *New York Times* said in an editorial, "but she has a right to express them without suffering abuse." Even old–line liberals came to her defense. "This is exactly what happened during the McCarthy years," Ira Glasser, the executive director of the New York Civil Liberties Union, told Nat Hentoff, the Village Voice columnist. Hentoff agreed, "This time," he wrote, "the victim is Anita Bryant."[14]

Anita lost her endorsements and was removed as spokesperson for the Florida Citrus Commission. Her marriage to Bob Green ended in divorce in 1980. The tactics learned during the APA struggle were applied to Anita Bryant and many others who would voice opposition to homosexuality.

---

14. Ibid., 328, 329.

In 1977, the United Church of Christ became the first mainline liberal church to ordain an openly homosexual woman. This would be but the first of many such moves on the part of liberal churches to attract homosexuals with a "come as you are, God does not ask you to change how you live and love" attitude.

In 1978, Harvey Milk, who called himself the "Mayor of Castro Street" in San Francisco, was elected to a position on the city Board of Supervisors, becoming the first openly homosexual in an elected position in the history of the city. Dan White, who was more politically conservative, had also just been elected to the Board, but after serving only ten months in office became disenchanted with local politics.

> Dan White resigned his seat on the Board of Supervisors. He almost immediately changed his mind and asked Mayor Moscone to reinstate him, a request Harvey Milk opposed. With a different, more liberal supervisor in White's place, Milk could envision a progressive majority on the council. He gave Moscone an ultimatum: if he appointed Dan White he could forget the gay vote.

> November 27, the day Moscone was to announce his decision about White's seat, Dan White climbed into a side window of city hall, avoiding the metal detectors at the main doors. Carrying his .38–caliber police revolver in its holster, he went to see the mayor. When the two were alone in the mayor's private inner office, he drew the gun and shot Moscone twice in the chest and twice in the head. Then he moved quickly across the hall, closeted himself in a room with Harvey Milk and shot the man he so despised five times in all.[15]

Harvey Milk became a martyr of the homosexual cause and had a movie made of his life and death in 2008.

The 1970s was a decade that witnessed a tremendous cultural shift from many directions. The homosexual movement was out in full view and had flexed some surprising political muscle. they were on daytime television with talk show host Phil Donahue and his in–your–face approach to the subject. Mainline liberal church membership continued to decline, while never seeming to question the

---

15. Ibid., 403.

morality of homosexuality. Conservative evangelical and charismatic churches saw tremendous growth as people longed for more than "it doesn't matter what you believe, as long as you love Jesus" teachings. In 1976, Harold Lindsell published his book *Battle for the Bible*, which caused a firestorm by naming seminaries and professors who were teaching the view that the Bible contained errors.

In October 1978, some three hundred scholars, pastors, and laymen met in Chicago to form the International Conference on Biblical Inerrancy (ICBI), which served to call the church back to this important doctrine. Churches were growing with memberships into the multiple thousands. Men like Pat Robertson and Jerry Falwell were reaching millions through television and radio.

The 1970s were a time of both loss and gain for the church. It was a chance for the church to reach out to the homosexual community, like they never did before, thanks to their higher visibility, but, sadly for the most part, the church relied on politics and the law to do the "heavy lifting" by keeping them at a safe distance. The church relied too much on the "shared morality" that had been eroding over the previous twenty years. The challenge for the church was to change the methods without changing the message. In 1968, singer Ed Ames recorded a song with lyrics that should challenge every believer. The words are as powerful today as they were nearly 50 years ago:

> *Hallelujah! Hallelujah! Hallelujah!*
> *From the canyons of the mind,*
> *We wander on and stumble blindly*
> *Through the often–tangled maze*
> *Of starless nights and sunless days,*
> *While asking for some kind of clue*
> *Or road to lead us to the truth,*
> *But who will answer?*
> *Side by side two people stand,*
> *Together vowing, hand–in–hand*
> *That love's imbedded in their hearts,*
> *But soon and empty feeling starts*
> *To overwhelm their hollow lives,*
> *And when the seek the hows and whys,*
> *Who will answer?*
> *On a strange and distant hill,*

A young man's lying very still.
His arms will never hold his child,
Because a bullet running wild
Has struck him down. And now we cry,
"Dear God, oh, why, oh, why?"
But who will answer?
High upon a lonely ledge,
A figure teeters near the edge,
And jeering crowds collect below
To egg him on with, "Go, man, go!"
But who will ask what led him to
his private day of doom,
And who will answer?
[Chorus:]
If the soul is darkened
by a fear it cannot name,
If the mind is baffled
When the rules don't fit the game,
Who will answer? Who will answer? Who will answer?
Hallelujah! Hallelujah!, Hallelujah!
In the rooms of dark and shades,
The scent of sandalwood pervades,
The colored thoughts in muddled heads
Reclining in the rumpled beds
Of unmade dreams that can't come true,
And when we ask what we should do,
Who . . . Who will answer?
'Neath the spreading mushroom tree,
The world revolves in apathy
As overhead, a row of specks
Roars on, drowned out by discotheques,
And if a secret button's pressed
Because one man has been outguessed,
Who will answer?
Is our hope in walnut shells
Worn 'round the neck with temple bells,
Or deep within some cloistered walls
Where hooded figures pray in halls?
Or crumbled books on dusty shelves,

Or in our stars, or in ourselves,
Who will answer?
[Chorus]
If the soul is darkened
by a fear it cannot name,
If the mind is baffled
When the rules don't fit the game,
Who will answer? Who will answer? Who will answer?
Hallelujah! Hallelujah! Hallelujah!
(Lyrics by Davis / Aute)

Jesus Christ not only has the answer, but IS the answer: ". . . but whoever drinks of the water that I will give him will never be thirsty again. The water that I will give him will become in him a spring of water welling up to eternal life" John 4:14.

"Again Jesus spoke to them, saying, 'I am the light of the world. Whoever follows me will not walk in darkness, but will have the light of life'" John 8:12.

"I have come into the world as a light, so that whoever believes in me may not remain in darkness" John 12:46.

4

The 1980s

A Slight Turn to the Right

The 1980s was a decade of growth, consumption, and high expectation. Eighty–three million got to see who shot J. R., and a President is elected who was a movie star. E.T. finally gets to phone home, and the Pope is seriously wounded in Rome. Space shuttle Challenger launched towards the heavens and took into eternity all of the seven. Superman would splash across the screen, but the real superheroes are the U.S. hockey team. Televangelists cried to be forgiven, and many of their followers kept on believin'. The stock market would have a great fall, but not as great as the Berlin Wall. "Just say no" was started by Nancy Reagan, while AIDS would hit and leave the country shaken.

AIDS: The Party's Over

During the "sexplosion" of the late 70s, there began to be rumors of an illness that seemed to be affecting only homosexual men. The illness, which was first named Gay Related Immune Deficiency Disorder (GRID), was reported by the Centers for Disease Control and Prevention (CDC) in July 1981. Not long after the disease was discovered, biologist Bruce Voeller (May 12, 1934 – February 1994) a founder of the National Gay Task Force, coined the name, Acquired Immuno Deficiency Syndrome (AIDS) and lobbied to change the name of the new disease from GRID to AIDS. Bruce Voeller died at the age of 59 of AIDS related illness. According to the CDC's Morbidity and Mortality Weekly Report (MMWR) AIDS: the Early Years and CDC's Response, of October 7, 2011: "By the end of 1981,

... seventy–five percent of cases were reported from New York City or California, and all but one case were in men. Within 6 months, it was clear that a new, highly concentrated epidemic of life threatening illness was occurring in the United States."

In the early days of the disease, as the number of cases began to rapidly increase, concern turned to fear and fear into almost panic as it was not known how the infection was spread. What was known was that almost 80% of the cases involved were homosexual men and most of the rest involved IV drug users.

As the death toll mounted, the media began to report more and more on the AIDS crisis, and in typical media fashion, the less facts available, the more speculation occurred. The AIDS crisis also threatened to have a negative effect on all the homosexual "rights" victories of the 1970s as people began to rethink their views. In November 1985, a Gallup poll "found that 37 percent of those questioned had changed their opinion about homosexuals for the worse since the disease became widely publicized."[1]

Private Acts, Public Consequences

Because of the intimate nature in the way the HIV virus that caused AIDS was spread, it raised difficult issues between the privacy of individuals and public safety concerns about the spread of a life–threatening illness. This was especially true of the homosexual community because any involvement of the government or even medical profession was viewed with suspicion. Ronald Bayer, gives an example of this distrust:

> Michael Lynch wrote in the *Body Politic,* a Canadian gay journal, "Gays are once again allowing the medical profession to define, restrict, pathologize us." To follow the advice of physicians would involve a renunciation of "the power to determine our own identity," and would represent "a communal betrayal of gargantuan proportions" of gay liberation founded upon a "sexual brotherhood of promiscuity." Doubts about the scientific foundations, on the basis of which the cautionary advice was being proffered, inspired others. "I feel that what we are being advised to do

---

1. Dudley Clendinen and Adam Nagourney, *Out for Good* (New York: Simon and Schuster, 1999), 524.

involves all of the things I became gay to get away from. . . .
So we have a disease for which supposedly the cure is to go
back to all the styles that were preached at us in the first place.
It will take a lot more evidence before I'm about to do that."[2]

AIDS Has a Face

In the early days of the AIDS crisis, it was mostly the gaunt faces
and emaciated bodies of homosexual men with AIDS that were seen
in magazines or on the evening news. In 1985, the nameless faces we
saw on TV would have a face that was recognized all over the world
when a famous movie star announced he had AIDS. Rock Hudson
(November 17, 1925 – October 2, 1985) who was a leading man in
many movies during the 50s and 60s, as well as numerous television
appearances, was diagnosed with HIV on June 5, 1984. Hudson's homosexuality was the gossip of Hollywood for years, but for the most
part he was able to keep his off–screen life hidden. In July 1985 he
traveled to Paris, France, to receive treatments for his disease. When
he returned, he had to be carried on a stretcher off the plane he had
hired. On July 25th, in a press conference, surrounded by Hollywood
friends, it was confirmed that Hudson had AIDS. He passed away on
October 2, 1985 at his home in California just shy of his 60th birthday.

The death of a beloved movie star helped to raise awareness
of AIDS and helped in raising money for the search for a cure. On
the political front, homosexual rights ordinances were bringing together Roman Catholics, Evangelicals, and Charismatic conservative
Christians as well as Orthodox Jews who were opposed to homosexual rights and used the AIDS epidemic as a sword in their opposition to the ordinances. By the mid–eighties, many of the ordinances
seeking passage were toned down and appealed more to those in the
middle such that, "In all, by the start of 1985, three states, eleven
counties, forty–seven cities and towns, and the District of Columbia
had adopted some form of gay rights legislation."[3]

The arrival of AIDS both hurt and helped the homosexual "rights"
movement. It hurt because in fact it is a deadly disease that mostly af-

---

2. Ronald Bayer, *Private Acts, Social Consequences* (New Brunswick: Rutgers
University Press, 1991), 26.

3. Clendinen and Nagourney, 526.

fected the group of men having sex with men. According to the CDC (Centers for Disease Control and Prevention) in 2010, new HIV infections among men having sex with men was 29,800, an increase of 12% from 2008. "Although MSM [Men who have Sex with Men] represent about 4% of the male population in the United States, in 2010, MSM accounted for 78% of new HIV infections among males and 63% of all new infections. MSM accounted for 54% of all people living with HIV infection in 2011, the most recent year these data are available." Since the epidemic began, an estimated 311,087 MSM with an AIDS diagnosis have died, including an estimated 5,380 in 2012" (CDC, HIV in the United States: At A Glance).

Although no one in his right mind would ask for help by wishing for a disease like AIDS, nonetheless, it did help in motivating people who would never think of getting involved with homosexual people, to reach out to those suffering and dying with AIDS. It put the topic on the nightly news and made for a more receptive audience. No one who understands Jesus' words in Luke 10: 30–37 could see the work of that horrible disease and not feel sympathy and compassion for the suffering even though it came about most of the time by their own free will.

Fear of the disease and concern about its spread prompted some less than thoughtful ideas. "In June 1985, Jerry Falwell, president of the fundamentalist Moral Majority, called for involuntary manslaughter charges against 'AIDS carriers' who knowingly infected 'a non–sufferer' with a deadly disease resulting in his or her death."[4] William F. Buckley suggested that AIDS infected persons could be tattooed on the upper forearm for identification. There were various laws and statutes put forward but they were rarely enforced. "Nevertheless, they stood as a symbolic statement of societal condemnation. It was from such symbolic significance that efforts to criminalize sexual intercourse by individuals with AIDS derived their attraction."[5]

Even with some setbacks because of the AIDS crisis (bathhouses in several major cities had been closed down), the 1980s was still a positive decade for homosexual "rights." Some people claimed that AIDS was God's punishment for a homosexual lifestyle, but many

4. Bayer, 180–181.

5. Ibid., 181.

more began to have sympathy for them especially when the media portrayed homosexuals on the nightly news as "victims." It is interesting to note that as medical treatments for HIV have improved, the practice of risky sexual behavior has increased. There were many homosexuals who felt that giving up their sexual practices would be worse than the disease itself, and the fact that most of those who got AIDS did so by an act of free will *even after* it was known how the disease was spread. For some reason this fact has just seems to have faded into the background.

Conservative Christians Deliver a Right Cross

Most observers in the early 1980s would not have guessed that conservative Christians would organize and get involved in the political process on local, state, and national levels. Jerry Falwell (August 11, 1933 – May 15, 2007) founder and pastor of Thomas Road Baptist Church and Liberty University in Lynchburg, Virginia, did just that. Falwell co–founded the political organization called the Moral Majority in 1979 to organize as well as to energize Christians to vote for candidates that endorsed traditional moral values. The Moral Majority is credited with helping to elect Ronald Reagan in 1980 and 1984. Falwell has been called "the Moses who led evangelicals out of the wilderness of isolation," and together with televangelist Pat Robertson, they energized their viewers and made a powerful political force. Falwell was an outspoken critic of homosexual "rights" and worked with Anita Bryant to help overturn homosexual "rights" laws in cities across the country. Despite the anger and hatred directed at Falwell for his views on homosexuality, he never argued for making homosexuality a crime, and he argued against discrimination of homosexuals in housing and employment.

In October of 1999, a historic meeting took place in Falwell's Thomas Road Baptist Church, which brought together 200 members of Thomas Road and 200 of Mel White's organization, *Soulforce,* which promoted homosexual rights. Mel White had been a ghost writer for several evangelicals including Falwell, Pat Robertson, and Oliver North until he announced his homosexuality in 1991. An article for the *New York Times,* October 23, 1999, noted, "Mr. Falwell said he thought the gathering was significant for its occurring at all, for the fact that conservative evangelicals who believe homosexual activity a grave sin would break bread with gay men, lesbians and their supporters." Falwell and White hoped the meeting would help tone down the shrill voices directed at each side. In another *New York Times* article dated November 6, 1999, we read, "Mr. Falwell said flatly to the Lynchburg gathering, speaking of the potential fall-out of 'reckless and dangerous language.' He vowed that he and his staff would vigilantly examine their 'characterizations and criticisms of the homosexual community' to avoid any 'statements that can be construed as sanctioning hate or antagonism against homosexuals.'"

In an interview on February 15, 2000 for *Frontline* on *PBS*, Falwell was asked about changes in attitude towards homosexuality, and he stated that he was worried that the state of Vermont was on the edge of passing a same–sex marriage law. Then Falwell predicted, "Unless the Supreme Court surprises me, maybe ten years from now there'll be a 5–4 vote at least, saying it's okay. When that happens, we have a modern–day Sodom and Gomorrah. We have a corrupt society where the family is trashed and where everybody loses."[6] Well, it took fifteen years. Before same–sex "marriage" would become legal, the laws against sodomy would be struck down. In 1980, the New York State Court of Appeals would rule in a 5–2 decision against the State's anti–sodomy laws. The final legal move came in 2003 with the 6–3 decision of the United States Supreme Court in the case of Lawrence v. Texas, which made anti–sodomy laws unconstitutional.

The New Age Movement –– Feeling the Force Flow

The New Age Movement, which became extremely popular in the 1980s, was a western version of eastern philosophy and religion. It stands as a testament to the fact that most people need something, *anything* transcendent in their lives.

One of the reasons for its popularity is that the god (or gods) of the New Age is a "tame god" as C. S. Lewis puts it, "The Pantheist's God does nothing, demands nothing. He is there if you wish for Him, like a book on a shelf. He will not pursue you. There is no danger that at any time heaven and earth should flee away at His glance. . . . a formless life–force surging through us, a vast power which we can tap–best of all. But God Himself, alive, pulling at the other end of

---

6. Jerry Falwell, interviewed by *Frontline* on *PBS,* February 15, 2000.

the cord, perhaps approaching at an infinite speed, the hunter, king, husband–that is quite another matter."[7]

Much of it was introduced in the late 1950s but became more generally known through the 1960s, and 70s through the efforts of famous entertainers. One of the best examples of this is the Maharishi Mahesh Yogi (January 12, 1918 – February 5, 2008) who founded the "Transcendental Meditation Movement." Maharishi was made known in the West by being the "guru" to such groups as *The Beatles,* and *The Beach Boys.*

With the introduction of Transcendental Meditation, Yoga, channeling, crystals, mystical consciousness, etc., the emphasis for many people shifted from facts and knowledge to intuition and feelings. This influence is seen in the very popular *Star Wars* films where the hero *Luke Skywalker* is told to "stretch out with your feelings," "your eyes can deceive you, don't trust them," and "you must unlearn what you have learned." The relevance of this is that such a view, when practiced weakens the Christians stand on doctrine. It shifts the focus from what does the text say, to how do I feel about the text. Feelings then will become the standard for understanding the Scripture rather than knowing what the text says and letting it change their hearts.

Even *Newsweek* magazine noted the influence that films like *Star Wars* was having on people. "People can croak, 'Entertainment! Entertainment!' until they're blue in the face. The fact remains that films like . . . 'Star Wars' have become jerry–built substitutes for the great myths and rituals of belief, hope and redemption that cultures used to shape before mass secular society took over."[8] People were walking right past the church into the cinema and along with rockets and ray–guns were receiving spiritual messages. The director of *The Empire Strikes Back,* Irvin Kershner, was up–front about it. "I wanna introduce some Zen here because I don't want the kids to walk away just feeling that everything is shoot–em–up, but that there's also a

---

7. C. S. Lewis, *Miracles, Preliminary Study* (New York: Macmillian Publishing Co., 1977), chap. 11.

8. *Newsweek*, January 1, 1979, 50.

little something to think about here in terms of yourself and your surroundings."[9]

Weaving the Threads Together

We began this part of the book with the questions, how did this happen, how did we get here? With this very brief look at the decades and some of the major players involved in changing American attitudes about homosexuals and homosexuality, we hope it has helped to answer those questions. Most of the time a major cultural shift occurs too slowly for those living at that time to see what is happening. It can be likened to standing on a glacier and being unable to feel any movement, yet with the aid of time–laps photography, it becomes clear that movement is indeed taking place. With this view of history, we can see the glacier's descent down the mountain, not as fast as stepping on a slippery slope, but a downward descent nonetheless. What was unthinkable sixty years ago is now considered the norm. With this perspective of history, we looked back through the decades to see some of the complex forces that changed the hearts and minds of American culture.

We began with Alfred Kinsey and his "scientific" study of the sexual habits of "everyday" Americans and the tremendous ripple effect that it had as the implications of his work became clear. Most people would never read through all 800 pages of graphs and charts and other data, but would rely on magazine articles, newspaper reviews and "office talk." Kinsey made dark sexual perversion appear normal by making it seem as though this is what your neighbors and friends are telling the sex researchers what they were doing behind closed doors. It makes for a kind of collective forgiveness; if "everybody's doing it," then the little thing I do is not so bad. Kinsey's work undermined the moral foundation of the laws governing sexual behavior by arguing that laws should be more in line with what people are in fact doing, rather than what they should do. From this would come the sexual revolution with its attack on faith, family, and marriage.

Hugh Hefner, whose life was changed after reading Kinsey, took the pin–up girls of the 1940s and went a step further to create a maga-

---

9. *Rolling Stone Magazine*, July 24, 1980, 37. For more, see Michael Medved, *Hollywood vs. America* (New York: HarperCollins, 1992) and Steve Allen, *Vulgarians at the Gate* (Amherst: Prometheus Books, 2001.

zine that put Kinsey's ideas into living color. The influence of *Playboy* went well beyond just the readers of the magazine as his philosophy and ideas of how the single man should view sex and relationships became part of the secular culture, which in turn influenced many in the church who knew little more than "don't do it; it's wrong." Margaret Sanger, who founded *Planned Parenthood*, would see her dream of an effective contraceptive come true that would make women as "free" as men in sex without the consequences. It would also help her in her eugenics vision of decreasing the ever growing population of non–white "human weeds."

The introduction of "the Pill" in 1960 changed everything and must be seen as a major cultural shifting event. The pill made temporary chemical sterilization possible and once the link between sex and reproduction had been removed, the effect on many was a profound change in attitude from what are the responsibilities that accompany sex, to what is the pleasure that can be received from it. Even in the church it had an effect on attitudes about the importance of marriage and faithfulness. It is interesting how little protest there was when colleges began to allow coed dorms because students demanded them, which in turn saw the beginnings of the "hook–up" mind set with its "it's only sex" attitude. Nine years after the Pill, came "No–Fault" divorce, which removed the need to prove fault in obtaining a divorce and allowed that only one party needs to desire the divorce. This, thus, undermined the "one flesh" union in marriage that was assumed by the law.

The main target of this decades' long assault was (and continues to be) the natural family, the *Ozzie and Harriet, Leave it to Beaver, Father Knows Best* type of family. We use the term "natural family" instead of "traditional family," because the word traditional carries with it the idea that something was done out of habit, that it was put in place by people, and it can be removed when people wish to start a new tradition. As the divorce rate increased and families were torn apart and thrown back together like a salad, fathers walking away from their responsibilities, leaving mothers to take care of the children, the definition of what family means was so hollowed out, that it was filled with whatever happened to be lying around. In order for "homosexual marriage" to succeed, the meaning of "marriage" must be changed and a new meaning poured into it, and by meaning we not only mean the dictionary definition of marriage, but what does marriage mean in our lives. The natural family has been so denigrated and distorted that many (even in the church) have come to settle for the bumper sticker definition, "Love makes a Family."

Faith and family are intertwined. Most of the time it is through family that faith is passed on. In her excellent book *How the West Really Lost God*, Mary Eberstadt uses the analogy of the DNA double helix to illustrate this interdependence. "What this book means to impress is that *family and faith are the invisible double helix of society––two spirals that when linked to one another can effectively reproduce, but whose strength and momentum depend on one another.*"[10]

As mainline denominations struggled with the issue of ever more empty pews, it also had to deal with the growing clamor for accepting homosexuality. As anti–supernaturalism crept in, they began to view the Scripture as less and less absolute and started viewing it more and more as just the words of men for a different time and different culture. With the political and cultural winds shifting towards greater acceptance of homosexual practice, the mainline denominations followed in large measure the culture while they ignored the words of Jude, verses 3 – 4, and looked for any wiggle room to allow for what God's Word said could not be allowed. They began to listen to interpretations of Scripture unknown in the 2,000 years of church history. Men like D. S. Bailey, Troy Perry, John J. McNeill, John Boswell and others, were telling homosexuals that "God loves them and doesn't ask them to change anything about their sex lives."

There were many important events that occurred after the 1980s with regard to the homosexual "rights" movement, but by that time, as the saying goes, *that train had left the station* and was not going to stop until they achieved what they considered "equality" and every dissonant voice was cowed into silence. We hope that this brief look at our cultural shift and the events that took place will help in understanding that this issue did not just fall out of the sky and land in the Supreme Court, but was *decades* in the making. We were watching the cultural subversion of the Christian faith, and most Christians did not realize it. Most of the people who relied on civil law to keep

---

10. Mary Eberstadt, *How the West Really Lost God* (West Conshohocken, PA: Templeton Press, 2013), 22.

homosexuality in check forgot that even though natural law and civil law may run in the same direction, when natural law is forgotten, then civil law can be changed by whoever has the loudest voices.

Stanton L. Jones, of Wheaton College, in the conclusion of his paper *Sexual Orientation and Reason,* writes,

> As moral and religious traditionalists face this profound polarization, it is important that we confess our own culpability in creating the mess we are in. We were complicit, even if ignorantly and passively so, in the cultural embrace of the disease conceptualization of homosexuality. We offloaded responsibility for the articulation of a thoughtful, caring, theologically rich and pastorally sensitive understanding of sexual brokenness onto the disease conceptualization, and thus were unprepared for the vacuum created by its timely demise. We have failed to articulate thoughtful understandings of human sexuality in light of evolving scientific findings and cultural developments.
>
> Perhaps most importantly, we failed and continue to fail to engage individuals who embrace homosexual identity with compassion, understanding, and love, and to seek to defend them against unjust discrimination and violence.[11]

As important as the Supreme Court decision of June, 2015 was, for the Christian the final "court of appeal" remains the Scripture and not the Church Fathers, not the latest "scientific" data from psychology or genetics or popular opinion, but the Scripture.

If we take a step back to look at the changes that took place in just these 4 decades (to say nothing of the decades since), it should become clear that we have witnessed something that is laughed at or discounted by many thinkers and writers of trends and changes in culture and that is the idea of the "slippery slope." The acceptance of ideas that in turn change attitudes and then actions is evident even in our brief study. The acceptance of same–sex "marriage" by our culture is the result of many ideas turned into action over the course of decades. Those who view God's design and laws as a prison will always seek a way of escape, believing they are free when in fact they

---

11. Stanton L. Jones, "Sexual Orientation and Reason," ChristianEthics.org (January 2012), 20, accessed July 12, 2014, www.christianethics.org.

are slaves. We need to remember the warning Paul gives to Timothy in 2 Tim. 3:13, ". . . while evil people and imposters will go from bad to worse, deceiving and being deceived."

Next, we will look at the attempted scientific justification for homosexuality.

We close this chapter with a quote from the English poet Alexander Pope (1688–1744) in his *An Essay on Man: Epistle II.* Notice how each step mirrors the change in attitude with regard to homosexuality.

> *Vice is a monster of so frightful mien*
> *as to be hated needs but to be seen;*
> *Yet seen too oft, familiar with her face,*
> *we first endure, then pity, then embrace.*

5

Searching for Scientific Justification

In this chapter we will take a look at the various theories and data that have been used in the search for a biological, genetic or natural cause of homosexuality. The quest for such an explanation has been of great interest and importance to those in the homosexual community and even many outside of it because it is felt by many that if a genetic or biologically determined cause can be found it, would place homosexuality in the same genetic category as eye color, skin color, or left–handedness, making any moral argument against it seems as though it is based on nothing but sheer bigotry.

During the mid–twentieth century, most Americans thought of science as *the* best way to determine if something was true or not. When Alfred Kinsey published the results of his research in 1948 and 1953 about the sexual habits of "average" Americans, it was not presented as some theory or speculation, but as data gathered from hundreds of people with thousands of hours of interviews. In his 800 pages of charts and graphs, Kinsey made it seem as though most of their friends or neighbors were involved in or thinking about sexual activities for which they could be arrested in any State in the country. Kinsey argued for a revision of sex laws that should be based not on any supposed morality, but on what in fact people were doing as long as no one was harmed or forced to do what they did not want to do. If enough people were doing something Kinsey argued, then it should be thought of as just a natural variation of the human sexual response.

Most of the general public's view of scientists at the time Kinsey published his work was of the scientist as a kind of "Mr. Spock" of Star

Trek, in a white lab coat, who was the objective researcher and would never let their personal feelings or philosophy influence their work as they try to push back the frontiers of ignorance. Unfortunately, as has already been shown, this was not true of Kinsey.

From Old Sin to New Species

For most of recorded history homosexual practice was considered to be a violation of God's laws or at least a perversion of the natural order. In the twentieth century we have seen homosexual practice go from being a sin, to being a crime, to being a mental illness, to being a life–style, to being "born that way," to being a parade down main street. The view that most Americans had about homosexuality being a moral issue was being replaced by the "scientific" understanding of homosexuality as a psychological condition with the majority of psychologists believing it was a mental maladjustment that needed to be treated so that even if the individuals were not "cured," at least they would be better able to cope with their condition. This was the majority view of psychologists until, Evelyn Hooker, (1907–1996) published her findings in 1957. Hooker studied a small group of 30 homosexuals and 30 heterosexual volunteers, matched them for age, education, and IQ, and conducted psychological tests. She found that the homosexuals were just as well– adjusted as the heterosexuals.[1] This *one* study of 30 homosexuals sent shock waves through the psychological profession because it was the majority view at that time that homosexuality itself was evidence of psychological maladjustment.

In her study, Hooker quotes from a report issued by the *Group for the Advancement of Psychiatry*: "When such homosexual behavior persists in an adult, it is then a symptom of a severe emotional disorder."[2] Prior to Hooker, most clinicians studying homosexuals obtained their subjects from individuals who came in for psychological help, from mental hospitals, or from prisons. Hooker wanted subjects that were not from any of those sources because she wanted people whom she felt were more in line with the general population. Hooker states, "No one knows what a random sample of the ho-

---

1. Evelyn Hooker, "The Adjustment of the Male Overt Homosexual," *Journal of Projective Techniques* 21 (1957): 18–31.
2. Ibid., 18.

mosexual population would be like; and even if one knew, it would be extremely difficult, if not impossible to obtain one. The project would not have been possible without the invaluable assistance of the Mattachine Society, an organization which has as its stated purpose the development of a homosexual ethic in order to better integrate the homosexual into society."[3] Hooker's work, along with Kinsey's and others, was used again and again as reasons for the removal of anti–sodomy laws as well as the removal of homosexuality as a mental disorder from the DSM II, which is the official "bible" of diagnosed mental disorders.

In her work Hooker knew that she did not have a representative sample of the entire male homosexual population, but she did not need one since all she needed was one example of a well–adjusted homosexual to overturn the absolute claim that *all* homosexuals must be maladjusted because the condition itself is the result of maladjustment. It seems amazing that just one study of 30 individuals could overturn the thinking of most psychologists of the day. The limitations of this study did not stop the homosexual affirming American Psychological Association from asserting (even when contrary data emerged) that homosexual persons have no more mental health issues than heterosexual persons. Dr. Stanton L. Jones makes the observation that the APA "has passed a number of resolutions asserting that homosexuality is a 'normal and positive variant of human sexuality.' But how this assertion of value could be established as a matter of 'scientific fact' is truly mystifying."[4] After Hooker there were multiple research papers to investigate if there is any difference for the risk of psychiatric disorders between homosexual and heterosexual persons. In a study published in 2001, it was reported that "our findings underscore the growing concern that homosexually active individuals are at increased risk for psychiatric morbidity in much the same way as people with other disadvantaged social statuses. Our results are consistent with previous investigations in showing that risks of some psychiatric disorders and of suicidal symptoms are ele-

---

3. Ibid., 19.

4. Stanton L. Jones, "Sexual Orientation and Reason: On the Implications of False Beliefs about Homosexuality" (January 2012), 5, accessed August 13, 2017, http://www.wheaton.edu/CACE/Print–Resources/~/media/Files/Centers–and–Institutes/CACE/articles/Sexual%20Orientation%20and%20 Reason%20%201–9–20122.pdf.

vated among homosexually active people compared with exclusively heterosexually active persons."[5]

In 2006, a large Dutch population survey involving almost 10,000 participants reported, "In general, though, self–reporting physical and mental health problems are systematically higher in the gay/lesbian group and, to somewhat lesser extent, the bisexual group. Gay and lesbian people reported more acute mental health symptoms than heterosexual people, and their general mental health also was worse. Gay/lesbian people also more frequently reported acute physical symptoms and chronic conditions than heterosexual people. Differences in physical health were partly explained by the higher prevalence of mental health problems among gay/lesbian people."[6]

An interesting and important thing to remember about the Dutch study is the fact that the usual reason given for the increase of mental health issues among homosexuals is attributed to the "societal stress" suffered by homosexuals in non–affirming countries. But with this study that explanation loses much of its credibility because these homosexuals are living in what has been for years one of the most liberal, socially tolerant and affirming countries in the western world.

A large systematic review of studies done between January 1966 to April 2005, with data on 214,344 heterosexual and 11,971 non–heterosexual people, concluded,

> In summary, there was an increased lifetime and 12 month risk of alcohol and drug dependency in all groups compared with heterosexuals with markedly higher risk in lesbian and bisexual women. LGB people are at higher risk of suicidal behavior, mental disorder and substance misuse and dependence than heterosexual people. The results of the meta–analyses demonstrates a two–fold excess in risk of suicide attempts in the preceding year in men and women, and a four–fold excess risk in gay and bisexual men over a

5. Steven E. Gilman et al., "Risk of Psychiatric Disorders among Individuals Reporting Same– Sex Sexual Partners in the National Comorbidity Survey," *American Journal of Public Health* 96, no.6 (June 2001): 937.

6. Theo G. M. Sandfort et al., "Sexual Orientation and Mental and Physical Health Status: Findings from a Dutch Population Survey," *American Journal of Public Health* 96, no. 6 (June, 2006): 1123.

lifetime. Similarly, depression, anxiety, alcohol and substance misuse were at least 1.5 times more common in LGB people. Findings were similar in men and women but LB women were at particular risk of substance dependence, while lifetime risk of suicide attempts was especially high in GB men.[7]

Later, the authors state the implications of their findings. "Although we cannot report on whether or not LGB people are at greater risk than heterosexuals for completed suicide, the elevated risk for all forms of mental disorder, DHS and substance misuse would suggest very strongly that this is the case."[8] So, while it is true there is no evidence that *all* homosexuals suffer from mental disorders, the research would seem to show that there is a higher risk for such disorders than in the heterosexual population.

Multiple studies have been done on the risk of a homosexual orientation to young people as it relates to mental health issues. A study published in 1999 was a 21 year longitudinal study of 1,265 children in New Zealand. "At 21 years of age, 1007 sample members were questioned about their sexual orientation and relationships with same-sex partners since the age of 16 years. Twenty–eight subjects (2.8%) were classified as being gay, lesbian, or bisexual sexual orientation. Over the period from age 14 to 21 years, data was gathered on a range of psychiatric disorders that included major depression, generalized anxiety disorder, conduct disorder, and substance use disorders. Data were also gathered on suicidal ideation and suicide attempts." They concluded, "Findings support recent evidence suggesting that gay, lesbian and bisexual young people are at increased risk of mental health problems, with these associations being particularly evident for measures of suicidal behavior and multiple disorder."[9]

The authors site 3 other studies that show a higher risk for suicide in gay, or bisexual men aged 18 to 27 years and 668 heterosexual men found that rates of suicide behavior were nearly 14 times higher

7. Michael King et al., "A systematic review of mental disorders, suicide and deliberate self harm in lesbian, gay and bisexual people," *BMC Psychiatry* 70, no. 8 (August 18, 2008): 8, 9.

8. Ibid., 10.

9. David M. Fergusson et al. "Is Sexual Orientation Related to Mental Health Problems and Suicidality in Young People?" *Archives of General Psychiatry,* 56, no. 10 (October 1999): 876.

among the gay or bisexual subjects. Garofalo et al. compared 104 GLB high school students with 4,055 high school students identifying themselves as heterosexual. They found rates of suicide attempts among the GLB subjects that were more than 3.5 times higher than among the control subjects. Similarly, Remafedi et al. compared 394 GLB high school students with 336 heterosexual controls. Their findings showed that the GLB subjects had odds of suicide attempts that were 7.1 times higher than heterosexual controls and odds of suicidal intent that were 3.6 times higher. The weight of evidence from these studies clearly supports the view that GLB sexual orientation acts as a risk factor for suicidal behaviors."[10]

In July 2012, Dr. Mark Regnerus of the University of Texas at Austin published an article in the journal *Social Science Research* that looked at the following: "I compare how young adults from a variety of different family backgrounds fare on 40 different social, emotional, and relational outcomes. In particular, I focus on how respondents who said their mother had a same–sex relationship with another woman–or their father did so with another man–compare with still–intact, two–parent heterosexual married families using nationally–representative data collected from a large probability sample of American young adults."[11] The article created a firestorm of controversy because the published results of the study were contrary to "consensus." The reaction was so strong, angry and vocal that someone might have thought that Dr. Regnerus suggested killing kittens for fun. So, what was it that was making sociologists and others so angry? His findings from the *New Family Structures Study* (NFSS) was "a large random sample of American young adults (ages 18–39) who were raised in different types of family arrangements."[12] Dr. Regnerus' results did not support the "no difference between homosexual / heterosexual family" studies that had previously used much smaller samples. He writes, "Small sample sizes can contribute to 'no difference' conclusions. It is not surprising that statistically–significant differences would not emerge in studies employing as few

10. Ibid.

11. Mark Regnerus, "How different are the adult children of parents who have same–sex relationships? Findings from the New Family Structures Study," *Social Science Research* 41, no. 4 (July 2012): 752.

12. Ibid.

as 18 or 33 or 44 cases of respondents with same–sex parents respectively. . . ."[13]

At the conclusion of his study he writes, "But the NFSS also clearly reveals that children appear most apt to succeed well as adults–on multiple counts and across a variety of domains–when they spend their entire childhood with their married mother and father, and especially when the parents remain married to the present day."[14] This conclusion was unacceptable to the "no difference" propagandists who even questioned how the reviewers could allow an article like this to be published in such a respected journal. In the August 2012 issue of the same journal, Dr. Regnerus published a reply to the major objections raised by the critics of his original paper but not backing down on his conclusions: "In other words, the original study muddied what had largely been, up to that time, a relatively consistent, positive portrait of child outcomes in gay and lesbian households (however defined)."[15] He concludes his reply with this, "Perhaps in social reality there are really two 'gold standards' of family stability and context for children's flourishing–a heterosexual stably–coupled household and the same among gay/lesbian households–but no population–based sample analyses is yet able to consistently confirm wide evidence of the latter. Moreover, a stronger burden of proof than has been employed to date ought to characterize studies which conclude 'no difference'. . . ."[16]

In December of 2013, a study by Douglas W. Allen was published based on a 20% sample of data from the 2006 Canadian census. In Canada, same–sex couples have had access to all government and taxation benefits since 1997 and been able to marry since 2005. At the conclusion of his study Dr. Allen writes, ". . . there is little hard evi-

---

13. Ibid., 754.

14. Ibid., 766.

15. Mark Regnerus, "Parental same–sex relationships, family instability, and subsequent life outcomes for adult children: Answering critics of the new family structures study with an additional analysis," *Social Science Research* 41, no. 6 (November 2012): 1368, accessed August 18, 2017, www.sciencedirect.com/science/journal/0049089x/41.

16. Ibid., 1377. See also Mark Regnerus, "The data on children in same–sex households gets more depressing," The Witherspoon Institute Public Discourse, June 29, 2016, accessed August 13, 2017, http://www.thepublicdiscourse.com/2016/06/17255/; also, "Hijacking science: How the "no difference" consensus about same–sex households and children works," The Witherspoon Institute Public Discourse, October 14, 2016, accessed August 13, 2017, http://www.thepublicdiscourse.com/2016/10/18033.

dence to support the general popular consensus of 'no difference.'" He then adds, "I have argued that the 2006 Canada census–though not perfect–is able to address most of these issues, and the results on high school graduation rates suggest that children living in both gay and lesbian households struggle compared to children from opposite sex married households. In general, it appears that these children are only 65% as likely to graduate from high school compared to the control group. . . ."[17] Of course the guardians of the temple of "no difference" did all they could not only to attack the study but Dr. Allen himself for daring to question what "everybody knows."

The controversy continues about Dr. Regnerus' study with the publication of a paper in 2015 in, *Social Science Research*, which attempted to "debunk" the data presented in Dr. Regnerus' original 2012 paper. He responded online in May, 2015,

> Every social situation involves attempts to persuade others of your definition of the situation. The stock photo of happy, young, white lesbian couple with two bubbly children that is by far the preferred download of the news media is an example of this phenomenon. It's also an illustration of what Max Webber labeled an "ideal type." It's not average–it's an image of what many hold to be ideal. In reality, however, white lesbians are among the *least* likely among LGBT couples to wish to have children, according to the National Study of Family Growth. This cheerful, photogenic presentation hides the dramatic inequality that is an open secret of the LGBT community, faulted only among friends. But such inequality remains backstage until political battles fought by (and for the primary benefit of) the wealthiest members of the LGBT community are won. The same goes for the LGBT movement's annexation of the civil rights movement's legacy, which–to those who have eyes to seen the disparity in power and access between the two–amounts to nothing more than cultural larceny.[18]

17. Douglas W. Allen, "High school graduation rates among children of same-sex households," *Review of Economics of the Household* 11, no. 4 (December 2013): 653.

18. Mark Regnerus, "Making differences disappear: The evolution of science on same-sex Households," *The Public Discourse*, May 12, 2015, accessed August 18, 2017, www.thepublicdiscourse.com/2015/05/14978/. For a more in-depth look at the issues conservatives face see Walter R. Schumm, "A conservative's view from the academic trenches: reply to Duarte, Crawford, Stern, Haidt, Jessim, and Tetlock," *Journal of Behavioral and Brain Sciences* 6 (April 2016): 149–166.

What About Children?

In June 2011, the Centers for Disease Control and Prevention (CDC), in their *Morbidity and Mortality Weekly Report* (MMWR), published the findings of a large 247 page report titled "Sexual Identity, Sex of Sexual Contacts, and Health–Risk Behaviors Among Students in Grades 9–12–Youth Risk Surveillance, Selected Sites, United States, 2001–2009."[19] This report has important information on risk behaviors of students. "This report summarizes results from YRBSs conducted during 2001–2009 in seven states and six large urban school districts that include questions on sexual identity (i.e., heterosexual, gay or lesbian, bisexual, or unsure), sex of sexual contacts (i.e., same–sex only, opposite sex only, or both sexes), or both of these variables. The surveys were conducted among large population–based samples of public school students in grades 9–12."[20] The survey looked at behaviors that contribute to unintentional injuries, behaviors that contribute to violence, behaviors related to attempted suicide, tobacco use, alcohol use, other drug use, sexual behaviors, physical activity and sedentary behaviors, and weight management.

The overall results and some specific behaviors that were studied are revealing. "Across the nine sites that assessed sexual identity, the prevalence among gay or lesbian students was higher than the prevalence among heterosexual students for a median of 63.8% of all risk behaviors measured, and the prevalence among bisexual students was higher than the prevalence among heterosexual students for a median of 76.0% of all risk behaviors measured."[21] Additionally, the study shows, "Across the nine sites that assessed sexual identity, the percentage of students who identified themselves as heterosexual ranged from 90.3% to 93.6% (median: 93.0%), as gay or lesbian ranged from 1.0% to 2.6% (median: 1.3%) and as bisexual ranged from 2.9% to 5.2% (median: 3.7%)."[22] The survey looked at multiple

---

19. Laura Kann et al., "Sexual Identity, Sex of Sexual Contacts, and Health–Risk Behaviors Among Students in Grades 9–12—Youth Risk Behavior Surveillance, Selected Sites, United States, 2001—2009 Center for Disease Control and Prevention," *Morbidity and Mortality Weekly Report*, June 10, 2011, 1.

20. Ibid., 2.

21. Ibid.

22. Ibid., 7.

behaviors and health risks. However, we will look at just those relevant to our study.

1. Seriously Considered Suicide: "Across the eight sites (Delaware, Maine, Massachusetts, Rhode Island, Boston, Chicago, New York City, and San Francisco) that assessed having seriously considered attempting suicide during the 12 months before the survey and sexual identity, the prevalence of having seriously considered attempting suicide ranged from 9.9% to 13.2% (median: 11.7%) among heterosexual students, from 18.8% to 43.4% (median: 29.6%) among gay or lesbian students, from 35.4% to 46.2% (median: 40.3%) among bisexual students . . . . The prevalence of having seriously considered attempting suicide was lower among heterosexual than gay or lesbian students in six sites . . . lower among heterosexual than bisexual students in all eight sites. . . . "[23]

2. Attempted Suicide: "Across the nine sites (Delaware, Maine, Massachusetts, Rhode Island, Vermont, Boston, Chicago, New York City, and San Francisco) that assessed having attempted suicide one or more times during the 12 months before the survey and sexual identity, the prevalence of having attempted suicide ranged from 3.8% to 9.6% (median: 6.4%) among heterosexual students, from 15.1% to 34.3% (median: 25.8%) among gay and lesbian students, from 20.6% to 32.0% (median: 28.0%) among bisexual students. . . . The prevalence of having attempted suicide was lower among heterosexual than gay or lesbian students in eight sites . . . lower among heterosexual than bisexual students in all nine sites. . . . "[24]

3. Had Sexual Intercourse before Age 13: "Across the nine sites . . . that asserted having had sexual intercourse for the first time before age 13 years and sexual identity, the prevalence of having sexual intercourse before age 13 years ranged from 4.3% to 11.2% (median: 4.8%) among heterosexual students, from 13.3% to 28.5% (median: 19.8%) among gay or lesbian students, from 9.0% to 23.3% (median: 14.6%)

---

23. Ibid., 18.
24. Ibid., 19.

among bisexual students. . . . The prevalence of having had sexual intercourse before age 13 years was lower among heterosexual than gay or lesbian students in seven sites . . . lower among heterosexual than bisexual students in seven sites. Across the 12 sites . . . that assessed having had sexual intercourse before age 13 years and sex of sexual contacts, the prevalence of having had sexual intercourse before age 13 years ranged from 5.3% to 17.8% (median: 12.4%) among students who only had sexual contact with the opposite sex, from 10.1% to 33.5% (median: 15.8%) among students who only had sexual contact with the same sex, and from 13.5% to 42.6% (median: 22.9%) among students who had sexual contact with both sexes.[25]

4. Had Sexual Intercourse with Four or More Persons during Their Life: "Across the nine sites . . . that assessed having had sexual intercourse with four or more persons during their life and sexual identity, the prevalence of having had sexual intercourse with four or more persons ranged from 7.6% to 20.7% (median: 11.1%) among heterosexual students, from 10.6% to 39.9% (median: 29.9%) among gay and lesbian students, from 22.9% to 37.0% (median: 28.2%) among bisexual students. . . . The prevalence of having had sexual intercourse with four or more persons was lower among heterosexual than gay or lesbian students in six sites . . . lower among heterosexual than bisexual students in all nine sites. . . .[26]

5. Currently Sexually Active: "Across the nine sites . . . that assessed having had sexual intercourse with at least one person during the 3 months before the survey (i.e., currently sexually active) and sexual identity, the prevalence of being currently sexually active ranged from 19.3% to 41.6% (median: 32%) among heterosexual students, from 25.0% to 62.9% (median: 53.2%) among gay or lesbian students, from 44.3% to 61.5% (median: 52.6%) among bisexual students. . . ."[27]

25. Ibid., 40.

26. Ibid., 41.

27. Ibid., 42.

Discussion / Conclusion

YRBSS is the only public health surveillance system in the United States that monitors, among interested states and large urban school districts, the prevalence of health–risk behaviors and selected health outcomes among population–based samples of sexual minority youths defined by sexual identity and by the sex of which sexual minority students practice many health–risk behaviors. This disparity is most apparent among students who identify themselves as gay or lesbian or bisexual. Across the nine sites that assessed sexual identity, the prevalence among gay or lesbian students was higher than the prevalence among heterosexual students for a median of 63.8% of all the risk behaviors measured, and the prevalence among bisexual students was higher than the prevalence among heterosexual students for a median of 76.0% of all risk behaviors measured. . . .[28]

Compared with students who are not sexual minorities, a disproportionate number of sexual minority students engage in a wide range of health–risk behaviors.[29]

There should be no need of concern for these students if we believe the guardians of "no difference" since they rely on the elevated wisdom of the American Psychological Association, which said in 2003, "Being Gay Is Just as Healthy as Being Straight."[30]

Is There Evidence of Environmental / Family Influence on Sexual Orientation?

There have been questions by researchers about the likelihood of children raised in a same–sex household adopting a homosexual orientation. Most of those researchers would answer NO because of their belief that homosexuality was mostly genetic in origin and could no more be influenced by a family environment than could the color of eyes or skin color. The "born this way" theory was the consensus of most researchers in this field.

---

28. Ibid., 60.

29. Ibid., 67.

30. "Being Gay Is Just as Healthy as Being Straight," American Psychological Association, May 28, 2003, accessed August 18, 2017, http://www.apa.org/research/action/gay.aspx.

In 2006, Dr. Paul Cameron published a paper putting forward the hypothesis that children raised by homosexual parents would be more likely to become homosexual themselves, a theory called *intergenerational transfer*.[31] As expected, a number of authors criticized Cameron and felt this was nothing more than some kind of anti–homosexual rhetoric designed to make people believe that children adopted by homosexual parents would automatically grow up to be homosexual.

In 2010, respected scholar Walter R. Schumm published a paper looking at the objections by the critics of Cameron's paper as well as taking a closer look at the data Cameron presented. After listing multiple cultures that accept or do not accept homosexuality, he states, "Therefore, it appears reasonable to conclude that sociological factors, such as general societal acceptance, could be associated with rates of expression of homosexual behavior and that therefore it is plausible that such might also operate at the family level. Such findings do not rule out genetic effects – rather they merely contradict the null hypothesis that social variables have *nothing* to do with expression of sexual orientation."[32] At the end of his paper, Schumm pulls the data together and concludes,

> Here, the evidence appears to support Cameron's (2006) hypothesis regarding the intergenerational transfer of sexual orientation, from a number of different directions, using narrative data, ethnographic data, and data from over two dozen previous studies on gay and lesbian parenting. Not only were these results statistically significant, but the percentages and odds ratios indicate substantive or clinical significance.

> It was surprising that Cameron's estimate of 35–47% of children of a homosexual parent becoming homosexual themselves was not as outrageous as some might have thought, given the percentages presented here, which range as high as 61% when data were restricted to lesbian mothers' older daughters whose sexual orientation had been clearly discussed or reported. Results from the 26 previous studies

---

31. Walter R. Schumm, "Children of Homosexuals More Apt to be Homosexual? A Reply to Morrison, and Cameron Based on an Examination of Multiple Source Data" *Journal of Biosocial Science* 42, no. 6 (November 2010): 721.

32. Ibid., 733, 734.

on gay and lesbian parenting confirm higher rates for gay and lesbian parents but at lower percentages (14–31%) than observed in the ten narrative sources. The higher rates of transfer observed for daughters of mothers may corroborate research by Bos et al. (2006) in which daughters of lesbian mothers were more likely than their sons to adopt more of a same–sex sexual orientation even before the age of 13.[33]

In a recent 2016, article published in *The Journal of Sex Research*, noted researcher Lisa Diamond (who is herself a lesbian) said the following,

> Arguably, the most supportive and accepting social context for same–sex sexuality would be a household headed by a same–sex couple: if same–sex sexuality can be enhanced by social acceptance, one would expect that children raised by same–sex couples would be more likely to consider and to pursue same–sex relationships themselves. In fact, this is the case. Long–term longitudinal research on lesbian–headed families (Gartrell, Bos, and Goldberg, 2011) found that late–adolescent girls who were raised from birth by lesbian parents were more likely than age–matched controls to report same–sex attraction and behavior. The most likely explanation (given that not all of the children were genetically related to their mothers) is that girls raised by lesbian mothers experience a family climate of acceptance regarding same–sex relationships and received less exposure (relative to the average female adolescent) to conventional societal pressures to pursue exclusively heterosexual relationships. As a result, they may have been more willing and able to consider–and to positively evaluate–their own propensity for same–sex sexuality.[34]

Of course, one of the oldest and strongest of "conventional societal pressures" would be a home and family life where Christianity is taught, believed, and lived out in daily life.

So what is the big controversy about the fact that children raised in a home where the father or mother are in a same–sex relationship

---

33. Ibid., 739.

34. Lisa M. Diamond and Clifford J. Rosky, "Scrutinizing Immutability: Research on sexual orientation and U.S. Legal advocacy for sexual minorities," *The Journal of Sex Research* 53, no. 4–5 (2016): 370, 371.

are more likely to be homosexual than in the general population? The reason for the controversy is that if a family environment can influence a child towards same–sex attraction, this would undermine the argument that homosexuality has a genetic cause in the same way as eye or skin color. We will see a little later how the latest scientific data is stacking up *against* the biological determination theory.

Another factor that makes the guardians of "can't change / no difference" nervous is the threat that such data would be a setback to the political and social gains of the past couple of decades, for example, the effort to have homosexuals designated as a class of people which would make them eligible for particular civil rights in the same way as a racial minority. If members of a class are coming into or going out of the class, it makes it difficult to determine what constitutes that class. The guardians of "no difference" can also play rough when they want to. One example is when allegations of scientific misconduct were raised by a writer named Scott Rose against Dr. Mark Regnerus' work in 2012. The University of Texas at Austin, where Dr. Regnerus teaches, determined that no formal investigation was warranted because there was insufficient evidence and "deemed the matter closed from an institutional perspective."[35]

What's So Important about the Same–Sex Parenting Studies?

Over the last few decades a growing list of studies have been done on the effects of children growing up in a same–sex household and comparing them to natural marriage heterosexual households. Most of the studies were small, involving about 30, 40, or 50 households, and from these generalizations were made and applied to same–sex households as a whole. These studies are then sited in the courts or various legislatures in an attempt to affect changes in public policy and laws. Few if any judges or lawmakers have the time or training to carefully look into the "nuts and bolts" of the studies in order to determine if they are based on good empirical evidence, sound methods of gathering data, or if the conclusions follow from the data presented.

---

35. Allen Price, The University of Texas at Austin, *UT NEWS*, August 29, 2012.

In a recent article, Dr. Douglas Allen pulls back the curtain and allows us to see what is really going on with the same–sex parenting literature. It will become clear from this that all is not as it seems or is reported.

> Despite the various differences in each study, most have the same conclusion: Children of same–sex parents perform at least as well as children from heterosexual families, and there is no difference in child outcomes based on family structure. This conclusion has played a major role in legal cases, legislation, and professional opinions on gay family rights. . . . Finally, most of the literature on same–sex parenting is based on weak designs, biased samples, and low powered tests. The result is a nascent literature that falls far short of normal social science empirical research standards. At its best, the literature contains interesting exploratory studies that raise provocative questions and observations. At its worst, it is advocacy aimed at legislators and judges, which may explain why, despite its weak scientific nature, the literature is characterized by strong recommendations for policy and legal changes to family regulations. . . . I argue that the flaws generally found within the current literature are fatal in terms of any ability to make generalizations regarding the population of same–sex parents, and therefore it is impossible and irresponsible to use literature to advance any recommendations regarding same–sex family legislation.[36]

Dr. Allen goes on to list some sources of bias and how in more mature areas of science there are various checks and balances that help minimize biases. However, "These conditions are generally not met within the same–sex parenting literature. As a result, the literature is flawed in terms of bias from a number of sources. These forms of bias make the general claims within this literature unreliable."[37]

He then uses this illustration of data bias: "A policeman sees a drunk searching for something under a street light and asks what the drunk has lost. He says he lost his keys, and they both look under the street light together. After a few minutes the policeman asks if he is

---

36. Doug Allen, "More Heat Than Light: A Critical Assessment of the Same–Sex Parenting Literature, 1995–2013," *Marriage and Family Review* 51, no. 2 (2015): 155, 158.

37. Ibid., 158.

sure he lost them here, and the drunk replies, no, that he lost them in the park. The policeman asks why he is searching here, and the drunk replies 'this is where the light is.' [Freedman, 2010]"[38]

Allen makes it clear, "The point cannot be overstated. A proper probability sample is a necessary condition for making a general claim about an unknown population, based on a sample. Within the same–sex parenting literature the street lamp effect abounds. Researchers have typically studied only those community members who are convenient to study. This means the results lack the integrity and validity that lead to any truth statements regarding out of sample same–sex parents and their children."[39] He then identifies researcher bias: "Thus, since the mid–1970s empirical research often had the objective of showing that gay and lesbian parents were on par with heterosexual parents. From its start then, researchers and participants in that research have had a social agenda over and above the simple social science pursuit of understanding same–sex households. From this starting point a type of researcher has emerged: mostly female, often lesbian, and strongly feminist and supportive of gay rights. Indeed, Stacy and Biblarz admit that 'few contributors to this [same–sex parenting] literature personally subscribe to [a hetero–normative] view. . . .'"[40] Allen adds, "Stacey and Biblarz (2001) point out that the desire to show gay and lesbian parents on par with heterosexual parents led 'sensitive scholars . . . to tread gingerly around the terrain of differences'. . . ."[41]

Allen makes this concluding statement about the same–sex parenting literature, "A consistent remark found within the same–sex literature relates to how large and growing it is. New studies are said to confirm many past studies, and there is a general impression that, like a snowball rolling down a hill, the evidence is mounting and becoming unchallengeable. This, of course, is not a scientific conclusion. A series of weak research designs and exploratory studies do not amount to a growing body of advanced research."[42]

---

38. Ibid., 159.
39. Ibid.
40. Ibid., 165.
41. Ibid., 166.
42. Ibid., 173.

The unscholarly and often shrill reaction by the "no difference" crowd against the conclusions of Allen, et al. is because they *cannot* allow any negative data as such data would undermine the picture of happy healthy homosexual "parents." The evidence shows that children flourish best when raised by their biological father and mother. Other arrangements are only done because of less than perfect situations, but they should never be seen as a good substitute for what God intended. So what does all this mean? For one thing, it means that the mountain of small studies along with all the problems of bias that Allen points out may not be worth the paper they are printed on *IF* we are trying to discover the truth about any difference between heterosexual and homosexual parents. But it is these small studies that are sited again and again as evidence of the "no difference" argument. These arguments are put before judges, lawmakers, and are used to sway public opinion on this important issue.

Do These Genes Make Me Look Gay?

The quest for the "gay gene" began in the early 1990s and has had about as much success as the SETI project (Search for Extraterrestrial Intelligence). This quest was motivated by more than just to increase our understanding of genetics and sexual behavior. If such a discovery were made, it would have profound implications for society far beyond the laboratory. If same–sex attraction and identity had evidence of being determined by genetics ("born that way") like eye or hair color, then moral arguments against homosexuality would appear to be based on no more than "I don't like it." There have been a number of different research projects looking for a possible genetic basis for homosexuality, this section will look at some.

Brain Structures

It was guessed that there might be actual brain structure difference between homosexuals and heterosexuals. In mid–1991, neurobiologist Simon LeVay published the results of a small study on the autopsied brains of forty–one individuals, 35 males and 6 females. Nineteen of the men who died from complications due to AIDS were assumed to be homosexual, six of the sixteen men who were assumed to be heterosexual died of AIDS from involvement with IV drug use, and all of the females were assumed to be heterosexual. The tiny area of the brain that LeVay investigated is called the third interstitial nucleus of the anterior hypothalamus or INAH3. LeVay found some *slight* difference in volume between some of the group assumed to be homosexual and those assumed to be heterosexual. But he did not ask if the difference in volume in INAH3 contributed to homosexual behavior or if homosexual behavior contributed to a smaller INAH3. It was also unknown what effect the AIDS virus might have on the brain.

When his results were published, the media lit up like a Las Vegas casino with stories about how the discovered differences in the brains of homosexuals were the cause of their sexual preference. In the March 1994 issue of *Discover Magazine*, LeVay tried to correct some of the misinterpretations of his work. "I did not prove that homosexuality is genetic, or find a genetic cause for being gay. I didn't show that gay men are 'born that way,' the most common mistake people make in interpreting my work. Nor did I locate a gay center of the brain–INAH3 is less likely to be the sole gay nucleus of the brain than part of a chain of nuclei engaged in men and women's sexual behavior."[43] In 2001, William Byne, et al. published a study of the hypothalamus variation as it relates to sexual orientation and concluded, "No sex difference in volume was detected for any other INAH. No sexual variation in neuronal size or density was observed in any INAH. Although there was a trend for INAH3 to occupy a smaller volume in homosexual men than heterosexual men, there was no difference in the number of neurons within the nucleus based on sexual orientation."[44]

To help illustrate this point Laurence S. Meyer and Paul R. McHugh, in a recent article use a hypothetical example. "Suppose we were to study the brains of yoga teachers and compare them to the brains of bodybuilders. If we search long enough, we will eventually find statistically significant differences in some area of brain morphology or brain function between these two groups. But this would not imply that such differences determined the different life

---

43. David Nimmons, "Sex and the Brain," *Discovery Magazine,* March 1993, accessed August 19, 2017, http://discovermagazine.com/1994/Mar/sexandthebrain346/.

44. William Byne et al. "The Interstitial Nuclei of the Human Anterior Hypothalamus: An Investigation of Variation with Sex, Sexual Orientation, and HIV Status," *Hormones and Behavior* 40, no.2 (September 2001): 86.

trajectories of the yoga teacher and the bodybuilder. The brain differences could be the result rather than the cause, of distinctive patterns of behavior or interests."[45]

Hormonal Influences

It has been known for some time that the differentiation between males and females occurs in the womb through the influences of hormones especially testosterone and estrogen. The hypothesis was that perhaps homosexual orientation might be the result of an imbalance of hormones in the womb. Due to the potential of harm during pregnancy, an indirect way was used by a comparison of digit (finger) length ratios. Studies had shown that these ratios could be predictors for some hormones like testosterone and estrogens. In women the index finger or second digit (2D) is nearly the same length as the ring finger or fourth digit (4), but in men the index finger is usually shorter than the fourth digit. It was theorized that differences in the 2D:4D ratio could indicate a difference in prenatal hormone levels which might cause homosexual orientation.

A study by Terrance Williams shows, "The right–hand 2D:4D ratio of homosexual women was significantly more masculine (that is, smaller) than that of heterosexual women, and did not differ significantly from that of heterosexual men . . . The 2D:4D ratio of homosexual men was not significantly different from that of heterosexual men for either hand."[46] Meyer and McHugh report, "Finally, a 2005 study of 2D:4D ratios in an Austrian sample of 95 homosexual and 79 heterosexual men found that the 2D:4D ratios of heterosexual men were not significantly different from those of homosexual men. After reviewing the several studies on this trait, the authors conclude that 'more data are essential before we can be sure whether there is a 2D:4D effect for sexual orientation in men when ethnic variation is controlled for.'[47] A recent paper by Lauren Holler looked at the amount of testosterone and estrogen in umbilical cord blood to see if

---

45. Lawrence S. Meyer and Paul R. McHugh, "Special Report: Sexuality and Gender," *The New Atlantis: A Journal of Technology and Society,* no. 50 (August 19, 2016): 40, accessed August 20, 2017, www.thenewatlantis.com/docLib/20160819_TNA50SexualityandGender.pdf.

46. Terrance J. Williams et al., "Finger length ratios and sexual orientation," *Nature* 404 (March 30, 2000): 455.

47. Meyer and McHugh, 38.

it was related to the 2D:4D ratios in adults. She reported, "The exact relationship between prenatal sex steroid exposure and digit ratio is unclear. . . . In conclusion, this population based study of umbilical cord sex steroids and adult digit ratio found no statistically significant relationship between late gestation sex steroid exposure and the adult hand digit ratio."[48]

Lisa Diamond, et al. writes about another steroid exposure when unborn females receive too much androgen or male hormones,

> Perhaps the most relevant evidence comes from studies of girls with congenital adrenal hyperplasia (CAH), a condition in which fetuses are exposed to unusually high levels of androgens in utero as a result of disruptions in the synthesis of cortisol by the adrenal gland. Girls with CAH have received so much fetal androgen exposure by the time that they are born that they typically have partially masculinized genitals, which may be surgically altered at birth. As a result, girls with CAH allow for the investigation of prenatal androgen effects on female sexual orientation: if prenatal androgen exposure is a primary contributor to female sexual orientation, one would expect *all* CAH girls to develop stable, robust, and consistent lesbian or bisexual orientations, given that they have received a far stronger "dose" of prenatal androgens than the average non–CAH lesbian or bisexual would be expected to receive. Yet this is not the case. Longitudinal research has found that although CAH girls are more likely than age–matched controls to same–sex attractions, the majority identify as heterosexual and report exclusively other–sex attractions and sexual behavior. . . . Hence, as with the genetic data, the evidence does not support straightforward causation.[49]

Something that should be kept in mind that people often gets confused when hearing about these scientific studies is the difference between *correlation* and *causation*. Correlation is when one event is often seen with another event. Causation is when this event is the cause of that event happening. Identification of the two is called the *post hoc* fallacy (after this, therefore, because of this). Just because

---

48. Lauren P. Hollier et al., "Adult digit ratio (2D:4D) is not related to umbilical cord androgen or estrogen concentrations, their ratios or net bioactivity," *Early Human Development* 91 (2015): 116.

49. Diamond, 367, 368.

the sun rises after the rooster crows does not mean that the sun rises because the rooster crows.

Another term that should be explained is *heritability*. Edward Stein explains it this way: "Heritability represents the extent to which a trait is caused by genetic factors. That a trait has high heritability is not the same as a trait being genetically determined. The heritability of a trait is context–sensitive and highly contingent."[50]

Twin Studies

One of the most promising areas of study in looking for the "gay gene" was thought to be in the study of twins. For researchers the study of twins has always been a fascinating one because of their genetic similarity. If homosexuality has a genetic cause, then the study of its occurrence in twins should provide strong evidence for that theory since they are the genetically closest human beings. Monozygotic (MZ) or "identical twins" are just that, identical right down to their DNA. The next closest are dizygotic (DZ) or "fraternal twins." The purpose of the study of twins was not only to look at a possible genetic connection to same–sex behavior, but also to try to understand to what degree environmental factors may have played in that behavior.

Beginning in the early 1990s, studies sought volunteers via ads in homosexual publications or by word of mouth. Using this method can raise some issues for the accuracy of the data. Noted researcher Michael Bailey, who has published multiple studies in this field explains, "Such sampling is likely to result in volunteer bias that affects twin concordances and heritability analyses. . . . Furthermore, respondents with exclusively homosexual orientations may be over-represented and those with modest levels of homosexual attractions, underrepresented. . . . "[51] Bailey conducted a large study of about 5,000 twins drawn from the Australian National Health and Medical Research Council Twin Register, with the average age for both men and women being 29 years. He reported,

---

50. Edward Stein, *The Mismeasure of Desire, The Science, Theory and Ethics of Sexual Orientation* (Oxford: Oxford University Press, 1999), 215, 216.

51. J. Michael Bailey et al. "Genetic and Environmental Influences on Sexual Orientation and Its Correlates in an Australian Twin Sample," *Journal of Personality and Social Psychology* 78, no.3 (2000): 523.

In a recent review the lowest concordances for single–sex MZ, samples were 47% and 48% for men and women respectively. . . . In contrast, our concordances were 20% and 24% respectively . . . This suggests that concordances from prior studies were inflated because of concordance–dependent ascertainment bias. . . . In those studies, twins deciding whether to participate in a study clearly related to homosexuality probably considered the sexual orientation of their co–twin before agreeing to participate.[52]

Kenneth Kendler, conducted a study based on a random survey of 50,000 households in which the presents of a twin was reported by 14.8% of the respondents of whom 60% gave permission to be contacted for the twin study. The study reported, "The concordance rate for nonheterosexual sexual orientation in monozygotic twins found in this sample (31.6%) is similar to that found in the one previous general population twin study . . . but lower than the approximately 50% concordance rates found in the two previous studies that ascertained twin pairs through hemophilic publications. . . . These results suggest that twin pairs concordant for sexual orientation may be more likely to respond to such ads than are twin pairs discordant for sexual orientation."[53]

What Bailey and the other twin studies are looking for is *concordances*, which is what percentage of the identical twins are BOTH homosexual. If homosexual orientation was genetically determined like that of eye or skin color, we would expect the concordances to be near 100% instead of the 20% as the Bailey study reported. After all, how many identical twins have one with blonde hair and one with black hair? Edward Stein comments on these twin studies,

Twin studies have no bearing on whether sexual orientation is directly or indirectly heritable, that is, whether sexual orientation is caused directly by genes or whether it is caused indirectly in the context of particular environmental factors, by the effects of some other trait, itself genetically caused. . . . Nothing in Bailey's studies establishes that sexual orientation is genetically determined or that it is the direct

---

52. Ibid., 533.

53. Kenneth S. Kendler, "Sexual Orientation in a U.S. National Sample of Twin and Non–twin Sibling Pairs," *American Journal of Psychiatry* 157, no. 11 (November 2000): 1845.

result of genetic factors. Bailey realizes that his studies do not prove that genes directly cause sexual orientation, but many who site his studies do not."[54] Bailey himself realizes the limitations of his studies, "Our male MZ concordance figures suggest, however, that any major gene for strictly defined homosexuality has either low penetrance or low frequency."[55]

Meyer and McHugh conclude,

> Summarizing the studies of twins, we can say that there is no reliable scientific evidence that sexual orientation is determined by a person's genes. But there is evidence that genes play a role in influencing sexual orientation. So the question 'Are gay people born that way?' requires clarification. There is virtually no evidence that anyone, gay or straight, is 'born that way' if that means their sexual orientation was genetically determined. But there is some evidence from twin studies that certain genetic profiles probably increase the likelihood the person later identifies as gay or engages in same−sex sexual behavior.[56]

Regardless of whether there is a genetic influence on one becoming gay, it is irrelevant. For even if one were born with an anti−gay gene, it would not justify their being anti−gay any more than being born with a propensity to hate or to kill justifies acts of hatred or murder by them (see Frank Turek, *Correct, Not Politically Correct,* Charlotte: CrossExamined, 2008).

Fraternal Birth Order Effect or My Big Brother Made Me Gay!

Researchers have observed that males who have multiple older brothers have a slightly higher chance of being homosexual than the general population. The hypothesis used to try to explain this observation is called *The Fraternal Birth Order Effect*. One of the leading advocates and defenders of this hypothesis is Dr. Ray Blanchard who explains what he believes is happening to produce this effect:

---

54. Stein, 216.

55. J. Michael Bailey, 534.

56. Meyer and McHugh, 31.

Cells (or cell fragments) from male fetuses enter the maternal circulation during childbirth or perhaps earlier in pregnancy. These cells include substances that occur only on the surfaces of male cells, primarily male brain cells. The mother's immune system recognizes these male–specific molecules as foreign and produces antibodies to them. When the mother later becomes pregnant with another male fetus, her antibodies cross the placental barrier to and enter the fetal brain. Once in the brain, these antibodies bind to male–specific molecules on the surface of neurons. This prevents these neurons from "wiring–up" in male–typical pattern, so that the individual will later be attracted to men rather than women.[57]

Blanchard himself urges caution about this hypothesis. "I hasten to add that the fraternal birth order effect is a relatively weak effect, as quantified by conventional measures of effect size."[58] These are some of the limitations of this hypothesis. First, there are many homosexual men who have no older brother so this hypothesis would not account for them. Second, the presence of having only one older brother does not seem to have this effect. Third, having an older sister or multiple older sisters does not have this effect. Andrew Francis offers a further critique. "Moreover, although having multiple older brothers has a positive effect, it is not significant at the 5% level. Not only does the empirical evidence appear to reject the assumption of linearity, but it also cast doubt on whether there is a significant effect of older brothers on male sexual orientation in the first place."[59] He continues, "Therefore, while the maternal immune hypothesis is consistent with the finding that having multiple older brothers may have a positive (albeit insignificant) effect on male sexual orientation, the theory is unable to explain the entire pattern of family–demographic correlates reported in this article using a nationally representative sample of young adult Americans."[60] So, what is the percentage of male homosexuals who could attribute their sexual orientation to the

---

57. Ray Blanchard, "Detecting and Correcting for Family Size Differences in the Study of Sexual Orientation and Fraternal Birth Order," *Archives of Sexual Behavior* 43 (July, 2014): 851.

58. Ibid.

59. Andrew M. Francis, "Family and Sexual Orientation: The Family–Demographic Correlates of Homosexuality in Men and Women," *Journal of Sex Research* 45, no.4 (2000): 376.

60. Ibid., 377.

fraternal birth order effect? According to Blanchard et al. it is about 15%.[61] To put this into perspective, the estimated male homosexual population is about 3%, so this would mean it affects 15% of the 3% of male homosexuals plus, it assumes that this theory is correct for which there is as yet no confirming data.

Does X Mark the Spot?

When researchers looked at family histories, they found that more homosexual male relatives came through the mother's side of the family than through the father's. The researchers used a method called Molecular Genetics to try to estimate which particular variations are associated with certain traits, whether behavioral or physical. In 1993 Dean Hamer and his team studied 40 pairs of homosexual brothers, and through their family histories, Hamer found a possible linkage between homosexuality in males and markers on the Xq28 region of the X chromosome.[62] In1999 researcher George Rice attempted to replicate Hamer's study but was unsuccessful. He concluded, "We agree with Hamer that our results do not exclude the possibility of genetic effects underlying homosexuality. But with the use of similar methods of family ascertainment, phenotyping, and genotyping, we were unable to confirm evidence for an Xq28–linked locus underlying male homosexuality. Sanders et al. (3) came to the same conclusion with their linkage study."[63]

In a multi–authored paper in 2010 titled *Male Homosexuality: Nature or Culture?* Dr. John Bancroft concludes, "At the present time, therefore, we have no clear evidence of a specific determinate of homosexuality, but indications that a number of factors, varying in importance across individuals, can interact to make same–sex interaction and attraction more likely, followed by the impact of sociocultural 'constructionism' on sexual identity formation."[64] Currently the method used for chromosome linkage studies is called GWAS

---

61. Brian S. Mustanski et al. "A Critical Review of Recent Biological Research on Human Sexual Orientation," *Annual Review of Sex Research* 13 (2002): 119.

62. Dean Hamer et al. "A Linkage between DNA Markers on the X Chromosome and Male Sexual Orientation," *Science* 261, no. 5119 (July 1993): 321.

63. George Rice et al., "Genetics and Male Sexual Orientation," *Science* 285 (August 1999): 803a.

64. John Bancroft et al., "Male Homosexuality: Nature or Culture?" *Controversies in Sexual Medicine* 7, no.10 (October, 2010): 3252.

(Genome Wide Association Studies) which is a highly technical and sophisticated method for linkage studies.

In 2012, at the annual meeting of the American Society of Human Genetics, E. M. Drabant, et al, presented an abstract of an unpublished study carried out by the genetic testing firm 23andMe. "We carried out GWAS stratified by sex in a cohort of 7887 unrelated men and 5570 unrelated women of European ancestry collected in the two months since the initial survey release. No clear genome–wide significant associations have been found thus far, and the current data do not show any direct associations for markers within chromosome band Xq28."[65] In a recent 2015 article, researcher A. R. Sanders concludes, "While our study results provide further evidence for early (prenatal) biological influences on variation in male sexual orientation, we also emphasize that genetic contributions are far from determinant but instead represent a part of the trait's multifactorial causation, both genetic and environmental."[66]

Science writer Kate O'Riordan writes about how the "gay gene" has taken on a life of its own despite the fact that no one has been able to find it. In her 2012 article she concludes,

> There is no more a biological materiality to the gay gene now than there was in 1993. However, despite this, the address of the gay gene has persisted. It has become embedded in science media cultures and lodged in databases that open up into information flows with greater porosity than ever. It is fed by aggregations of noise that contribute to the erroneous signal strength of the message that there is a gay gene. . . .The combination of scientific journals promoting research in this area, together with science news media, reviews of popular science writing, and online databases, provides a substrate in which the gay gene has materialized and has a life story of its own. This materialization operates as an effective address that speaks to people but lacks real accountability.[67]

---

65. E. M. Drabant, "Genome Wide Association Study of Sexual Orientation in a Large, Web–based Cohort," Abstract presented at the American Society of Human Genetics Annual Meeting, 2012, 23andMe, Mountain View, CA.

66. A. R. Sanders et al., "Genome–wide scan demonstrates significant linkage for male sexual orientation," *Psychological Medicine* 45 (2015): 1386.

67. Kate O'Riordan, "The Life of the Gay Gene: From Hypothetical Genetic Marker to Social Reality," *Journal of Sex Research* 49, no. 4 (2012): 376.

Edward Stein agrees, "The terms 'gay gene' and 'homosexual gene' are, therefore, without meaning, unless one proposes that a particular gene, perhaps through a hormonal mechanism, organizes the brain specifically to support the desire to have sex with people of the same-sex gender. No one has, however, presented evidence in support of such a simple and direct link between genes and sexual orientation. . . ."[68] A quote from Meyer and McHugh is a fitting conclusion to this section: "So, again, the evidence for a genetic basis for homosexuality is inconsistent and inconclusive, which suggests that, though genetic factors explain some of the variations in sexual orientation, the genetic contribution to this trait is not likely to be strong and even less likely to be decisive."[69]

Is There Evidence That Sexual Orientation Can Change?

For decades one of the arguments used by advocates of homosexuality is that change in their sexual orientation either cannot or does not occur. Their mantra has been "once gay, always gay." Researchers began to study self-identified groups of heterosexual, homosexual, and bisexuals through a questionnaire process. In order for the researchers to identify any change in sexual orientation, the studies had to be conducted over a period of 5, 10, or more years in what is called a "longitudinal study. . . ." The results of these studies surprised many of the researchers as they discovered that changes in sexual attractions, sexual behaviors, and sexual identity took place in more people than they expected. *Sexual Fluidity* is the name given to these observations because of people reporting change in their sexual orientation usually from homosexual or bisexual to heterosexual, but on occasion they reported changes in the opposite direction. These changes occurred most often with adolescents and young adults, but they seem to become more stable by their early to mid-thirties.

With mounting evidence for sexual fluidity, researchers have difficulty knowing just how many members of any self-identified group there are. As Ritch Savin-Williams explains, "Yet, researchers readily acknowledge the existence of such groups ("gay youth") with little evidence that these individuals will be in the same group a month, a

---

68. Stein, 221.

69. Meyer and McHugh, 33.

year, or a decade henceforth. Evidence to support sexual orientation stability among nonheterosexuals is surprisingly meager."[70] Williams sites another study that covered a five year period from ages 16–20.

> Although most (97%) heterosexuals maintained their identity, nonheterosexuals frequently changed their identity label over the life course: 39% of gay males, 65% of lesbians, 66% of male bisexuals, and 77% of female bisexuals. The dimensional assessments of fantasy, attraction, and behavior reflected similar trends. Although roughly 90% of heterosexually identified individuals had none or one point changes during their lifetimes, the majority of gay (52%), lesbian (80%), and bisexual (90%) identified individuals had multiple changes on the dimensional variables. For nonheterosexuals, sexual behavior changed more often than romantic attraction and for all sexual identity categories, except bisexuals, women changed more than men.[71]

Williams concludes, "Thus, the answer to the question 'how many gays are there?' depends on which component of sexual orientation (behavior, attraction, identity) is used, how much of a component must be present to determine the cut–off point, and which biologic sex is being assessed."[72]

One of the leading researchers in the field of sexual fluidity is Dr. Lisa Diamond, of the University of Utah. She has authored multiple articles in peer–reviewed journals and is a respected researcher in this field. In an article published in 2008, she reports on her ten–year longitudinal study of female bisexuality with T1 being at the beginning of the study and T5 at the ten year mark.

> By T5, 60% of T1 lesbians had had sexual contact with a man, and 30% had been romantically involved with a man. Many of these women resolved the resulting contradiction between their lesbian identity and their other–sex attractions/behavior by switching to unlabeled or bisexual identities. Such "post–coming–out" identity changes challenge the longstanding

---

70. Ritch C. Savin–Williams et al. "Prevalence and Stability of Sexual Orientation Components during Adolescence and Young Adulthood," *Archives of Sexual Behavior* 36 (June 2007): 386.

71. Ibid., 387.

72. Ibid., 393.

assumption that sexual identity questioning is permanently resolved as soon as the individual replaces his or her initial heterosexual identity with a gay/lesbian/bisexual identity. For many women, this may be only the first of several such transitions; two thirds of women changed their identity label after T1, and approximately half of these women did so more than once. Hence, identity *change* is more common than identity *stability*, directly contrary to conventional wisdom. Furthermore, these changes do not appear attributable to social or developmental factors such as psychological immaturity, instability, or fear of stigmatization. If this were so, then one might expect a greater likelihood of identity change among younger women, women with a history of family disruption, and women who have experienced antigay stigmatization, but this is not the case.[73]

In a recent publication, Dr. Diamond reports on one of the longest longitudinal studies involving about 1,000 New Zealanders from their early 20s to their late 30s.

Given the multiple assessments, these data permit us to examine changes between ages 21 and 26, between ages 26 and 32, and between ages 32 and 38. . . . [R]ates of change do not appear to decline as respondents get older. Rates of change in attractions among same-sex attracted men ranged from 26% to 45%, and rates of change in same-sex-attracted women ranged from 55% to 60%. Among the same-sex attracted men reporting change, between 67% and 100% of the changes were towards heterosexuality, and this also was true for 83% to 91% of the same-sex-attracted women undergoing changes. Overall, changes among men who identified as heterosexual were observed in 1% to 2% of men and ranged from 4% to 12% among heterosexual women. Given the consistency of these findings, it is not scientifically accurate to describe same-sex sexual orientation as a uniformly immutable trait.[74]

Another recent study of 118 female and male young adults (18–26) with same-sex orientation reported, "Change in attractions was reported by 63% of females and 50% of males; of those reporting a

---

73. Lisa M. Diamond, "Female Bisexuality from Adolescence to Adulthood: Results From a 10-Year Longitudinal Study," *Developmental Psychology* 44, no. 1 (January 2008): 13.

74. Diamond and Rosky, "Scrutinizing Immutability," 370.

change in attractions, 48% of females and 34% of males reported that the change in attractions resulted in a change in sexual orientation identity labels used to describe their sexual orientations."[75]

Diamond concludes, "Several such studies have now been completed, and they unequivocally demonstrate that same–sex and other–sex attractions *do* change over time in some individuals. The degree of change is difficult to reliably estimate, given differences in study measures, but the occurrence of change is indisputable. . . . (It bears noting, however, that the majority of individuals seeking to change their sexual orientation report doing so for religious reasons rather than to escape discrimination . . ."[76]

The impact and importance of environmental, (in this case family) *influence* can have on behavior and attractions in an individual's life is illustrated in a study by Peter A. Lee and Christopher P. Houk.

> Two histories of physically normal men with persistent gender issues highlight the major impact played by parental input on sexual and gender development of children. Both men had been subjected to firm, harsh behavior modification by their parents, particularly their mothers, during childhood in response to effeminate behavior. While both men continue to manifest major gender/sexual issues as adults, their outcomes have been dramatically different. The first man takes female hormones and denies any satisfaction from his sexuality. This individual remains convinced that he has female internal sex organs and monthly internal menstrual bleeding. Although he has a career, he has become alienated from his family and is a social cripple.
>
> The second man has a successful career, lives a heterosexual life with his children and wife of 20 years and is involved in his community. He is visually attracted to men and remains obsessed with male pornography. This individual credits his mother with directing him towards a successful heterosexual life, which he feels has prevented the emotional burden of an active homosexual life. These two cases illustrate the

---

75. Sabra L. Katz–Wise, "Sexual Fluidity and Related Attitudes and Beliefs among Young Adults with a Same–Gender Orientation," *Archives of Sexual Behavior* 44 (July, 2015): 1465.

76. Diamond and Rosky, 368, 369.

tremendous influences played by environmental and parental input on the sexual perspectives of developing children.[77]

We have looked at the various theories and attempts to find a biological or genetically determined cause of homosexual orientation or behavior and found them to be a bit of a leaky bucket. William Byne, when looking at the evidence for biologically deterministic theories, states, "It is concluded that support for these theories derives as much from their appeal to prevailing cultural ideology as from their scientific merit. This appeal may explain why seriously flawed studies pass readily through the peer review process and become incorporated rapidly into the biologically deterministic canon where they remain viable even when replication attempts repeatedly fail."[78] Edward Stein argues, "In fact, it is more plausible that changes in attitudes about homosexuality have made biological theories seem more palatable and made psychological theories seem less so: a person who is favorably inclined towards lesbian and gay men may be more willing to accept biological theories than psychological ones; a person who is not so inclined might have the reverse dispositions. . . ."[79]

With so much of the discussion being carried on in the lofty towers of science, we would do well to listen to the words of Mark Twain: "There is something fascinating about science; one gets such wholesale returns of conjecture from such a trifling investment of fact."[80]

The conclusion of this section is summed up well by Lisa Diamond. "First, arguments based on the immutability of sexual orientation are unscientific, given that scientific research does not indicate that sexual orientation is uniformly biologically determined at birth or that patterns of same–sex and other–sex attractions remain fixed over the life course."[81] As we have seen, science has not removed the element of choice for those involved in homosexual practice. Some might be tempted to say, "I don't remember making

77. Peter A. Lee et al. "Impact of environment upon Gender Identity and Sexual Orientation: A Lesson for Parents of Children with Intersex or Gender Confusion," *Journal of Pediatric Endocrinology and Metabolism* 18, no. 7 (2005): 625.

78. William Byne, "Science and Belief: Psychobiological Research on Sexual Orientation," *Journal of Homosexuality* 28, no.3–4 (February 1995): 304.

79. Stein, 230.

80. Mark Twain, *Life on the Mississippi* (1883).

81. Diamond, "Female Bisexuality," 364.

a choice to be gay," but this assumes that the inability to remember a choice means that no choice was made. For example, most people cannot remember what they ate for breakfast 5 years ago, and yet they know that choices were made, so simply being unable to remember a choice is not proof that no choices were made.

When it comes to human sexuality we need more than a simplistic view of choice because there are many subtle factors involved, but in the end, these influences do not remove the moral nature of our choices. For many, homosexual practice was and remains a moral issue in much the same way that abortion is a moral issue. Walking into an abortion clinic is a choice. Who you get into bed with is a choice, and both have profound moral implications not only for the persons involved, but for our society as a whole.

Facts and Figures

We have looked at a number of attempts to determine if sexual orientation is the result of genes or environmental factors or both. We have looked at data on drug use, depression, suicide, and high risk sexual behavior. We want to take a look at some other data that paints a picture of homosexuality that is virtually never reported on the evening news or in the popular print media.

One statistic that we don't hear of is that of *Intimate Partner Violence* (IPV) among homosexuals. In their report, Meyer and McHugh give figures from a number of studies. A 2013 study by UCLA's Naomi Goldberg and Ilan Meyer collected data from a large probability sample of almost 32,000 people from the California Health Interview Survey.

> All three LGB groups had greater lifetime and one–year prevalence of intimate partner violence than the heterosexual group, but this difference was only statistically significant for bisexual women and gay men. Bisexual women were more likely to have experienced lifetime IPV (52% of bisexual women vs. 22% of heterosexual women and 32% of lesbians) and to have experienced IPV in the preceding year (27% of bisexuals vs. 5% heterosexuals and 10% of lesbians). For men, all three non–heterosexual groups had higher rates of lifetime and one–year IPV, but this was only statistically significant for gay men, who were more likely to have experienced IPV

over a lifetime (27% of gay men vs. 11% of heterosexual men and 19.6% of bisexual men) and over the preceding year (12% of gay men vs. 5% of heterosexual men and 9% of bisexual men).[82]

Another study cited by Meyer and McHugh is one conducted by Gregory Greenwood, published in 2002 based on telephone interviews with 2,881 men who have sex with men (MSM) in four cities from 1996 to 1998.

> Of those interviewed, 34% reported experiencing psychological or symbolic abuse, 22% reported physical abuse, and 5% reported sexual abuse. Overall, 39% reported some type of battering victimization, and 18% reported more than one type of battering in the previous five years. . . . The five–year prevalence of physical battering among this sample of urban MSM was also "significantly highe" than the annual rate of severe violence (3%) or total violence (12%) experienced in a representative sample of heterosexual women living with men, suggesting that the estimates of battering victimization for MSM in this study "are higher than or comparable to those reported for heterosexual women.[83]

A study published in 2015 by Taylor N.T. Brown and Jody L. Herman focused on Intimate Partner Violence (IPV) and Intimate Partner Sexual Abuse (IPSA). "We reviewed 42 studies, from 1989 to the present, that include findings on the prevalence of IPV and IPSA. . . . Most studies reviewed for this report found a lifetime prevalence of IPV among lesbian and bisexual women, gay and bisexual men, and transgender people that is as high as or higher than the U.S. general population."[84]

A possible link between childhood sexual abuse (CSA) and later intimate partner violence has also been reported for men who have sex with men (MSM),

---

82. Meyer and McHugh, 72.

83. Ibid., 73.

84. Taylor N.T. Brown and Jody L. Herman, "Intimate Partner Violence and Sexual Abuse among LGBT People," *The Williams Institute*, UCLA School of Law (November 2015): 2.

MSM who initially disclosed male sex partners reported significantly . . . higher rates of early physical abuse (36%) and lifetime abuse (49%) compared with non–MSM (15 and 22%), respectively. These MSM reported significantly higher rates of sexual abuse by age 11, age 21, and over a lifetime compared with non–MSM. . . . Early life physical and sexual abuse was higher among MSM who disclosed male sex partners compared with heterosexual men; however, all MSM who experienced early–life abuse were more likely to be IPV victims or perpetrators.[85]

Another study looked at the associations of sexual identity and same–sex behaviors of those with a history of Childhood Sexual Abuse (CSA). "

Overall, 14.9% of women and 5.2% of men reported CSA. Among women, bisexuals, lesbians, and heterosexuals with same–sex partners had 5.3 times, 3.4 times, and 2.9 times the odds, respectively, for CSA occurring sometimes/ more frequently (vs. never) compared with heterosexuals not having same–sex partners or attractions. Among men, bisexuals, gay men, and heterosexuals with same–sex partners had 12.8 times, 9.5 times, and 7.9 times the odds, respectively, for CSA. Men and women sometimes or frequently abused had significant increases in odds for HIV/STI incidence compared with those not abused. Among women, sexual minorities had 3.8 times the odds and heterosexuals had 2.8 times the odds, whereas among men, sexual minorities had 4.2 times odds and heterosexuals had 1.5 times the odds. Extraordinarily high rates of CSA were observed for sexual minorities, and sexual minorities were more likely to have incident HIV or STIs, in this U.S. population survey.[86]

HIV and AIDS

The first clinically observed cases of AIDS in the U.S. came in 1981. It was a new and frightening disease of unknown origin that

---

85. Seth L. Welles et al. "Intimate Partner Violence among Men Having Sex with Men, Women, or Both: Early Life Sexual and Physical Abuse as Antecedents," *Journal of Community Health* 36 (June 2011): 477.

86. Thersa Sweet and Seth L. Welles, "Associations of Sexual Identity or Same–Sex Behaviors with History of Childhood Sexual Abuse and HIV/STI Risk in the United States," *Journal of Acquired Immune Deficiency Syndrome* 59, no. 4 (April 1, 2012): 400.

was largely seen in homosexual men, and because of this, it was soon named "GRID" or gay–related immune deficiency. An article was published in *The New York Times* on May 11, 1982 by Lawrence K. Altman with the title "New Homosexual Disorder Worries Health Officials." It reads in part,

> A serious disorder of the immune system that has been known to doctors for less than a year–a disorder that appears to affect primarily male homosexuals–has now affected at least 335 people, of whom it has killed 136, officials of the Centers for Disease Control in Atlanta said yesterday. Federal health officials are concerned that tens of thousands more homosexual men may be silently affected and therefore vulnerable to potentially grave ailments. . . . The cause of the disorder is unknown. Researchers call it A.I.D., for acquired immunodeficiency disease, or GRID, for gay–related immunodeficiency. It has been reported in 20 states and seven countries. But the overwhelming majority of cases have been in New York City (158), elsewhere in New York State (10), New Jersey (14) and California (71).[87]

In 1983 the virus that causes AIDS was discovered and was given the name HIV (human immunodeficiency virus). Shortly thereafter (with some political pressure) the designation for the disease was changed from GRID to AIDS (acquired immunodeficiency syndrome). The disease would go on to have a devastating impact beyond what anyone could have imagined in 1983. Let's look at some of the facts and figures from the CDC.

According to a CDC fact sheet dated March 2015, "By the end of 2011, an estimated 311,087 gay and bisexual men with AIDS had died in the United States since the beginning of the epidemic, representing 47% of all deaths of persons with AIDS."

"In 2013, in the United States, gay and bisexual men accounted for 81% (30,689) of the 37,887 estimated HIV diagnoses among all males aged 13 years and older and 65% of the 47,352 estimated diagnoses among all persons receiving an HIV diagnosis that year."[88] Keep in mind that most estimates put the male homosexual popula-

---

87. Lawrence K. Altman, "New Homosexual Disorder Worries Health Officials," *The New York Times*, May 11, 1982.

88. "HIV among gay and bisexual men," *CDC Fact Sheet*, March 2015.

tion at about 3%. In a 2016 CDC Fact Sheet, the rate of new HIV diagnoses among MSM is "more than 44 times that of other men"[89]

A study published in 2011 found that men who have sex with men (MSM) have a 140-fold increased risk for HIV and syphilis compared to heterosexual men (MSW) in New York City.

> MSM HIV and P&S syphilis rates were 2526.9/100,000 and 707.0/100,000, each of which was over 140 times MSW rates. Rates were highest among young and black MSM. Over 4 years, HIV rates more than doubled and P&S syphilis rates increased 6-fold among 18-year-old to 29-year-old MSM. . . . Our analysis adds to this body of work by examining trends in newly diagnosed HIV and P&S syphilis among sexually active MSM in New York City (NYC), an epicenter of the US HIV epidemic. In NYC, the proportion of reported male HIV diagnoses that were among MSM increased 19% in just 5 years. MSM have also been disproportionately affected by P&S syphilis since the outbreak began in 1999. In 2008, 87% of male P&S syphilis cases in NYC reported sex with other men.[90]

Another problem for those suffering from HIV is that many are aging before their time. As Alan Landay, chair of the immunology and microbiology department at Rush University Medical Center of Chicago explains, "What we are now realizing is that HIV as a disease is really a disease of inflammation. We are able to control the virus, but what remains are the immune dysfunction and dysregulation in patients that are leading to the diseases of aging such as cardio-vascular disease, bone disease, cancer and diabetes."[91] Landay, who has been speaking at various sessions of the Sixteenth International Congress of Immunology in Melbourne, calls this new concept "inflammaging," referring to the "accelerated immune senescence or

---

89. Ibid., August 2016.

90. Preeti Pathela et al, "Men who have sex with men have a 140-fold higher risk for newly diagnosed HIV and syphilis compared with heterosexual men in New York City," *Journal of Acquired Immune Deficiency Syndrome* 58, no.4 (December 1, 2011): 408.

91. Alan Landay, "HIV Patients 'Getting Old before Their Time,'" August 30, 2016, accessed August 20, 2017, http://www.scidev.net/global/hiv-aids/feature/hiv-patients-old-ageing-disease.html.

the cells are getting old before their time," which they are seeing in HIV patients.[92]

Divorce

In the wake of the U.S. Supreme Court's decision concerning homosexual "marriage," it would seem wise to find out if there are any significant differences that have been observed between homosexual and heterosexual marriages in countries that have allowed same–sex "marriages" for a number of years. In 1989, Denmark became the first country to give legal recognition to same–sex unions under the term *registered partnership.* In 1993, Norway gave same–sex couples this same legal status as Denmark, which was followed by Sweden in 1995. Then in 2001, the Netherlands amended their marriage laws to give same–sex couples the same marriage legal status as heterosexual couples. This was followed by Belgium in 2003, and then Spain and Canada in 2005.

In a study of same–sex marriages in Norway and Sweden published in 2006 we read,

> We found that divorce risks are higher in same–sex partnerships than opposite–sex marriages and that unions of lesbians are considerably less stable, or more dynamic, than unions of gay men. In Norway and Sweden, the divorce risk for female partnerships is practically double that for male partnerships. . . . In Norway, 13% of partnerships of men and 21% of female partnerships are likely to end in divorce within six years from partnership registration. In Sweden, 20% of male partnerships and 30% of female marriages are likely to end in divorce within five years of partnership formation. These levels are higher than the corresponding 13% of heterosexual marriages that end in divorce within five years in Sweden. . . .[93]

Another study, this time of British same–sex couples and different–sex couples published in 2012, found that "compared to married couples, the dissolution rates for male and female same–sex cohabiters were seven and five times higher, respectively. Among

---

92. Ibid.

93. Gunnar Andersson et al. "The Demographics of Same–sex Marriages in Norway and Sweden," *Demography* 43, no.1 (February 2006): 95.

cohabiters, the differences were smaller: The dissolution rate for male and female same-sex cohabiters was approximately double the rate for different-sex cohabiters."[94] Another recent study in 2014, of Norwegian same-sex marriages found, "For instance, after 7 years, 26% of female partnerships had dissolved, compared with 20% of male partnerships. At the end of the observation period (18 years) 45% of female and 40% of male partnerships contracted in 1993 had dissolved. In comparison, 31% of opposite-sex marriages contracted in 1993 had dissolved by 2011"[95]

If this is the case for Sweden, Norway, and Britain whose laws have been changed for nearly 20 years and who have a much lower level of "homophobia" than the United States, what should we expect the stability of homosexual "marriages" to be? These studies should tell us to expect the divorce rate to be even greater than what we are experiencing with natural marriage couples.

Divorce is like an acid that weakens the very institution of marriage because as Jesus said in Matthew 19:8, it was never intended by God that married couples would divorce and the boundary for that marriage was, and remains, one man and one woman for life. Human beings who desire to "expand" that boundary are setting themselves up as the creator, claiming that they know what is best for human relationships. For the Christian a true marriage between persons of the same sex is as impossible to achieve as it is to be a married bachelor. True, deep, and lasting friendships between members of the same sex should be sought and cherished, and even though there are many similarities between close same-sex friendship and marriage, we must never allow ourselves to confuse the two regardless of whatever feelings we may struggle with.

Conclusions

We have looked at multiple attempts to locate the "gay gene" or some other mechanism which could be shown to be biologically deterministic for homosexual behavior only to find that genes or expo-

---

94. Charles Q. Lau, "The stability of same-sex cohabitation, different-sex cohabitation and marriage," *Journal of Marriage and Family*, 74 (October 2012): 984.

95. Kenneth Aarskaug Wiik, "Divorce in Norwegian Same-sex marriages and Registered Partnerships: The Role of Children," *Journal of Marriage and Family* 76 (October 2014): 923.

sure to prenatal hormones have no more than a weak to moderate *influence* and do not in any known way determine behavior. We saw how data continues to increase for the observation of *sexual fluidity* with regards to both sexual orientation and sexual behavior especially for the early to late teen years. There is no solid scientific basis for the belief that homosexual are "born that way" or that their sexual orientation is immutable ("once gay, always gay"), a mantra that even researcher and self–identified lesbian Dr. Lisa Diamond has urged the homosexual community to drop.

The search for the scientific justification of homosexual behavior is motivated by more than just pure research. The discovery of a genetic determination for homosexual behavior would have a profound effect on the moral discussion of the issue. Most of the researchers quoted in this chapter are either sympathetic to or supportive of homosexual "rights" or are themselves homosexual (e.g. Simon LeVay, and Lisa Diamond). The discovery of a "gay gene" that determined behavior would be welcome news for those seeking to reinterpret Scripture, as it would give solid footing to the "God made me this way" argument that would force those of the traditional interpretation to be in a more defensive position. It would in other words be the long sought for, moral escape hatch.

Science is telling us from the view of the natural world what the Bible has long said, namely that there is something intrinsically wrong with same–sex sexual relationships. Of course, we can always find some people who have adapted to "unnatural" living conditions just like there are people who have adapted to living in the Arctic, but this in no way proves that it's the best place for human flourishing. After the intimate relationship between Adam and Eve and the Lord was broken because of disobedience, they hid themselves (Genesis 3:8). Human beings have been hiding themselves from God ever since.

In a recent 2016 study published in *Culture, Health & Sexuality*, titled "Struggling to Be the Alpha," lead author Tamar Goldenberg suggests that one of the ways to reduce the high incidence of intimate partner violence in male homosexual relationships would be to redefine the gender roles. This would mean that one of the partners should take on a more feminine role because two 'alpha' males tend towards violence in an intimate relationship. This is more evidence for the *unnaturalness* of intimate same–sex relationships because as Robert Gagnon has pointed out, there is too much sameness and not enough complimentary difference that you have in opposite–sex relationships, which is what God intended at creation for human beings.[96]

The scientific information presented here gives witness to what Paul wrote in Romans that people suppress or hold down and reject the truth about what may be known about God because of their sinful behavior. Paul writes in Romans 1:19, 20, ". . . what may be known about God is plain to them, because God has made it plain to them. For since the creation of the world God's invisible qualities–his eternal power and divine nature–have been clearly seen, being understood from what has been made, so that men are without excuse." It is plain for anyone to see what God's intention for human sexuality was and is. One example of how our society is suppressing the truth is the effort to blur the distinctions between male and female–women in frontline combat units, gender "neutral" bathrooms, removing "Father" and "Mother" from birth certificates and replacing them with "Partner 1" and "Partner 2." These and many more are examples of the attempts to blur the God created distinctions, distinctions that help keep us in a right relationship with Him. Imagine the dangerous effect there would be if distinctions between the medicines in your medicine cabinet were removed. Removing or blurring the God created differences will have just as disastrous and long lasting results. The importance of distinctions is put forcefully by Isaiah in chapter 5 verse 20, "Woe to those who call evil good and good evil, who put darkness for light and light for darkness, who put bitter for sweet and sweet for bitter."

The purpose of this chapter is not to clobber those involved in homosexuality with facts, figures, and statistics, but to use it to remove the shield that is often used to hide behind when confronted with God's truth. God's Spirit calls us all to drop our shields and stop our hiding to allow His Spirit to begin the help, hope, and healing we

---

96. See Robert Gagnon, "The Scriptural Case for a Male–Female Prerequisite for Sexual Relations: The New Testament Perspective," in *Homosexuality, Marriage, and the Church*, edited by Roy E. Gane et al. (Berrien Springs, MI: Andrews University Press, 2012), 74.

need. This won't be easy, but then Jesus never promised it would be (Matthew 16:24).

PART 2

WHAT DOES THE BIBLE SAY?

6

Homosexuality in Ancient Greece and Rome

In this chapter we will take a look at how the two most influential cultures at the time of the New Testament writers viewed homosexuality and marriage. It is sometimes argued that the authors of Scripture were unaware of loving, committed, and monogamous homosexual relationships and that most of them in ancient times were exploitive in nature, and, therefore, the prohibitions listed against homosexual behavior do not apply.

First, a couple of terms need to be clarified so we can better understand how the ancient Greeks and Romans viewed sexuality. There is no word in the ancient world for the term "homosexual" or "homosexuality." These terms were invented in the mid–nineteenth century. Their focus is on orientation whereas the ancient Greeks and Romans were more focused on gender. The term *paederasty* or "boy love" or to love boys has a bit different understanding in ancient times than for us today. For us the term "boy" means a very young male between maybe 3 to 11 years old, but for the ancients that would be a child. In ancient Greece the age for a boy to begin being tutored by an older man was just after entering puberty until the age of 17 or 18 or until he could grow a full beard.[1] When a young man reached maturity, he was expected to find a wife (which had most likely been prearranged) and begin a family. He would end the pupil/teacher relationship, which had often involved sexual intercourse between them.

---

1. Hans Licht, *Sexual Life in Ancient Greece* (New York: Dorset Press, 1993), 416.

The ancient Greeks had a different view of what was "natural" and "unnatural" about sex between males than most people in the present Western world. The Greeks worshiped form and beauty, and since they believed in the inherent superiority of males, they found the beauty of the young athletic male to be an object of natural desire. Litcht explains, "As time went on, Hellenic culture became more and more occupied with male sex, as is shown by the fact that an actual education is only spoken of in the case of boys. The most necessary elementary knowledge in reading and writing, and likewise skill in female handiwork, the most important of which were spinning and weaving, was taught girls by their mothers."[2]

In his classic study of Greek homosexuality, Kenneth Dover explains the Greek idea of homosexuality. It was considered natural or unnatural based upon the belief that because women do not have the same level of moral insight as a man, together with the belief that women enjoy sexual intercourse more intensely than a man, a woman would be more likely to give in to a potential lover. This was one of the reasons for sexual segregation. The Greeks thought it unnatural for a man to desire the submissive (female) role in sexual intercourse as it was not physically enjoyable and was a demeaning role for an adult male to assume. "All the evidence which tends to support the hypothesis that the Greeks regarded male homosexual desire as natural concerns the active partner, and we have yet to consider the abundant evidence that for them the differentiation between the active and the passive role in homosexuality was of profound importance."[3]

In the male dominated culture of ancient Greece marriages were mostly prearranged and there was a kind of moral duty or expectation for a man to find a wife and have children. Women were for the most part second class citizens who had no real say in local government and were not allowed to speak in an assembly of civic leaders. Most of a woman's life was spent in the home raising children and directing slaves. It was the prescribed role of women to be inseminated and bring forth the next generation of citizens. As Licht points out, "That men took wives mainly for the sake of begetting children, not only follows from the official formula of betrothal, 'for the pro-

---

2. Ibid., 28.

3. Dover Kenneth, *Greek Homosexuality* (Cambridge: Harvard University Press, 1978), 67–68.

creation of legitimate offspring,'. . . but is also frankly admitted by several Greek authors. . . ."[4]

Given this cultural setting and mindset, homosexual relationships between a man, who was married, and an adolescent male whom he was teaching would have been almost expected. It would have also been common for the master of the house to engage in sex with any slaves he might own since slaves were not considered citizens but property. They had no rights, and the master could do with them as he wished. Dover explains the cultural thinking of the time, ". . . it was taken absolutely for granted that close contact with a beautiful, grateful, admiring young male was a virtually irresistible temptation. It is equally easy to see why an eros which perpetually restrained itself from bodily gratification should be homosexual: it was after all the prescribed role of women to be inseminated, whereas popular sentiment romanticised and applauded the chastity of an eromenos and the devotedly unselfish erastes."[5] The *eromenos* is the young male "loved one" and *erastes* is the older male "lover." This idea was even incorporated into Greek myth with Zeus lusting after and carrying away the young man Ganymede. This sent the message that if the gods approved of this kind of relationship, who could argue against it.

To be sure, there were laws in some city/states that prohibited the seduction and sexual use of young free born males by older ones but they varied from one city/state to another and were often not enforced. There is some evidence that on occasion the relationship between the older male and young pupil would continue beyond the time it was expected to stop. Such a relationship would be thought of as "unnatural" and irresponsible if there was no marriage to a wife and children were not produced.

Rome

The Romans had a view similar to that of the Greeks with regard to homosexuality in that it was not considered a moral issue as long as the regulations regarding who, when, and how you had sex with were observed. Both Greece and Rome were honor / shame based

---

4. Licht, 33.

5. Dover, 164.

societies with a strong masculine domination and belief in the inferiority of women, slaves, and non–Romans. Craig Williams gives us some insight into the thinking and conduct of sexual matters of the ancient Romans. "As we shall see, the sources left to us from ancient Rome make it abundantly clear that Roman traditions fell squarely in line with the worldwide trend: homosexual behavior was not condemned per se, and a citizen male could admit to sexual experience with males in certain contexts and configurations without fear of ridicule or reprisal, without the threat even of a raised eyebrow."[6] Williams neglected to mention a notable group that did not follow this "worldwide trend" that being the Hebrews (and Christians after them) who condemned all sexual activity outside of man and woman marriage.

Kyle Harper gives some more insight into the "nature" of a man attracted to boys.

> Whereas pederasty was a type of passion, in the Roman world the man who wished to be loved by men was a type of person. Nothing brings this out quite so clearly as the astrological literature of the high empire. The Roman era was the first great age of popular astrology in the west. Study of the stars was a serious science; Ptolemy was, after Galen, the greatest scientist of his century. His handbook of astrology was meant for learned practitioners of the craft. Astrology was a predictive science not because it provided a mystical insight into the future but rather because it could account for the individual's physical and mental constitution. Sexual traits were determined by the composition of the soul. Ptolemy imagines an extraordinary array of sexual phenotypes; the stars could make people erotic, frigid, passionate for women, passionate for boys, aggressive, pathic, impotent, incestuous, adulterous and so on. Desire for boys was an expression of the same underlying passions for girls, and it could exist in normal or excessive quantities.[7]

Williams gives us the sexual protocols for a Roman man.

---

6. Craig A.Williams, *Roman Homosexuality*, 2nd ed. (Oxford: Oxford University Press, 2010), 1.

7. Kyle Harper, *From Shame to Sin, The Christian Transformation of Sexual Morality in Late Antiquity* (Cambridge: Harvard University Press, 2013), 31–32.

First and foremost, a self–respecting Roman man must always give the appearance of playing the insertive role in penetrative acts, and not the receptive role: to use popular terminology often unfortunately replicated in the language of scholarship, he must be the "active," not the "passive," partner. This can justly be called the prime directive of masculine sexual behavior for Romans, and it has an obvious relationship to hierarchical social structures. . . . A second protocol governing men's sexual behavior concerned the status of their partner, and here too the rule applied regardless of their partners' sex: apart from his wife, freeborn Romans both male and female were officially off–limits sexual partners for a Roman man. . . . According to the rules, freeborn Roman males and females other than his wife were excluded as acceptable partners, thus leaving slaves, prostitutes, and noncitizens of either sex as persons with whom a Roman man could have sexual relations without causing eyebrows to rise–provided always, of course, that the man observed the prime directive of maintaining the appearance of playing the insertive role in these sexual encounters.[8]

This view of sexual restraint or lack thereof, by Roman men made for a dramatically different view of marriage and the role of women in Roman social life. Love often had little place in getting married and staying married. Otto Kiefer remarks,

These accounts, especially Plutarch's, show us this at least– what we call love had hardly any part in these marriages. In addition, the husband and wife were very often betrothed to each other by their parents in early youth, for one motive or another; the reason was usually an economic one. The earliest age at which a man could marry was 15 to 16; a woman could marry when she was 12. . . . If real love developed between husband and wife in these conditions it was generally a fortunate accident rather than the general rule. . . . Above all, the Romans married to have children to succeed them–that was their free and natural way of regarding sexual matters.[9]

What we have pointed out should not be taken to imply that there was no romance and love between men and women and they were

---

8. Williams, *Roman Homosexuality,* 18–19.

9. Otto Kiefer, *Sexual Life in Ancient Rome* (New York: Barnes & Noble, 1953), 24–25.

just in the business of begetting children, but it should be understood that the man of the house had the power of life and death over even the children born to him. If he welcomed the child into the house, it would live, and if not, it was exposed and left outside for "the gods" to decide. Archaeological evidence for this type of treatment of infants has been found in Ashkelon, Israel where 100 baby skeletons were found under a former Roman bathhouse, and in Hambleden, England in 1912, the Roman era remains of 97 infants that had been killed were found at that site.[10]

So, from Israel to England, from one end of the Roman Empire to the other, we see one of the results of when human beings turn away from God. As the apostle Paul states in Rom. 1:21–23, "For although they knew God, they neither glorified him as God nor gave thanks to him, but their foolish hearts were darkened. Although they claimed to be wise, they became fools and exchanged the glory of the immortal God for images made to look like mortal man and birds and animals and reptiles."

It must have been a bit of a shock for Greek and Roman men who came to the Lord to hear the words of Paul in Ephesians chapter 5 about loving their wives as Christ loved his church. Nothing would have been more counter–cultural for them than the command for husbands to love their wives as Christ loved the Church.

With this very brief look at both the Greek and Roman view of homosexuality as well as marriage, we now look at an objection to the traditional understanding of the biblical statements about homosexual activities.

Objections to Traditional Biblical Position on Homosexuality

It has been argued by some who wish to blunt the force of the Bible's very pointed words about homosexuality that the New Testament authors were unaware of the loving, kind, caring and monogamous relationships modern homosexuals desire and that they knew only of "exploitive" types such as boys taken as slaves or pros-

---

10. April Holloway, "Accounts of Roman Infanticide and Sacrifice All Just Myth and Legend?" September 5, 2016, accessed September 18, 2017, http://www.ancient-origins.net/news–history–archaeology/accounts–roman–infanticide–and–sacrifice–all–just–myth–and–legend–006591.

titutes. First, this "new knowledge" argument assumes (against the evidence) that ancient people had not yet experienced the full range of human emotions as modern people have and therefore the biblical writers could not have known about the loving and deeply committed types of same–sex relationships some have today.

Kyle Harper points out, "It scarcely needs saying that same–sex marriages between women, or men, had no standing or consequences in public law, but that fact hardly diminishes the extraordinary testimony we do have for durable forms of same–sex companionship. In a peaceful and prosperous society, amid a highly urbanized and remarkably interconnected empire where marriage was valorized as an institution of the greatest moral and emotional fulfillment, same–sex pairs openly claimed, and ritually enacted, their own conjugal rights."[11]

We should not assume that biblical writers, like the apostle Paul who traveled all over the Mediterranean, had contact with travelers who visited still more cities all of whom had been conquered by Rome, who spoke the language, and lived in that culture should know less about the sexual situation of his day and accepted the assumptions of the pagan culture of that time as to what constitutes "natural" or "unnatural" sexual relations. Pottery, paintings, and parchments help us to see that Paul could very well have known of long term same–sex relationships and still found them sinful.[12]

The "new knowledge" argument assumes that the biblical writers were mainly concerned with true loving and non–exploitive types of relationships, when in fact they were most concerned with righteous and holy relationships after the pattern that had been established by God in Genesis 1 and 2.

---

11. Harper, 36.

12. For a scholarly study of the accuracy and detail in the book of Acts, see Colin J. Hemer, *The Book of Acts in the Setting of Hellenistic History,* 2nd ed. (Warsaw, IN: Eisenbrauns, 2001).

7

God's First Revelation

The Witness of Creation vs God's Plan and Pattern for Sex

The Bible is accepted as an authority by both many Jews and Christians. Indeed, it was cited by many of our founding Fathers as the basis for our society. And the first words of the Bible declare, "In the beginning, God created the heavens and the earth" (Gen. 1:1). This declarative statement of God as Creator of all things will be crucial to the understanding of our relationship to God as well as our relationship to others, especially between that of men and women. As the Creator, God sets the limits, boundaries, and functions for everything He creates, and everything He created was "very good" (Gen. 1:31). As the Creator of all things, it is God who determines the functions and boundaries not just of living things but of all of the cosmos.

In Gen. 2:18, we read that it is God who pronounces the first "not good," saying, "It is not good for the man to be alone." It is God who brings the created animals to Adam for him to name. He does this for at least two reasons. First, naming the animals shows he has dominion over them, and second, when all the animals had been named, no suitable helper, no one like Adam was found. God made it clear what Adam was lacking. It is God who causes Adam to fall into a deep sleep, and taking a portion of Adam's side, He creates a woman. It is God who brings the woman to Adam, who then exclaims, "This is now bone of my bone and flesh of my flesh; she shall be called woman, for she was taken out of man" (Gen. 2:23).

In Gen. 1:27, 28, we see this summed up: "So God created man in his own image, in the image of God he created him; male and female he created them. God blessed them and said to them, 'Be fruitful and increase in number, fill the earth and subdue it.'" Notice in all this that it is God who is the actor, the Creator, the one who sets the patterns and the boundaries. There is no hint that there was a "suggestion box" somewhere in Eden where Adam could make his own ideas known.

What is being emphasized in the creation account is the complementary nature of the man and the woman–she is not just *like* him; she is *from* him. She is his sexual "other" and as such is the only one who can complete him. Their physical joining is a reminder of God's intention for them when He created them, in a similar way to how our "naval" reminds us we were joined to a mother at one time. Donald Wold explains, "God created woman, not from the earth as he did the beasts, thus to emphasize the division between species, but from the man himself. . . . The union between a man and a woman thus recreates the natural order of creation. . . . Unnatural acts, that is, cross–species and same–gender sexual relations, ultimately deny the creative work of God and offend the design of the human species, which is patterned after the image of God."[1]

This "otherness" cannot be completed by adding another male for him or another female for her, which is why feelings and desires, as important as they are in relationships, are not the basis for the rightness or wrongness of sexual actions, but creation, the way God made us, is. The sexual union, the "one flesh" joining in marriage of a man and a woman, allows us to participate in the privilege of making another human being, a being made in the image and likeness of God. Dr. Robert Gagnon, in his excellent book *The Bible and Homosexual Practice,* says, "So great is the complementarity of male and female, so seriously is the notion of 'attachment' and 'joining' taken, that the marital bond between man and woman takes precedence even over the bond with the parents that physically produced them. . . . Attention is focused not on the goal of procreation (childbearing receives mention only in 3:16) but rather on the relational (including physical/sexual) complementarity of the male and female,

---

1. Donald J. Wold, *Out of Order* (Grand Rapids: Baker Books, 1998), 131.

that is, on the companionship and support provided by heterosexual marriage."[2]

It would seem clear from this that God as the Creator of heaven and earth, who sets the boundaries of day and night, of days and years, of even the boundaries of the oceans as in Job 38:11, this God has set the pattern and limits of human sexual relationships within the marriage between one man and one woman for life. It is this pattern that will be assumed throughout all of Scripture. It is the rock upon which human sexual morality will be built and why homosexuality will be referred to as "contrary to nature" as it is contrary to God's created order. James B. De Young puts it this way: "The creation of humans as male and female (Genesis 1) and the heterosexual union that constitutes marriage (Genesis 2) lie at the basis of the rest of Scripture and its comments about sexuality and marriage. A proper understanding of, and submission to, the record of Creation will guide the inquirer to the truth about homosexuality and heterosexuality. Genesis 1–3 clearly is foundational to other Bible texts."[3]

Homosexuality violates the order of creation on at least two levels, a symbolic level and a physical level. On the symbolic level homosexual sex mocks the male/female distinction created by God and attempts to substitute what cannot be substituted. On the physical level it attempts to complete the design of human sexual nature by simply adding sameness instead of the complimentary and completing differences designed by God. Whether it is homosexual sex, adultery or fornication, the feelings of love and companionship experienced are irrelevant to God's order of creation, and this order will be the boundary to *all* human sexual activity. It is objective and outside of the individual and is not based on their feelings. God's pattern of perfection became twisted and distorted when created human beings felt they knew more than the Creator of how best to meet their needs.

---

2. Robert Gagnon, *The Bible and Homosexual Practice* (Nashville: Abingdon Press, 2001), 61.

3. James B. De Young, *Homosexuality: Contemporary Claims Examined in the Light of the Bible and Other Ancient Literature and Law* (Grand Rapids: Kregel Publications, 2000), 32.

The Sad Story of Sodom

The story of Sodom in Genesis 19 is one of the most well–known and in modern times one of the most controversial accounts in the Bible. The story begins in chapter 18 when the Lord and two angels who appear as men meet Abraham. As a good host, Abraham offers them food and drink and a chance to rest. When they have rested they start towards Sodom, and the Lord tells Abraham why He is there: "Then the Lord said, 'The outcry against Sodom and Gomorrah is so great and their sin so grievous that I will go down and see if what they have done is as bad as the outcry that has reached me. If not, I will know" (Gen. 18:20, 21). Abraham bargained for the life of the righteous, asking the Lord if there were fifty righteous (in a city of thousands) would He still destroy the city to which the Lord said, no, He would not. Abraham seems to have had some idea of the wickedness of the city because he asks God if He will spare the city if there are only forty–five righteous, and then forty, and then thirty, and then twenty, and finally ten, where we read in verse 32, "He answered, For the sake of ten, I will not destroy it." In chapter 19, the two angels have arrived at Sodom where they are met by Lot who was Abraham's nephew. Lot strongly insists that they stay with him for the night. In verse 4 and 5 we read, "Before they had gone to bed, all the men of the city of Sodom both young and old–surrounded the house. They called to Lot, 'Where are the men who came to you tonight? Bring them out to us so that we can have sex with them.'" Most of the controversy hinges on *one* word, which the King James Version translates as *know*, instead of what modern translators translate as *sex*. "Bring them out that we may *know* them." The Hebrew word for *know* is *yadah* and occurs over 900 times in the Old Testament with the majority of the time meaning "to get acquainted with." But, the issue is not how many times the word appears, but, what is the *context* in which it appears. The controversy arose with the 1955 publication of Derrick Sherwin Bailey's book, *Homosexuality and the Western Christian Tradition* in which Bailey attempted to show that the men of Sodom really intended no harm and just wanted to "get acquainted with" the visitors that Lot brought into his house and that it was really a case of "inhospitality" rather than a case of attempted homosexual rape.

Hospitality is a virtue that is important in many cultures even in our own day. In Scripture, it is based on the fact that all people are made in the image of God and therefore deserve to be treated with dignity and respect. As such, it is an act of righteous behavior. This is what Abraham showed to the strangers who visited his tent. When the strangers arrived in Sodom, it was Lot who approached them and urged them to stay at his house rather than the city square. Apparently, Lot knew that the degree of inhospitality in Sodom was so bad that it could be physically dangerous for the strangers, which was in fact demonstrated when the men of the city pounded on Lot's door and demanded to have sex with them.

It should also be remembered that before any visit by the angels to Sodom, the men of that city were described in this way: "Now the men of Sodom were wicked and were sinning greatly against the Lord" (Gen. 13:13). This was before the law was given, so what the men of Sodom had was the witness of creation. This is exactly the point the apostle Paul makes in Rom. 1:18–20.

The reinterpretation by pro–homosexual theologians raises some interesting questions about the story such as why would the people of Sodom not send a small group of say 6 or 10 men to "get acquainted with" Lot's guests rather than all the men of the city both young and old that surrounded the house? Why would Lot compare "get acquainted with" to "Don't do this wicked thing"? What was so "wicked" about the men of the city wanting to "get acquainted with" Lot's guests? Why would Lot offer his two daughters who had "not *known* a man" to the men of Sodom in place of the two men in Lot's house if he knew that all they wanted was just to "get acquainted with" them? Why were the men of Sodom so desperate to "get acquainted with" these guests that even after being struck with blindness they became weary trying to find the door?

Something else that should be kept in mind is that the cities of the plain were judged *before* the angels ever arrived. They were there to bring Lot and his family out; they were not on some kind of "fact finding mission" to find out if the city was that bad. We should also remember that Scripture never claims that homosexual practice was the *only* sin of the people of Sodom (see Ezek.16:49–50). The violence against Lot and the intention of the men of Sodom are simply an example by the writer of Genesis of the level of evil to which the people of Sodom had sunk. Another question to be asked is where in the rest of Scripture is inhospitality declared a capital offense so as to warrant the harshest judgment since the flood, with the complete destruction of the cities of the plain?

The strongest linguistic argument for translating *yada* as meaning sexual intercourse comes from the Septuagint. The Septuagint is a translation of the Hebrew Scriptures into Greek that was completed about two centuries before Christ. The translation (also known as the LXX) was made so that the Jews living in Egypt could read the Scriptures in a language they were more familiar with. Donald Wold tells us what word the Jewish translators choose to render the word *yada* in Gen.19:5. The Greek word in question in Genesis is *syngenometha* . . . a form of the verb *synginomai*. . . . Proper hermeneutical method dictates that we examine all of the occurrences of this word in the Septuagint to determine its range of meaning. When this is done, it will be apparent that the word means nothing short of sexual intercourse."[4] According to Wold, the only other time the Hebrew word *yada* was translated as *syngenometha* in the Septuagint is in Gen. 39:10, when the Egyptian, Potiphar's wife, attempts to seduce Joseph. "And though she spoke to Joseph day after day, he refused to *go to bed* with her or even be with her."

The weight of evidence seems clear: the word *yada* in Gen. 19:5 should be understood to mean "have sex with," unless we are willing to admit that Potiphar's wife just wanted to take a nap with Joseph. One other important thing to keep in mind is the fact that Bailey did not believe that the destruction of Sodom and Gomorrah was even a supernatural event.

> . . . but the evidence of the Bible and of ancient writers, interpreted in the light of modern archaeological and geological discovery, allows us to envisage what probably took place. A great earthquake, perhaps accompanied by lightning, brought utter ruin and a terrible conflagration to Sodom and the other communities in the vicinity. The destructive fire may have been caused by the ignition of gases and the seepages of asphalt emanating from the region, through lightning or the scattering of fires from hearths. So sudden and complete a devastation of these prosperous cities

---

4. Wold, 86.

would create an indelible impression upon the people of that time who, being ignorant of the scientific explanation, would inevitably tend to ascribe the disaster to supernatural agencies. In this way, no doubt, began the theory of a Divine visitation and judgement for sin, which developed into the familiar Sodom story of the Bible.[5]

There we have it; the destruction of the cities was not the result of Divine judgment for wickedness and sin, but was merely an unfortunate case of excess bad gas. This serves to point out that what we assume at the beginning, most often influences what we conclude at the end.

Judges 19:22–25
Another "Get Acquainted With" Story?

This account has some similarities to that of Genesis 19 in that a certain Levite who took a concubine from Bethlehem in Judah was headed home with her. On their journey they stopped for the night at Gibeah in Benjamin. An old man greeted them and showed hospitality by inviting them to stay at his house. In verse 22–25 we read,

> While they were enjoying themselves, some of the wicked men of the city surrounded the house. Pounding on the door, they shouted to the old man who owned the house, "Bring out the man who came to your house so we can have sex with him." The owner of the house went outside and said to them, "No, my friends, don't be so vile. Since this man is my guest, don't do this disgraceful thing. Look, here is my virgin daughter, and his concubine. I will bring them out to you now, and you can use them and do to them whatever you wish. But to this man, don't do such a disgraceful thing." But the men would not listen to him. So the man took his concubine and sent her outside to them, and they raped and abused her throughout the night, and at dawn they let her go."

Bailey rejects the interpretation of the demand for homosexual sex in verse 22 and yet accepts the heterosexual sex interpretation of verse 25 even though the same word *yada* is used. Wold states, "The Septuagint renders *yada* in both verses with a form of the verb *ginos-*

---

5. Derrick Sherwin Bailey, *Homosexuality and the Western Christian Tradition* (London, England: Longmans, Green and Co., 1955), 7.

ko, the same verb it used to translate *yada* in Genesis 19:8 . . . Once again there is no doubt that the Gibeahites were inhospitable, but this cannot be derived from the meaning of the verb *yada*. The inhospitality is reflected in their attempt at homosexual rape. Inhospitality and homosexuality are not mutually exclusive in these stories. . . ."[6] Gagnon adds, "How is it possible to reasonably argue that homosexual intercourse *per se* did not add to the dimension of horror for the old man, for the Levite, and for the narrator of the story? Repugnance for male penetration of males must have been a significant factor in twice designating the demand for sexual intercourse with the Levite as a *nebala* much greater than that involving intercourse with the old man's daughter and the Levite's concubine."[7] It is interesting to note that Bailey and many of the other pro– homosexual interpreters after him dispute the interpretation of the word *yada* when it would involve homosexual intercourse as in Gen. 19:5 and Judges 19:22 but do not dispute the interpretation of the same word when it would involve heterosexual intercourse as in Gen.19:8 and Judges 19:25.

Leviticus 18:22 and 20:13
God's Love Expressed through Law

God is the one who spoke to Moses from the Tent of Meeting, giving instruction to the Israelites on how He is to be worshiped, how the people are to keep themselves holy, what to do for the forgiveness of sin, laws concerning sacrificing, laws concerning relationships between people, and laws concerning sexual relationships. It was necessary for God to give worship and moral laws to His people who had been brought out from under the dominance of pagan Egypt after 400 years. God demonstrates the special relationship His people have with Him by taking them out of the most powerful nation in the world at that time. God also tells them that this special relationship is not only between Himself and the people, but also between the people and the land. If they listen to God and obey His laws, the land will prosper; if they are disobedient, the land will "vomit" them out as it did the inhabitants before them.

---

6. Wold, 85.

7. Gagnon, 95.

The verses concerning homosexuality are found in Lev. 18:22 and 20:13 which say, "Do not lie with a man as one lies with a woman; that is detestable." "If a man lies with a man as one lies with a woman, both of them have done what is detestable. They must be put to death; their blood will be on their own heads." It is interesting to note that 18:22 is sandwiched in between sacrificing children to Molech and having sexual relations with an animal. One profanes the Creator God, and the other perverts the created order of God. Likewise, 20:13 is in the middle of a list of sexual prohibitions beginning with verse 10 and ending at verse 21. These practices are not wrong *because* the pagan nations around them practiced them, but they are wrong in and of themselves, *and* the pagan nations practice them.

Many of the pro–homosexual scholars attempt to argue that what God is prohibiting in Leviticus is cultic and ritual practices like male temple prostitution in the nations surrounding Israel. The word translated "detestable" in the NIV and "abomination" in the King James Version is the word *toebah* in Hebrew. The word came to have a wide meaning for offences in the Old Testament and is often linked to idolatry, but what the homosexual revisionists seem to fail to see is that forbidden sexual practices *are* a form of idolatry because the individual places his or her desire above that of the God ordained created order. There does not have to be a carved piece of stone or wood for an act of sex that is forbidden by God to be idolatry. The practice of homosexuality or adultery or bestiality will in time turn the heart away from God. The moral prohibitions in Leviticus 18 assume or are based on the order that God set at creation. James De Young, writes,

> All of the sins of chapter 18 seem to be wrong for all people everywhere at all times. All fall under the designation *toebah* in chapter 20, homosexuality, is also universal in application, as well as those common to both chapters. That is to say, some of the sins of chapter 20 are not universal in their application by this test. Note that *toebah* does not occur in references to unclean animals (20:25) nor for spiritism and harlotry (v.6), nor for cursing parents (v.9). The one sin designated *toebah* in the two chapters is homosexuality. The writer is placing

emphasis here. It is not circumstantial, incidental, or limited to Israel.[8]

We can see from this that the main reason for the prohibition of homosexuality in Israel is not because of the temple prostitution or cultic worship of pagan nations, but because it mocks the image of God in human beings and is sterile both spiritually and physically.

It is interesting to note how the revisionists seem to assume that the worship of idols appeared before the practice of homosexuality, rather than the possibility that homosexuality began to be practiced as everyone did what was right in their own eyes, and then they invented gods to give approval of their behavior. The reason they don't want to consider this possibility is this would make homosexuality wrong in and of itself and not as a result of worshiping an idol. Belief and behavior go hand in hand.

Old Testament scholar G. J. Wenham points out the differences between Israel's complete rejection of homosexual practice and that of the surrounding cultures.

> Lev. 20:13 states, "If a man lies with a male as with a woman, both of them have committed an abomination; they shall be put to death, their blood is upon them." Lev. 18 prohibits various acts but proscribes no penalties. Lev. 20 does mention how offenders should be treated. Sometimes human punishment is decreed, sometimes it is left to God. Homosexuality here attracts the death penalty, which puts it on par with adultery (Lev. 20:10) or the worst case of incest (Lev. 20:11, 12). These were offences that nations outside Israel did view with extreme seriousness: but they never put homosexuality on the same level. Secondly it should be noted that both parties in homosexual intercourse are punished equally: the passive partner and the active are both put to death. The use of the term 'lie' (here and in Lev. 18:22) without any qualifying verb, e.g. 'seize and (lie)', and the equal punishment shows that consent to intercourse is assumed between the partners. . . . In other words the Old Testament bans every type of homosexual intercourse, not just forcible as the Assyrians did, or with youths (so the

---

8. De Young, 50.

Egyptians). Homosexual intercourse where both parties consent is also condemned.[9]

Wenham concludes,

> It therefore seems most likely that Israel's repudiation of homosexual intercourse arises out of its doctrine of creation. God created humanity in two sexes, so that they could be fruitful and multiply and fill the earth. Woman was man's perfect companion, like man created in the divine image. To allow the legitimacy of homosexual acts would frustrate the divine purpose and deny the perfection of God's provision of the two sexes to support and complement one another.[10]

We have looked at several verses concerning God's pattern and program for human sexuality as well as the most infamous example of what happens when people turn away from what God designed. The moral laws in Leviticus are based on what God set up at creation with regard to sexuality, and since God's nature is expressed through creation and morality is based in God's nature, it follows that any sexual activity that is contrary to created nature is in fact immoral. There is not the slightest hint that any other sexual activity than what is found in Genesis 2:24, has the blessing of God. In Scripture, we learn that the city of Sodom is mentioned over 20 times and always as an example of what might be called the "gold standard" of wickedness, sin, rebellion, pride, greed, and yes, inhospitality. Here are a couple of examples:

- "The look on their faces testifies against them, they parade their sin like Sodom, they do not hide it. Woe to them! They have brought disaster upon themselves" (Isaiah 3:9).

- "And among the prophets of Jerusalem I have seen something horrible: They commit adultery and live a lie. They strengthen the hands of evildoers, so that no one turns from his wickedness. They are all like Sodom to me; the people of Jerusalem are like Gomorrah" (Jeremiah 23:14).

- Jesus compares the destruction of Sodom with that of the Flood, both of which were God's judgement for sin: "It was

---

9. G. J. Wenham, "The Old Testament Attitude to Homosexuality," *The Expository Times* 102, no. 12 (September 1991): 362.

10. Ibid., 363.

the same in the days of Lot. People were eating and drinking, buying and selling, planting and building. But the day Lot left Sodom, fire and sulfur rained down from heaven and destroyed them all" (Luke 17:28–29).

In the chapter *answering objections*, we will look at the argument that based on 1 Samuel Jonathan and David had a homosexual relationship.

8

God's Final Revelation

Did Jesus Really Say Nothing About Homosexuality?

For the followers of Christ, Jesus Christ is the ultimate authority and final revelation of God for those who put their hope and
faith in Him. Jesus applied different titles to Himself and accepted
titles to be placed on Him. Jesus proclaimed, "I and the Father are
one" in John 10:30. Jesus claimed to forgive sins, something only God
could do (Mark 2:5–7). He raised the dead (Luke 7:15; Mark 5:41;
John 11:44). When He is asked directly "Are you the Son of God?" in
Matthew 26:64 and Luke 22:70, Jesus replies, "Yes." Jesus even takes
the very name of God from Exodus 3:14 and applies it to Himself in
John 8:58, "I tell you the truth," Jesus answered, "before Abraham
was born, I am!" Jesus accepted worship, something reserved for
God alone when Thomas says to the risen Christ in John 20:28, "My
Lord and my God."[1]

With this kind of authority, it's easy to see why in a theological dispute everyone wants Jesus on his side. In the mid–seventies,
the Metropolitan Community Church, started by Troy Perry in Los
Angeles, handed out a small track–like paper with the statement
"What Jesus Christ Said about Homosexuality" on the front. As you
opened it up, the inside was blank, and then on the back it read,
"That's right; He said nothing about it." While it is true that Jesus
never used the word "homosexuality" since that word wasn't invented until the mid–nineteenth century, it doesn't follow that he has

---

1. See also Norman Geisler, *To Understand the Bible Look for Jesus* (Grand Rapids:
Baker Books, 2002).

nothing to say about sexual ethics that would include homosexual activities.

Those who argue that Jesus had a "less rigid" view of sexual ethics than the rabbis of his day, usually point to the encounter with the woman caught in adultery in John 8:3–11. The whole scene is really an attempt set up by the Pharisees to trap Jesus in something he might say. A woman is brought to Jesus by some Pharisees. They claim she was caught in the act of adultery, and they remind Jesus what the Law of Moses says, asking him, "Now what do you say...?" Jesus replies, "If any one of you is without sin, let him be the first to throw a stone at her." The crowd breaks up, and Jesus asks her, "Woman, where are they? Has no one condemned you?" "No one, sir," she said. "Then neither do I condemn you," Jesus declared. "Go now and leave your life of sin." Notice that there is no question about whether a sexual sin has been committed, but it is a demonstration of the authority Jesus has to forgive sin (Mark 2:10, 11) and that he is the "lamb of God, who takes away the sin of the world" (John 1:29). His tenderness towards her is not one of overlooking sin, but of giving her a chance for repentance, repair, and restoration, which would be impossible if she were executed.

Jesus and the Question of Marriage and Divorce

Jesus on no less than four occasions states His position on marriage and divorce (Matt. 5: 31–32, 19: 3–9; and Mark 10: 2–9, 11–12. In both Matt. 19:3–9 and Mark 10: 2–9, Jesus, in response to the question of why Moses allowed them to give a certificate of divorce, says it was because of the hardness of their hearts (Deut. 24:1–4). He then goes back before Moses and back before Abraham, to the pattern and purpose God set at creation. In Matt. 19:4–6 we read, "'Haven't you read,' He replied, "that at the beginning the Creator 'made them male and female'" and said, 'For this reason a man will leave his father and mother and be united to his wife, and the two will become one flesh'? So they are no longer two, but one. Therefore what God has joined together, let man not separate.'" Enfolded in the word "marriage" is the assumption of a sexual relationship, which Jesus makes plain in Mark 10:11 after the disciples asked him about what he had just said to the Pharisees. "He answered, 'Anyone who divorces his wife and marries another woman commits adultery against her. And if she divorces her husband and marries another man, she commits adultery.'" Jesus, far from being "soft" or "accommodating" actually goes back to God's pattern of one male and one female becoming "one flesh" for life. Even the one exception of marital unfaithfulness in Matt. 19:9 and 5:32 does not *require* divorce, but instead repentance, reconciliation, and repair should be sought as demonstrated by Jesus with the woman caught in adultery. Jesus closed a loophole in the law and restored marriage to the pattern set by God in Genesis. One mention should be made about the Greek word *porneia,* which has been translated as "marital unfaithfulness" or "sexual immorality" in many English translations, with the King James Version translating it as "adultery." As Donald De Young, points out, "By the time of the New Testament, *porneia* had become a broad term meaning "sexual immorality," including various sexual sins."[2] By using such an "umbrella" term, Jesus does not have to list all the sexually immoral acts one by one, which would have included homosexuality.

Jesus not only knew what the Scriptures said, he participated in creation itself. We read in John 1:1–3, "In the beginning was the Word, and the Word was with God, and the Word was God. He was with God in the beginning. Through him all things were made, without him nothing was made that has been made." This means that the view of sexual ethics (marriage) that Jesus had was not based in the culture of his time or the various schools of rabbinic thought, but in the fact of his being there at the creation of the world.

What does this mean with regard to Jesus and homosexuality? Jesus was in complete accord with Scripture and the teaching of his day that the only approved, legitimate human sexual relationship is that of the Genesis model, one male, one female, united for life. By doing this Jesus closes the door on *ALL* other forms of human sexual activities and therefore does not need to mention sex with animals, sex with children, sex with one's father or mother, or men having sex with men, none of which would have been an issue like one of multiple wives through serial divorce and remarriage. Robert Gagnon makes this point:

---

2. James B. De Young, *Homosexuality, Contemporary Claims Examined in the Light of the Bible and other Ancient Literature and Law* (Grand Rapids: Kregal Publications, 2000), 225, 226.

There is no need for him to comment on whether homosexual unions should be permitted and, if so, whether his stance on divorce and remarriage should apply to them too. The creation text authorized only one type of sexual union. It would have been a foregone conclusion for him that homoerotic relationships and human–animal unions, both proscribed in Leviticus, were unacceptable. The whole point of Jesus' stance in Mark 10:1–12 is not to broaden the Torah's openness to alternative forms of sexuality but rather to narrow or constrain the Torah's sexual ethic to disallow any sexual union other than a monogamous, life–long marriage to a person of the opposite sex.[3]

Given the evidence presented, there should be no doubt about the answer to the question, "Did Jesus really say nothing about homosexuality?" At the end of his earthly ministry, Jesus said in Matt. 28:18, "Then Jesus came to them and said, 'All authority in heaven and on earth has been given to me.'" For those who claim to know Jesus, to love Jesus, and to follow Jesus, it means dying to self and taking up our cross daily, whatever that cross happens to be. Jesus created the pattern for human sexuality at creation, he reaffirmed it during his earthly ministry, and he continues to affirm it through the writings of his apostles.

Paul and Creation's Echo in Romans

Romans 1: 18–27

No passage in the whole of Scripture speaks more directly to the issue of homosexuality than Rom. 1:18–27, and no passage has received more discussion, debate, and dissection on this issue than this section of Paul's letter to the Romans.

Paul had not yet been to Rome, but he wrote the letter to prepare the way. In 1:11–13 he says, "I long to see you so that I may impart some spiritual gift to make you strong–that is, that you and I may be mutually encouraged by each other's faith. I do not want you to be unaware, brothers, that I planned many times to come to you (but have been prevented until now) in order that I might have

---

3. Robert Gagnon, *The Bible and Homosexual Practice* (Nashville: Abingdon Press, 2001), 194.

a harvest among you, just as I have had among the other Gentiles." Paul was writing to a mostly Gentile house church or churches of whom Paul says, in verse 8 "your faith is being reported all over the world." So Paul is writing to a group of mostly Gentile believers who have been together long enough that word of their faith has spread far from Rome.

Paul begins his indictment of the Gentile world in verse 18 and 19. "The wrath of God is being revealed from heaven against all the godlessness and wickedness of men who suppress the truth by their wickedness, since what may be known about God is plain to them, because God has made it plain to them." It's clear that God is not revealing His wrath from heaven in the *same way* that He revealed it to the cities of Sodom and Gomorrah, so how is it being revealed? Verse 20 explains, "For since the creation of the world God's invisible qualities–his eternal power and divine nature–have been clearly seen, being understood from what has been made, so that men are without excuse." The creation, which God has placed before their eyes, reveals God's "eternal power and divine nature" through what has been created. Anyone who creates pottery, paintings, etc. imparts something that may be known of them through what they make.

God never leaves Himself without a witness, and His universal witness is creation. This is the same type of argument Paul uses in Acts 17: 23–28 when speaking with the Greek philosophers in Athens. However, this is not to say that knowledge of God through His creation is enough for salvation, but it should prepare them for, point them to, and persuade them of the full and final revelation of the Gospel's good news. "Now what you worship as something unknown I am going to proclaim to you" (Acts 17:23). Creation, as we shall see, plays a central role in Paul's indictment of the pagan world and the sexual acts they commit. In verse 19, Paul says that men "suppress the truth." To suppress the truth is an act of the will, which means that they don't want to know the truth about God or His created order and as a result in verse 21, "their thinking became futile and their foolish hearts became darkened." Jesus tells us in John 3:19 why they stay in that condition. "But men loved darkness instead of light because their deeds were evil." Paul in Rom. 1:23 tells us the result of their foolish thinking: "and they exchanged the glory of the immortal God for images made to look like mortal man and birds and animals and reptiles."

Several scholars have noted the parallels between Gen. 1:26–27 and Rom. 1:23, 26–27. C. K. Barrett in his commentary *The Epistle to the Romans* says, "In the obscene pleasures to which he refers is to be seen precisely that perversion of the created order which may be expected when men put the creation in place of the Creator."[4] M. D. Hooker writes, "Further indications that Paul had the Genesis narrative in mind when writing this passage are found in the vocabulary which he uses. We have already noted that several words in Rom. i. 23 are used also in Gen. i. 20–6. Other echoes of Gen. i. are found. . . ."[5] S. Lewis Johnson Jr. states, "The terminology of verses 22–23 points fairly clearly to the Genesis account. . . . It seems that Paul was thinking of the Genesis record in the Romans passage, ..."[6] Robert Gagnon has shown in his lectures, 8 points of correspondence between Gen. 1: 26–27 and Rom. 1: 23, 26–27 as follows:

GENESIS	ROMANS
God's likeness and image in humans	
1. Human (Gen. 1:26)	1. Human (Rom. 1:23)
2. Image (Gen. 1:26)	2. Image (Rom. 1:23)
3. Likeness (Gen. 1:26)	3. Likeness (Rom. 1:23)
Dominion over animal kingdom	
4. Birds (Gen. 1:26)	4. Birds (Rom. 1:23)
5. Cattle (Gen. 1:26)	5. Quadrupeds (Rom. 1:23)
6. Reptiles (Gen. 1:26)	6. Reptiles (Rom. 1:23)
Male – Female Differentiation	
7. Male (Gen. 1:27)	7. Males (Rom. 1:27)
8. Female (Gen. 1:27)	8. Females (Rom. 1:26)

4. C. K. Barrett, *The Epistle to the Romans* (New York: Harper and Row Publishers, 1957), 39.

5. M. D. Hooker, "Adam in Romans 1," *New Testament Studies* 6, no.4 (July 1960): 303.

6. S. Lewis Johnson Jr., "God Gave Them Up," *Bibliotheca Sacra* 129 (April 1972): 132.

In verses 24, 26, and 28 we find the words "God gave them over" in each. This is one form of "the wrath of God" for God to step back and withhold His restraining Spirit so they may follow "the sinful desires of their hearts to sexual impurity" (Rom. 1:24), "to shameful lusts" (Rom. 1:26), and "to a depraved mind" (Rom. 1:28). "Hearts," "lusts," and "mind" are all inward where decisions are made and then the body follows. There is strong evidence that Paul is reminding his readers of the Genesis account and the boundaries set there in the same way Jesus referred back to Genesis in Matt. 19:4–6. It seems clear that when human beings suppress the truth about what may be known of God in the creation all around them, the sexual boundaries and pattern set at creation will also be suppressed. This is exactly what Paul illustrates in verses 26 and 27, "Because of this, God gave them over to shameful lusts. Even their women exchanged natural relations for unnatural ones. In the same way the men also abandoned natural relations with women and were inflamed with lust for one another. Men committed indecent acts with other men, and received in themselves the due penalty for their perversion."

As state earlier, for the Romans (and Greeks) of Paul's time, "natural" and "unnatural" with regard to sexual relations would be based on observation and the obvious biological and functional differences between males and females, but they would also allow for individual preferences as long as the adult male did not become the receiving partner and take on the role of the woman so as to degrade his masculine nature. That would bring shame. Romans were not nearly as concerned with the gender of their sex partner as they were in maintaining the societal expectations.

Paul's view of "natural" and "unnatural" would include the biological and functional differences and the natural "fit" of men and women that enable them to become "one flesh," but his view would also go beyond that back to the order of creation. As Robert Gagnon states, "All of this explains why Paul selects female and male homosexual conduct as 'exhibit A' of culpable gentile depravity. First and foremost, along with idolatry, same–sex intercourse represents one of the clearest instances of conscious suppression of revelation in nature by gentiles, inasmuch as it involves denying clear anatomical gender differences and functions (leaving them 'without excuse').".[7] Some have argued that what Paul is saying in Romans, is that the focus is not on human beings, but on God and His eternal power and divine nature that are known through creation. But human beings *are* part of the creation through which we know something about God's nature ,and since God's nature is expressed through His creation (Rom. 1:20), and morality is based in God's nature, it follows that any activity that acts contrary to that created nature is in fact immoral. This is the truth about God that they exchanged for a lie and worshiped and served created things (including themselves) rather than the Creator (Rom. 1:25). When human beings for whatever reason, act contrary to the created (natural) order, they assume the role of the creator in deciding what is best for them.

In their recent book *Unchanging Witness* S. Donald Fortson III and Rollin G. Grams sum up what Paul says in Rom. 1:18–27.

> All this points to the fact that Paul is speaking of homosexual unions *per se*. He is addressing the failure to live in conformity to nature and not narrowing his comments to particular forms of homosexuality, such as pederasty or homosexual acts associated with idol worship or homosexual acts committed by heterosexual persons or homosexual acts committed due to out–of–control passions or unclean homosexual acts in which the penis comes into contact with fecal matter or bisexual abuse of slaves or homosexual sex outside of committed, loving relationships–or any other nuanced variety of homosexual practice. Paul's focus is rather on how males and females were created: God made them for each other, and the male and female sexual organs were created to be joined together.[8]

The wholeness and completeness experienced between a man and a woman whose differences God made to complete each other cannot be "reengineered" to suite the desires or heart felt feelings of the creature. Sex is too sacred, too intimate, too powerful, and too devastating when misused to leave to finite, sinful human beings to decide how they feel they should express themselves through it.

---

7. Gagnon, *The Bible and Homosexual Practice*, 264.

8. S. Donald Fortson III and Rollin G. Grams, *Unchanging Witness* (Nashville: B&H Academic, 2016), 341.

Paul writes in Col. 3:5, "Put to death, therefore, whatever belongs to your earthly nature: sexual immorality, impurity, lust, evil desires and greed, which is idolatry." "Earthly nature" is our old sinful nature before coming to Christ. "Sexual immorality" is the word *porneia,* which we saw is a broad term covering any sexual activity outside of male / female marriage, including men having sex with men (homosexuality). Paul ends the verse with "which is idolatry," meaning those who practice or engage in these activities are practicing idolatry, which puts the desires of the created ahead of their loving Creator. James Brownson tries to argue against the traditional understanding of the word "nature" in Romans 1 by injecting the modern concept of "orientation" in order to reinterpret Paul.

> For early Jews and Christians, the true meaning of "nature" could only be discerned in the ways that "nature" converged with the will of God revealed in the Torah. If this analysis is correct, however, it also suggests that the whole modern concept of sexual orientation and the contemporary evidence of its deeply rooted persistence, both in some humans and in some animals, represent an important range of empirical data about the natural world that was not considered by the ancient Jewish or Christian writers."[9]

So according to Brownson, it seems God, writing through the authors of Scripture, had to wait 2,000 years for modern science to reveal some vital missing information about human nature for the church to say, "Ah ha!! Now we understand what the Scripture *really* teaches." If we were to accept Brownson's argument, would we not have to reinterpret Scripture to allow for some men to have multiple wives because of their "orientation"? Would we not also have to embrace the changing cultural attitude that would move us to a "deeper" reading? We devoted an entire chapter to the evidence from genetics and biology for the "born that way" argument and found it to be very thin. The majority of evidence for "orientation" comes mostly from the subjective study of psychology than from the more objective field of biology.

---

9. James V. Brownson, *Bible, Gender, Sexuality* (Grand Rapids: William B. Eerdmans, 2013), 230.

Paul's Concern for a Confused Church
1 Corinthians 6:9

The city of Corinth was a major city in Greece that was situated about 48 miles west of Athens. It had a very busy port through which cargo and goods headed for Asia to the east or the Mediterranean Sea to the west. Corinth decided to attempt to oppose the expanding Roman Empire and was utterly crushed by the Roman army in 146 BC, which laid waste to it and enslaved or killed most of its people.

It remained in ruins until Julius Caesar made it a Roman colony in 44 BC after which it once again became a thriving port of trade and commerce. Corinth also had a reputation of being the "Las Vegas" of Greece when it came to the subject of sexual vice. In fact, the term *Korinthiazomai* ("to act like a Corinthian") became a synonym for the pursuit of sexual pleasure. Paul established a church in Corinth after leaving Athens (Acts 18: 1–11) in about AD 51 and wrote First Corinthians while he was in Ephesus at around AD 56. Paul lived and worked in Corinth for 18 months, so he was very familiar with how much the city was given over to idol worship and sexual sin.

Paul addresses sexual disorders in the church in chapters 5 and 6 of First Corinthians and makes it abundantly clear what the word of the Lord says. In 1 Cor. 5:1 we read, "It is actually reported that there is sexual immorality among you, and of such a kind that does not occur even among pagans: A man has his father's wife. And you are proud! Shouldn't you rather have been filled with grief and have put out of your fellowship the man who did this?" Paul reminds the Corinthians of what God said in Lev. 18:8, "Do not have sexual relations with your father's wife; that would dishonor your father." Without quoting the verse, Paul invokes the authority of the prohibition in Leviticus and is horrified that the church would allow this relationship to continue. Notice that there is not the slightest hint in Paul's condemnation of this relationship that feelings of love and commitment could transform this into a God approved union. In chapter 6, verses 9 and 10, Paul gives a "vice list." "Do you not know that the wicked will not inherit the kingdom of God? Do not be deceived: Neither the sexually immoral nor idolaters nor adulterers nor male prostitutes nor homosexual offenders nor thieves nor the greedy nor slanders nor swindlers will inherit the kingdom of God."

The issue in recent years has focused on two words Paul uses in this list, *malakoi* (male prostitutes) and *arsenokoitai* (homosexual offenders). The word *malakoi* in Greek literature has a broad general meaning of "soft," soft food, soft clothing, and is sometimes used to describe effeminacy. What's important is its context, how a given author. In this case Paul uses the word for the audience to whom he is writing. The list that Paul places *malakoi* in is very serious because those who continue to practice these things will not inherit the kingdom of God. It would seem most likely that the "soft men," as the word *malakoi* can be translated, would involve a moral issue since it is placed in a list of moral sins and specifically sexual sins with no indication that Paul was restricting it to activities such as pederasty. Fortson and Grams, in their book, point out how the first century AD Jewish philosopher Philo describes "soft men": "Without using the word *malakos,* Philo demonstrates precisely what is involved in this concept. It is a man who has abandoned his masculine nature to pursue womanly ways, including sex with other men and boys."[10] The late first and early second century satirical Roman poet Juvenal commented on the "soft men," as Fortson and Grams point out, "Juvenal also speaks of a tightly knit homosexual community: "Great is the concord among soft men" (Satire II.47) He uses the Latin word *molles,* which would be the direct translation of the Greek *malakoi,* as both words mean "soft men." A tightly knit group of individuals who are sexually active with persons of the same gender seems what is today termed the LGBT (lesbian, gay, bisexual, transgender) community."[11] Fortson and Grams conclude, "'Soft men' committed homosexual acts even though the term includes other nuances. The primary source evidence indicates that participation in homosexual acts was central to the definition of 'soft men', even though the term was not a mere synonym for 'homosexuals'. Also, softness referenced not only inability to control oneself. It characterized a man who is unnaturally nonmale, and therefore also oriented to the feminine side of life. It entails being soft, womanly, boyish, a eunuch, and interested in feminine things."[12] It seems clear from the context that

---

10. Fortson and Grams, *Unchanging Witness,* 286.

11. Ibid., 287.

12. Ibid., 293.

Paul is stating that these "soft men" *function* as females not only in manners and dress but also sexually.

Arsenokoitai

1 Corinthians 6:9–10

Paul writes: "Do not be deceived; neither the sexually immoral ... nor men who practice homosexuality ... will inherit the kingdom of God." The word translated "homosexuality *(arsenokoitai)* by the ESV is a very interesting word that has been the subject of a lot of speculation on the part of various interpreters especially those defending the view that the word has nothing to do with the modern understanding of homosexuality. Paul in 1 Tim. 1:10, writes, "For adulterers and perverts, for slave traders and liars and perjurers–and for whatever else is contrary to sound doctrine" One of the issues with this word is that there is no indisputable reference to the word prior to the time of Paul's usage. David E. Garland, in his commentary on 1 Cor. 6:9, translates *arsenokoitai* as "males who sexually penetrate males"[13]

Since *arsenokoitai* does not appear before Paul, it is plausible that Paul actually coined the term, but from where? James De Young gives the most likely answer.

> The evidence suggests that Paul coined the term, based on the juxtaposition of the two words *arsenos* and *koiten* in the LXX of Leviticus 20:13 (cf. similar phraseology in 18:22). We cannot prove this supposition, but style, practice, familiarity with the LXX, and literary context make this theory very plausible. Scholars have long pointed out words that seem to originate with Paul. Some 179 words found in his writings are seen nowhere else in pre–Christian Greek literature. Of these, eighty–nine occur only one time. . . . Paul displays considerable dependence upon the LXX. He quotes more frequently from the LXX than from the Hebrew Old Testament. . . . Obviously Paul was familiar with, and preferred to use the LXX.[14]

---

13. David E. Garland, *1 Corinthians* (Grand Rapids: Baker Academic, 2003), 211.

14. De Young, 195.

Fortson and Gram make the same argument. "Significantly, the Greek translation of Leviticus 20:13 offers the words needed to understand how the word *arsenokoitai* came in existence. . . . Not only are the words found together, but a Greek manuscript in Paul's day would not have separated them with spaces. While Paul would have known the two words were distinct, he would have seen them together in Leviticus 20:13 and apparently chose to keep them that way."[15]

By using the term "male/bed" (*arsenokoitai*) Paul implies that the prohibition of Lev. 20:13 against males having sex with males is applicable to the church at Corinth. This prohibition is in turn founded on the male–female distinction established by God at creation. The biblical emphasis on the necessity for an opposite sex sexual relationship is the exact opposite of what Roman society considered important in sexual matters. As Roman historian Craig Williams explains, "As we will see, Roman texts certainly show an awareness that just as there are males and females, men may engage in sexual acts with males or females or both; and that just as males and females exhibit physical differences, sexual practices between persons of the same sex may be compared or contrasted with such practices between persons of different sexes. But ancient writers consistently fail to suggest that these practices are significantly or essentially different. Rather, they are portrayed as two sides of one coin, differing mainly is surface detail."[16]

1 Timothy 1:10

Many scholars think 1 Timothy was written by Paul sometime around AD 63 and that he probably was martyred during a time of persecution under the Roman emperor Nero in about AD 67. Paul writes in 1 Tim. 1: 8–10, "We know that the law is good if one uses it properly. We also know that the law is made not for the righteous, but for lawbreakers and rebels, the ungodly and sinful, the unholy and irreligious; for those who kill their fathers or mothers, for murderers, for adulterers and perverts, for slave traders and liars and perjurers–and for whatever else is contrary to the sound doctrine. . . ."

---

15. Fortson and Grams, 295.

16. Craig Williams, *Roman Homosexuality*, 2nd ed. (Oxford: Oxford University Press, 2010), 6.

Paul uses the same word *arsenokoitai* (perverts) that he used in 1 Cor. 6:9. It seems unlikely that Paul would use a word *twice* that he probably coined unless he felt it conveyed exactly what he wanted to say. Paul places the word right after adultery, which is a broad term covering sexual activities outside of marriage (which always assumes male and female) and then uses a term drawn from Lev. 20:13 that prohibits sexual activities between males. Robert Gagnon makes this point, "The term does not appear or has not been found in any non–Jewish, non–Christian text prior to the sixth century AD. This way of talking about male homosexuality is a distinctly Jewish and Christian formulation. It was undoubtedly used as a way of distinguishing their absolute opposition to homosexual practice, rooted in the Torah of Moses, from more accepting views in the Greco–Roman milieu." Gagnon continues, "The appearance of *arsenokoitai* in 1 Timothy 1:10 makes the link to the Mosaic law explicit, since the list of vices of which *arsenokoitai* is a part are said to be derived from 'the law' (1:9)."[17]

It is interesting to note that of all the Greek words available to Paul to describe sexual activity between males (and there were many) he instead chooses to coin a term taken from the LXX translation that covers any such activity and thus eliminates the need for him to list out all of the various forms such activities might take.

We have looked at the main verses that speak to the biblical view of men having sex with men and found that the Scripture is clear and understandable in its placing male with male sex in the same category as that of adultery, incest, and bestiality. One of the first and most often repeated objections to the Bible's categorical rejection of men having sex with men as being acceptable to God is the idea that the biblical writers had no concept of loving, committed, monogamous, sexual relationships between members of the same sex. First, this objection assumes that God's involvement in the writing of Scripture was almost on the level of "advisor" instead of author and Creator.

Second, it assumes that ancient people in Greece and Rome had no experience of men who had long term loving and committed relationships with other men or that they had no knowledge of men who

---

17. Robert Gagnon, "The Scriptural Case for a Male–Female Prerequisite for Sexual Relations: The New Testament Perspective," in *Homosexuality, Marriage and the Church*, edited by Roy E. Gane (Berrien Springs, MI: Andrews University Press, 2012), 87.

had had a preference for men from a very early age that continued for all of their life. This assumption is demonstratively false as any deep reading of Greek or Roman sexuality would show. (See chapter 6.) It is only modern arrogance that believes that just because ancient peoples did not use technical language to express what they felt about sexuality does not mean they did not experience the full rainbow spectrum of love and sexuality. It also assumes that the biblical writers had no knowledge of this even though the pagan people all around them to whom they preached and with whom they interacted did.

Third, it assumes that deep heart felt love and commitment in a non–exploitive relationship is what gives God's stamp of approval on it. But we have reason to doubt this assumption if we look at 1 Cor. 5:1 where Paul addresses a committed, non–exploitive relationship of a man with his stepmother, and the church seems to have been both welcoming and affirming this openly sinful relationship. There is no indication that Paul cares about how "right" it feels to them, but only about the fact that the relationship violates God's law revealed in Lev. 18:8 and Deut. 22:22. It seems clear that Paul considered these prohibitions still binding on the church, or he would have had no authoritative moral ground to stand on. This church had wrong-headed spiritual pride when they should have been filled with grief over this openly sinful relationship that was sending the wrong message to those outside the church.

The clear message of Scripture from Genesis to Christ, to Paul– all of Scripture–is that God set the pattern and prerequisite of male / female becoming "one flesh," and all other possible combinations of sexual expression are locked out. God set the pattern for the heavens and humans, which comes through Scripture clearly despite the efforts of those who twist the Scripture into shapes that would make a yoga master envious.

Prison or Fortress?

As Creator and loving Father, God set the boundaries and context for the gift of human sexuality that is for His glory and our good. Our attitude towards God's boundaries reflects our level of commitment to serve God or serve ourselves. A question might help illustrate this. What is the difference between a prison and a fortress?

Both have high thick walls, and both have strong heavy doors, but one is meant to restrict freedom, and the other to protect it. The degree to which we view God's boundaries as a prison reflects the degree to which we lack faith, trust, and understanding, which in turn results in disobedience. We all live in a sex soaked society that both shouts and whispers at us, "If it feels good do it, as long as no one gets hurt." Here is how Paul put it: "Don't you know that when you offer yourselves to someone to obey him as slaves, you are slaves to the one whom you obey–whether you are slaves to sin, which leads to death, or obedience, which leads to righteousness? But thanks be to God that, though you used to be slaves to sin, you wholeheartedly obeyed the form of teaching to which you were entrusted" (Rom. 6:16–17).

The gospel is about repentance, return, and restoration (Luke 15: 11–32).

9

Answering Objections

In this chapter we will respond to the objections raised against arguments in our book that are raised by the anti–natural marriage advocates.

Objection 1: Today we consider slavery to be a moral evil, but in biblical times it was considered just a fact of life. In fact, there is not a single outright condemnation of slavery in all of Scripture. If the church has "evolved" in its understanding of something that was not condemned as morally wrong, why can't we say that the church should "evolve" its understanding of loving, caring, committed homosexuality as morally right?

Answer: The first thing that should be noticed about the comparison between slavery and homosexuality is that the main argument against homosexual practice is anchored in the Genesis account of creation whereas slavery is not. There is no account of God creating a slave race whose created purpose was to be slaves. As the saying goes, *God created man, and man created slaves.*

The problem with talking about first century slavery is that the term *slavery* carries with it visions of how slavery was used and conducted in the pre–Civil War South of the United States. This is not in any way to defend the existence of slavery in first century Israel, for there were real differences between them which will help in our understanding of the difference between slavery and homosexual practice and our understanding of how a change in our view of the first does not mean a change in our view of the other. S. Scott Bartchy, in his dissertation: *First–Century Slavery and 1 Corinthians 7:21,* says,

The unquestioned acceptance of the institution of slavery in the first century A.D., the improving conditions of slaves-life during that period, the respective places of slaves and freedmen in society, and the slave's view of his own situation clearly indicate that the person in Greek or Roman slavery in the first century A.D. led an existence which differed in many significant ways from the slavery practiced in modern times. Perhaps the most significant difference between that ancient slavery and modern slavery is the manumission [formal emancipation from slavery] anticipated by first century slaves. In nineteenth-century America, a slave had no hope of being set free; in first century Greece, a slave reasonably expected to be set free after a number of years of labor. . . . Other significant differences between first-century Greco-Roman slavery and nineteenth-century American slavery are: Nineteenth-century owners were forbidden by law to educate their slaves; thus slaves did not advance to "responsible" positions; slaves were not able to own property; they had no hope of ever having a "normal" family life.[1]

Robert Gagnon puts it this way: "Relative to the surrounding cultures of the ancient Near East and of Greece and Rome, the biblical witness on slavery moves in the direction of curtailing that institution."[2]

In Paul's letter to Philemon, we see that the emphasis is not on forcing change from the outside but from the inside, from a changed heart. Philemon was slave-holder and believer whose slave Onesimus, had run away and became acquainted with Paul, who led him to faith in Christ. Paul had the authority as an apostle to order Philemon to free Onesimus but chose to use persuasion. As we read in verse 8–10, "Therefore, although in Christ I could be bold and order you to do what you ought to do, yet I appeal to you on the basis of love. I then, Paul–an old man and now also a prisoner of Christ Jesus–I appeal to you for my son Onesimus, who became my son while I was in chains." Paul then drops a "hint" in verse 15 and 16. "Perhaps the reason he was separated from you for a little while was

---

1. S. Scott Bartchy, "First-Century Slavery and 1 Corinthians 7:21," *Society of Biblical Literature,* Dissertation series, number 11 (1973), 87.

2. Robert Gagnon, "The Scriptural Case for a Male-Female Prerequisite," in *Homosexuality, Marriage and the Church,* ed. by Roy E. Gane (Berrien Springs, MI: Andrews University Press, 2012), 130.

that you might have him back for good–no longer a slave, but better than a slave, as a dear brother. He is very dear to me but even dearer to you, both as a man and as a brother in the Lord.'"

In first–century Israel becoming the slave of a household could mean the difference between starvation and eating with the expectation of eventual freedom. David M. Cobin, quoting David Brion Davis, points out, "The ease and frequency of manumission would seem to be the crucial standard in measuring the relative harshness of slave systems. If we had to be slaves and were allowed to choose the time and place of our servitude, we should obviously prefer a society that held out some hope of eventual freedom."[3]

Some homosexualist authors claim that the biblical writers could not imagine the possibility of the end of slavery and so only wrote of how slaves should conduct themselves. It's interesting to note that those authors are a little more careful about saying that Jesus could not possibly have seen the end of slavery even though he made no mention of its end, or even that masters should free their slaves. James V. Brownson in his book *Bible, Gender, Sexuality* states, "For example, the church of the nineteenth century had to reread the biblical texts on slavery in a more deep and penetrating way. Even the biblical writers, particularly in the New Testament, had simply assumed, without question, that the institution of slavery existed and would continue to exist. So much of the advice offered by the New Testament had to do with "humanizing" the master–slave relationship."[4] So, should we assume that the church in the nineteenth century understood in a "more deep and penetrating way" what the apostles wrote than the apostles who wrote it or is there another answer.

We should ask, would the gospel be helped or hampered by preaching that those in slavery who become Christians are now free and should run away as soon as possible. How would saying something like this in a world under Roman rule help the gospel to spread? It certainly didn't help the slave revolt of Spartacus in 79 BC with an army of 50,000 runaway slaves under his command. Furthermore, Paul says in Rom. 13:1–8 that we are to obey the government. The

3. David M. Cobin, "A brief look at the Jewish law of manumission," *Chicago–Kent Law Review* 70, no. 3 (April 1995): article 13, 1339.

4. James V. Brownson, *Bible, Gender, Sexuality: Reframing the Church's Debate on Same–Sex Relationships* (Grand Rapids: Eerdmans Publishing Co., 2013), 277.

gospel is not about the overthrow from the outside, but of the "overthrow" of the inside, of a changed heart, and renewed mind. This is in fact how slavery ended. The same cannot be said for sex between men or sex between women because slavery is an immoral system that was invented and imposed on persons from the outside, whereas the practice of same–sex sexual relations is chosen as a desire against God's created order from inside the heart. No amount of cultural change can make it right.

Objection 2: Isn't the main concern of the Bible with regard to sex between men and sex between women about its association with idolatry, pagan practices, and wrongful lustful desires?

Answer: The Bible's main concern has always been holiness, righteous living, and loving according to the way God intended for human beings. That pattern was established at creation in Gen. 1:27 and 2:24, which was reaffirmed by Christ in Matt. 19: 4–6 and Mark 10: 5–9. There is *no* positive statement or teaching in Scripture that departs from the pattern that Jesus refers to in Matthew and Mark which is one man, one woman becoming one flesh for life. With regard to idolatry, too often we limit what idolatry is to visions of worshiping carved images of birds, reptiles, animals of various sorts, or even human beings (Rom. 1:23), but there are other forms of idolatry as Paul states in Col. 3:5, "Put to death, therefore, whatever belongs to your earthly nature: sexual immorality, impurity, lust, evil desires and greed, which is idolatry." It could be read this way: *sexual immorality is idolatry, impurity is idolatry, lust is idolatry, evil desires and greed are idolatry.*

The word Paul uses that is translated sexual immorality is the word *porneia,* which as we saw, is an umbrella term that by the first century meant any sexual activity outside of man–woman marriage. Sexual immorality (which includes sex between men and sex between women) is an act that grows out of evil desires, but it does not have to be organically connected to the worship of an idol. It is the act *itself* that is idolatrous by placing the creature's happiness ahead of God's holiness.

Those who argue that sexual immorality is always linked to idolatry confuse correlation with causation. While it's true that both are often found together, it does not mean that one *causes* the other. Idolatry is not the cause of sexual immorality; it is the excuse for it.

Objection 3: When the biblical authors wrote about sex between men, they only knew of exploitive forms of male with male sex such as tutor/student, master/slave, and those involved in idol worship or male prostitutes, most of which were short term relationships of younger serving older or where money was exchanged for sex. The biblical writers had no knowledge of loving, caring, long term monogamous same–sex relationships like we have today.

Answer: According to historians of ancient Greece and Rome, there is evidence that there were life–long romantic sexual relationships between adult males that included "marriage" with a complete ceremony. There is simply no good reason to believe that ancient men who preferred men over women should not have had life–long relationships. The concern for them was not about gender, but more about their standing in society and maintaining the expected masculine role as well as who would be the "woman" in the relationship. Historian Thomas K. Hubbard writes about some of the evidence for adult male relationships found in Greek vase paintings. "Scenes of lovemaking or courtship between adult men in the record of Greek vase painting are uncommon, but they do exist. . . . It surely must indicate, like Tyrrhenian ware, that there actually were some adult men, whether in Attica or Italy, who preferred other men rather than adolescent boys. The Affecter himself may have shared this preference, or he may have produced work to please one or more patrons who liked adult partners. Queer as they might be in the Athenian context, such men surely existed and were the focus of at least one Athenian painter's study."[5]

Roman historian Craig Williams writes about "marriage" between men in Roman times. "It may be equally worthwhile to insist on an important distinction: marriage between men were [sic] represented as anomalous not because of homophobic anxieties regarding intimacy between males, but rather because of hierarchical, androcentric assumptions regarding the nature of marriage. The fundamental problem was not that two men joined themselves

---

5. Thomas K. Hubbard, *A Companion to Greek and Roman Sexualities* (West Sussex, UK: Wiley–Blackwell Publishing, 2014), 144.

to each other, but that one man was thought necessarily to play the role of the bride."[6] Craig concludes, "In sum, it seems clear that some Romans did participate in formal wedding ceremonies in which one male was married to another . . . and that these men considered themselves joined as spouses."[7] What reason do we have to believe that the heartfelt desire of these men to be "married" to each other was less innate and genuine than those involved with same–sex attraction today?

It would seem clear the argument that the biblical authors *could not* have known about long term committed relationships between men is not supported by the evidence. Take a look at the apostle Paul who was raised in the Roman city of Tarsus, traveled all over the Near–East to such cities as Ephesus, Corinth, and even preached to the philosophers in Athens quoting their own poets to them (Acts 17:28). Does it make sense to believe that such a man would have no knowledge of the sexual practices of the culture around him? We do have an example in Scripture of a committed, long term (heterosexual) relationship that was deemed immoral by a biblical author. That author is the apostle Paul who writes about this relationship in 1 Cor. 5:1–3, "It is actually reported that there is sexual immorality among you, and of a kind that does not occur even among pagans: A man has his father's wife. And you are proud! Shouldn't you rather have been filled with grief and have put out of your fellowship the man who did this? Even though I am not physically present, I am with you in spirit. And I have already passed judgment on the one who did this, just as if I were present." Paul is invoking God's law found in Lev.18:8, "Do not have sexual relations with your father's wife; that would dishonor your father." That law is also found in Deut. 22:22, "If a man is found sleeping with another man's wife, both the man who slept with her and the woman must die. You must purge the evil from Israel."

For Paul and the church the immorality of the act transcends culture because it is based in Genesis. Only the means of discipline has changed. We need to ask if Paul had met the couple face to face and saw their love and commitment to each other and to the church, would he have given his blessing to that relationship? It seems clear

---

6. Craig A. Williams, *Roman Homosexuality,* 2nd ed. (Oxford: Oxford University Press, 2010), 281.

7. Ibid., 286.

that he would not because love and commitment are not a magic potion that transforms an immoral act into a moral one. If this is the case for a wrongly ordered loving heterosexual relationship, why should we believe it to be any different for a homosexual one?

Objection 4: The Inconsistency Objection. Why do those who use the Old Testament passages in Leviticus and Deuteronomy to show the immorality of homosexual practices, ignore the other verses about wearing mixed fiber clothing, or sowing two types of seed, or engaging in sexual intercourse during a woman's menstrual cycle?

Answer: The inconsistency argument is not a valid argument against the use of the sexual prohibitions in the Old Testament. First, we need to decide if one set of regulations is no longer in effect, does it nullify all the others. We need to look at the nature and or grounding as well as a possible purpose for the various prohibitions and whether as a result of new revelations that purpose has been fulfilled. In the case of the sexual prohibitions in Leviticus and Deuteronomy, you would need to show that they are no longer binding on the Christian in the same way that the prohibitions against mixed fiber, two types of seed, or sex during a woman's period were.

God has revealed through His Son Jesus Christ and His divinely appointed apostles what types of prohibitions are carried over and what types fulfilled their purpose after the coming of Christ. The fact is that no mention is made in the New Testament of the necessity of presenting an offering for sin at the temple after Christ's resurrection. With that change the various rituals and purity requirements for approaching God set forth in Leviticus and Deuteronomy have changed as God fulfilled all those requirements in Christ through His sacrifice on the cross. Heb. 8:5 talks about the "sanctuary that is a copy and shadow of what is in heaven." Paul says the same thing in Col. 2: 16, 17. "Therefore do not let anyone judge you by what you eat or drink, with regard to a religious festival, a New Moon celebration or a Sabbath day. These are a shadow of the things that were to come; the reality however, is found in Christ."

Purity rituals like not wearing mixed fiber clothes or sowing two types of seed stress purity and unity just like the bringing of a sacrifice without spot or blemish. The sacrificial system was never intended to take away sin on a permanent basis but was a covering like a "band–aid" that had to be applied again and again, all the while pointing towards the coming Messiah. With regard to a woman's monthly cycle (Lev. 20:18), it should be noted that nothing about the cycle itself is evil since God is the one who created it. The issue has to do with blood since blood is a very powerful symbol of the sacrificial system and remained powerful even after Christ's sacrifice for our sins. Another factor may be that when the blood leaves her body, it dies and bringing dead human blood into the tabernacle would be to violate the purity of the tabernacle. It would be similar to touching a corps and not purifying. Num. 19: 11–13 explains, "Whoever touches the dead body of anyone will be unclean for seven days. He must purify himself with the water on the third day and on the seventh day; then he will be clean. But if he does not purify himself on the third and seventh days, he will not be clean. Whoever touches the dead body of anyone and fails to purify himself defiles the Lord's tabernacle. That person must be cut off from Israel. Because the water of cleansing has not been sprinkled on him, he is unclean, his uncleanness remains on him."

Some anti–natural marriage advocates have argued that the penalty for having sex with a woman during her period was for both the man and the woman to be "cut off from their people" and that the term "cut off" means to execute them. The term "cut off" occurs multiple times in the Old Testament and about 12 times in Leviticus (7:20, 21, 25, 27, 17: 4, 9, 10, 19:8, 20:3, 6, 18, 23:29). The question of the application of a literal (cut off from life) or metaphorical (cut off from the people or community) interpretation of the punishment is not always clear and scholars continue to debate as to which type of punishment applies to which offense. However, the punishment in Lev. 20:13, is clear "If a man lies with a man as one lies with a woman, both of them have done what is detestable. They must be put to death; their blood will be on their own heads." After the coming of Christ, the immorality of men having sex with men remains, but the immediate loss of earthly life has now been replaced by an even greater loss, the possibility of losing the inheritance of the kingdom of God (1 Cor. 6:10). The door is left open for repentance, recovery and restoration as death would close the door for that opportunity.

Moral laws concerning sexual behavior are different than ritual or ceremonial laws because moral laws are grounded in God's nature as expressed in the order of creation. The pagan nations around Israel were not condemned by God because they did not observe the Sabbath, or because they ate forbidden foods. They were condemned because of their worship of idols *and* their sexual practices. God clearly left a witness through His creation which they chose to ignore (Rom. 1: 19, 20). So, despite what the defenders of anti–natural marriage might say about those who defend natural marriage, we are not "cherry picking" verses like some sort of "Bible verse buffet." There are real reasons why some verses of Scripture carry over to today and others have fulfilled their purpose and do not carry over. Notice that in the "vice lists" in the New Testament, none mentions things like wearing clothes of mixed fiber, sowing two types of seed, having sex with a menstruating woman, indicating that some things in the Law had been fulfilled. If not, why would they not be listed as impure or unholy behavior? Sexual morality in all of Scripture is grounded in the creation and was reaffirmed by the Son of God in Matt. 19:4–6 and Mark 10: 6–9, which closed the door on all other forms of human sexual expression and crosses over all times and cultures. Notice what the Jerusalem Council determined in Acts 15:20; Gentile believers should "abstain from the things polluted by idols, and from sexual immorality." Clearly the apostles believed that the sexual standards of the Old Testament were valid for Gentile Christians. Jesus pointed to the creation of Adam and Eve as the standard against which *all* marriage relationships are measured as one man and one woman for life. It is only because of human sin that the standard has been distorted in the attempt make it bend it to the will of man.

Objection 5: Loneliness is for most people one of the worst things in life to be endured. It seems clear from Gen. 2:18 that God did not intend for people to be alone, so why can't a loving, monogamous, same–sex relationship be one of the answers to the first "not good" of creation in the same way as an opposite–sex relationship?

Answer: The only "not good" in the creation account is in Gen. 2:18. "The Lord God said, 'It is not good for the man to be alone. I will make a helper suitable for him.'" Some anti–natural marriage advocates have argued that this situation takes God by surprise. Jay Michaelson puts it this way, "Yet suddenly something is not good. Suddenly, God realizes there is something within the world as we find it that is insufficient, something all of us experience in our own lives and strive to transcend: the existential condition of being alone."[8] Matthew Vines in his book *God and the Gay Christian* writes, "Animals could offer Adam some companionship, but that wasn't enough. God was looking for someone more *similar* to Adam than the animals were, someone with whom Adam could form a "one-flesh" bond. That had to be another human being. . . . Adam and Eve were right for each other, not because they were different, but because they were alike."[9]

There are several things "not good" with this understanding of the Genesis account. First, nothing in all of creation can take God by surprise. God cannot by His very nature come to "realize" something in creation is missing as a kind of "oops, I forgot something." "It is not good for the man to be alone" is a declaration of God continuing His work in creation. Notice two things after God creates the animals. First, He brings them to Adam to have Him name them because in the ancient Near East naming something indicates dominion over it (Gen. 1:26, 28). We still do something like this today. For example, if a new species, or fossil, or star is discovered, the discoverer is given the right to name it. Second, after all the animals had been brought before Adam and been named, there was not found a suitable helper for Adam. All of this was God's design for Adam. God knew all along that Adam needed a "helper" and what that helper needed to be like, but Adam did not until God showed him his need.

Next, God causes Adam to fall into a deep sleep and takes a rib (or part of his side) and fashions a woman out of it. Then God brings her to the man, and the man exclaims, "This is now bone of my bone and flesh of my flesh; she shall be called 'woman' for she was taken out of man." (Gen. 2:23). Notice it is *God* who is the initiator and God who is setting up His creation the way He intends for it to be. Some anti-natural marriage advocates try to down play the sexual differences between Adam and Eve and focus on their sameness. For example, Matthew Vines argues, "And the Genesis text focuses only on what these two have in common. Adam and Eve's sameness, not

---

8. Jay Michaelson, *God vs. Gay? The Religious Case for Equality* (Boston: Beacon Press, 2011), 5.

9. Matthew Vines, *God and the Gay Christian* (New York: Convergent Books, 2014), 46.

their gender differences, was what made them suitable partners."[10] We need to ask, what was created in Gen. 2:22, just another person or the missing part of what was taken out of Adam? It is their differences biologically, psychologically, and emotionally not their sameness that makes the marriage bond that God designed unique, special, and that cannot be duplicated with members of the same sex even when deep emotions are involved.

Robert Gagnon puts it this way, "The specific expression '*one flesh*' does not appear anywhere else in the Old Testament or in early Jewish or early rabbinic texts apart from a reference to Gen. 2:24. This makes it unlikely to have been an expression for denoting covenant bonds outside of a context of man–woman marriage. . . . The principle of two sexes becoming one flesh is correlated with the picture of two sexes being formed from one flesh."[11]

So here's the picture: God creates one flesh (Adam) from whom He takes a piece and creates one flesh (Eve). She is one flesh with him because she is taken *out of* him and for him. When they join together in sex, it is a physical reminder of their one flesh origin, and when the DNA material from each of them combine, the two make one flesh (child), so from one to two and back to one. Each whole human has only half of what is needed to create more humans, and through the beauty of joining as expressed in physical love, they become more than just the sum of their parts. Even though the ancients did not understand this process like we do, that does not change its truth. We should remember that when Jesus is asked a question about breaking apart a marriage in Matt. 19: 4–6, and Mark 10: 6–9, he refers back to Gen. 1:27 and 2: 23–24 as God's original intent and standard for marriage. For the Christian, Christ's statement should be the final authority because as John 1:3 states, "Through him all things were made; without him nothing was made that has been made."

Objection 6: Doesn't Jesus' encounter with the centurion in Matt. 8: 5–10, and Luke 7: 2–10 show that Jesus was more concerned with healing the centurion's servant than the almost certain man/boy sexual relationship that was going on between them, and since

---

10. Ibid., 47.

11. Robert Gagnon, "A Book not to Be Embraced: A Critical Appraisal of Stacy Johnson's *A Time to Embrace*," *Scottish Journal of Theology* 62, no. 1 (February 2009): 72.

nothing was said by Jesus or Matthew about it, isn't their silence an indication of approval? As Daniel Helminiak argues, "Still, the real probability of homosexual relationships in the lives of important biblical characters suggests that the Bible may be more open to same–sex love than most ever imagine."[12]

Answer: This argument is put forward by several anti–natural marriage advocates and is indeed one of the most imaginative to be found. Several things are being assumed with this argument. For example, there is the assumption that the centurion and his "boy" or servant were in a sexual relationship. It is true that a sexual relationship between Romans and their slaves was a common practice, but that does not mean every Roman did so. In Luke's account of the meeting, we read in verse 3–5, "The centurion heard of Jesus and sent some elders of the Jews to him, asking him to come and heal his servant. When they came to Jesus, they pleaded earnestly with him, 'This man deserves to have you do this, because he loves our people and has built our synagogue.'" This officer of the conquering Roman army showed his love of the Jewish people and paid to have their synagogue built, also showed great respect for Jesus and did not even feel worthy to have Jesus enter his house. He *may* have been closer to the kingdom of God than anyone knew with the exception of Jesus.

If by healing the "boy"/ slave and saying nothing about a possible same–sex relationship, Jesus would have been endorsing homosexual rape since by definition sex with a slave is nonconsensual. Jesus would be seen as having no problem with such an exploitive form of sexual relationships, but Jesus did not in any way "push the envelope" of God's standard for sexual relationships. Instead he raised the standard for marriage above that of his culture by returning to Gen. 1:27, 2:24 and took away every excuse for divorce except for sexual immorality (Matt. 19:9).

Another point that undermines the approval theory is the fact that Jesus ate meals with tax collectors and those involved in sexual immorality, which upset the religious leaders of the time. Jesus, however, never approved of the economic exploitation of the tax collectors or the sexual immorality of the prostitutes but called them

---

12. Daniel A. Helminiak, *What the Bible Really Says about Homosexuality* (Tajique, NM: Alamo Press, 2002), 127.

to repentance, to a loving, forgiving, and restoring God. So, even *if* there was a sexual relationship between the centurion and his slave, it does not follow that Jesus must have approved of it. By healing the centurion's "boy" / slave, Jesus is demonstrating that healing and forgiveness has arrived for the Gentiles and that Jewish prejudice against them was unacceptable. This kind of theory about Jesus and the centurion uses the type of imagination that people use to see the profile of Elvis in a potato chip.

Objection 7: Some re-interpreters of Scripture see in the re-lationship of Jonathan and David in 1 Sam. 18: 1–5 and following the clearest example in Scripture of a same–sex sexual, loving rela-tionship that is not condemned in any way. Former Jesuit priest and long–time advocate of homosexuality, John J. McNeill, writes, ". . . in a few instances where a loving homosexual relation is presented it is dealt with approval and respect. The most important example of this is the story of David and Jonathan in 1 Samuel."[13]

Author Jay Michaelson agrees with McNeill and devotes an entire chapter to the topic. ". . . this part of the book would not be complete if we did not discuss the Bible's clearest expression of same –gender love, the story of David and Jonathan. No, David was not 'gay.' He had numerous love affairs with women (often troubled and ethically dubious), as well as one with a man. But labels are not the point; this is a tale of two men who were in love with one another, who expressed that love physically, and who are an essential part of the Bible's overall depiction of love between people."[14]

Answer: This objection is an example on the part of those who favor the reinterpretation of Scripture to find something–anything that can be used to show a favorable same–sex relationship recorded in the Bible. To assume that they were "in love" as opposed to "loved him as himself" is to read something *into* Scripture.

Let's set some context for the verses on Jonathan and David. Because of Saul's abuses the Lord "was grieved that he had made Saul king over Israel" (1 Sam. 15:35). The Lord chooses David and anoints him as the king of Israel (1 Sam. 16: 12), David becomes one of Saul's armor–bearers and Saul is pleased with him in verses 21, 22,

---

13. John J. McNeill, *Sex as God Intended* (Maple Shade, NJ: Lethe Press, 2008), 39.
14. Michaelson, 94.

David defeats Goliath in chapter 17 verse 49, 50 and becomes a hero. Now we come to the references about Jonathan and David beginning in chapter 18. Jonathan is King Saul's eldest son and the heir to the throne. In 1 Sam. 18: 1, 3, 4 we read, "After David had finished talking with Saul, Jonathan became one in spirit with David and loved him as himself. . . . And Jonathan made a covenant with David because he loved him as himself. Jonathan took off the robe he was wearing and gave it to David, along with his tunic, and even his sword, his bow and his belt." In chapter 19:1 we read, "Saul told his son Jonathan and all the attendants to kill David. But Jonathan was very fond of David . . ." (20:17). "And Jonathan had David reaffirm his oath out of love for him, because he loved him as he loved himself."

In chapter 20 verses 41 and 42, we read, "After the boy had gone, David got up from the south side of the stone and bowed before Jonathan three times with his face to the ground. Then they kissed each other and wept–but David wept the most. Jonathan said to David, 'Go in peace, for we have sworn friendship with each other in the name of the Lord, saying, The Lord is witness between you and me, and between your descendants and my descendants.'"

Finally in 2 Sam. 1:26, after the death of Jonathan, David grieves for Jonathan. "I grieve for you, Jonathan my brother; you were very dear to me. Your love for me was wonderful, more wonderful than that of a woman." This is the scriptural evidence that is used to try to turn the record of a deep, lasting friendship into proof of an accepted intimate same–sex sexual relationship. Let's look at the words used to describe this relationship. Three times the phrase "loved him as himself" occurs with reference to Jonathan's love for David, but the same word "loved" is used to describe the feelings of Israel and Judah for David in 1 Sam. 18:16, "But all Israel and Judah loved David, because he led them in their campaigns." The terminology used in 1 Sam. 18:1 is the same in Hebrew as that in Gen. 44:30 of Jacob's love for is son Benjamin, ". . . who's life is closely bound up with the boy's life." As Richard Davidson explains, ". . . by using precisely the same phraseology regarding David and Jonathan, the narrator of their story also undoubtedly intended to describe a legitimate non–homosexual bond of affection between the two men."[15]

---

15. Richard M. Davidson, "Homosexuality in the Old Testament," in *Homosexuality, Marriage, and the Church* (Berrien Springs, MI: Andrews University Press, 2012), 31.

The problem is reading the wrong sense of the word "love" into the texts and assuming that it must have a romantic or sexual connotation. This is something that modern readers in our sex soaked society have done by assuming that statements of affection between members of the same sex must mean there is some sort of sexual desire involved.

What about Jonathan giving David his robe, tunic, sword, bow, and belt in 1 Sam. 18:4? Jonathan, who was the biological heir to the throne, had made a covenant with David, who was the Lord's anointed. By removing the emblems of royalty and then giving them to David, he symbolized David's right to the throne. There is nothing in the text that implies that Jonathan took off all his clothes as this was a political gesture on Jonathan's part.

As for the kissing between Jonathan and David, we need to ask what *kind* of kissing the text is talking about. Kissing as a demonstration of deep feelings and fondness between friends was (and remains) a common gesture in much of the Mid–East and has no romantic or sexual connotation when done between members of the same sex. There are several examples of this such as 1Sam. 10:1. "Then Samuel took a flask of oil and poured it on Saul's head and kissed him, saying, "Has not the Lord anointed you leader over his inheritance?" Also, 2 Sam. 14:33 says, "So, Joab went to the king and told him this. Then the king summoned Absalom, and he came in and bowed down with his face to the ground before the king. And the king kissed Absalom." Joab said to Amasa, "'How are you my brother?' Then Joab took Amasa by the beard with his right hand to kiss him" (2 Sam. 20:9). In 2 Sam. 19:39, David kissed the eighty year old Barzillai: "So all the people crossed the Jordan, and then the king crossed over. The king kissed Barzillai and gave him his blessing, and Barzillai returned home."

Most men in the modern western world sadly must hide their feelings for a good friend who dies or leaves for fear of it being misunderstood as having a sexual connotation, but in a large part of the Near–East, you can see men walking down the street holding hands which indicates nothing more than a close friendship. David and Jonathan had such a friendship. As 1 Sam. 20:41 says, "Then they kissed each other and wept together–but David wept the most." They were on the run hiding from a crazy king bent on killing David, and they bonded like soldiers in the life and death struggle of combat. We can see an example of this kind of emotion in the New Testament in Acts 20: 37. When the apostle Paul gets ready to leave for Jerusalem, the elders from the church at Ephesus wept at Paul's leaving. "They all wept as they embraced him and kissed him."

The statements of weeping and kissing between Jonathan and David are evidence of a close deep friendship and not a sexual relationship. What about David's lament over the death of Jonathan? In 2 Sam.1:26, we read, "I grieve for you, Jonathan my brother; you were very dear to me. Your love for me was wonderful, more wonderful than that of women." It is not difficult to understand how two men, two soldiers fleeing a king bent on their destruction, like minded, who enjoyed each others company with each one knowing that the other "has their back" could develop such a relationship. To see this one need only visit a war memorial to watch the emotions of men who, upon seeing the name of a comrade lost in battle even after decades and never speaking of it, weep and morn at the loss not of a lover, but of a friend.

Even with hundreds of wives and concubines, with them David did not experience the connection that he had with Jonathan. This does not imply sexual activities but a deep emotional friendship between them. David may not have had many true male friends. Modern readers tend to equate deep love feelings with sex and often view with suspicion someone who expresses deep feelings of love for someone who may be of the same sex. This is what modern readers are reading into the text of Scripture when they claim that David and Jonathan were sexual lovers. Richard Davidson summarizes it this way. "The whole setting of this narrative reveals that despite the political issues that should have interfered with their relationship (with Jonathan, by birth heir to the throne, realizing that David was chosen by God to rule instead), an amazingly close friendship developed between the two, Jonathan the tender and faithful friend of David, shielded David's life at the peril of his own and gave eloquent witness to the existence and power of unselfish love. This is not a portrait of homosexual relationship but of friends who rose to the heights of self–abnegation."[16]

---

16. Ibid., 33.

Objection 8: When Paul says in Gal. 3:28 "There is neither Jew nor Greek, slave nor free, male nor female, for you are all one in Christ Jesus," isn't he saying that the most fundamental distinctions between people are now done away with for those in Christ, which would allow for loving, committed, same–sex relationships since even the gender difference has been removed?

Answer: A careful reading of the verse in the context of Galatians along with looking at the totality of Paul's writings would be the best way to answer this objection. Some revisionists especially feminists authors try to use this verse out of its setting as the "lens" through which we should view all of Paul's writings about male and female, as well as marriage. Author Luke Timothy Johnson, in an article published in *Commonweal* argues, "The challenge, therefore, is to discern what constitutes the positive and negative in sexual behavior. A start would be to adapt Galatians 3:28 and state that "in Christ there is neither gay nor straight. . . ."[17]

Paul never intended that this verse was to wipe out *all* distinctions in daily life right down to the created distinctions between male and female, which would make his commands to husbands and wives in Eph. 5:22–33 and Col. 3:18–19 virtually unintelligible. Because of our unity in Christ, His light will shine through even with national distinctions (Jew and Greek), social distinctions (master and slave), and sexual distinctions (male and female). For Paul there are no upper or lower spiritual levels in Christ with Jews, masters, and males on the upper level and Greeks, slaves, and females on the lower level. The context of Gal. 3:28 is about salvation. The claim that same–sex sexual relations and opposite–sex sexual relations are now the same for those who are in Christ is simply absurd.

Objection 9: Jesus said in Matt. 7:15–20 "Watch out for false prophets. They come to you in sheep's clothing, but inwardly they are ferocious wolves. By their fruit you will recognize them. Do people pick grapes from thornbushes, or figs from thistles? Likewise every good tree bears good fruit, but a bad tree bears bad fruit. A good tree cannot bear bad fruit, and a bad tree cannot bear good fruit. Every tree that does not bear good fruit is cut down and thrown into

---

17. Luke Timothy Johnson, "Homosexuality and the Church," *Commonweal,* June 11, 2007.

the fire. Thus, by their fruit you will recognize them." When you see homosexual men and women who call Jesus their Lord and Savior, when you hear their testimony of what God has done and is doing in their lives, when you hear songs of praise and hands raised in worship, when you see their outreach to the helpless and hopeless in their community, is this not the evidence of the fruit from a good tree that Jesus spoke of to show that God was working through them?

Answer: This is a persuasive argument that has changed the minds of many conservative Christians, not because it is theologically convincing but because it is emotionally compelling. The testimony of Christians who have changed their views about the Bible and homosexuality are recounted in books by authors like Kathy Baldock in *Walking the Bridgeless Canyon*, where she tells how she met and befriended a Native American lesbian named *Netto* while walking on some hiking trails. Over the course of time as Kathy was introduced to more of Netto's homosexual friends, she found herself questioning many of her assumptions about them. In talking to Christians about her homosexual friends ,she began to dislike the distinction she always had to make between her and "them." She recalls a pivotal moment at a women's retreat, "During the Sunday service at the end of the women's retreat, I took my turn, as many did, to walk to the front of the room and share an "aha" moment from the retreat. I made a declaration to God and the women in my church: 'God, I don't know what you're doing in my life, but I recognize I have a lot of gay friends. I'm tired of cautiously validating my friendships.' Looking to the women, I continued, 'I really don't care what any of you think of me. God's doing something with these friendships, and I'm ready.' I raised up both my hands in submission. 'So, God, whatever this thing is, let's do it! Let's get this thing going. I'm ready.'"[18]

Sometime later she discovered there were people who called themselves "gay Christians," and she decided to attend one of their conferences. "On the first night of the conference, I stood alone in the back of the darkened room. I was bewildered. Undeniably, the Holy Spirit, who had been moving in my life for decades, was in the room and in the lives of the gay worshippers. Would it be possible to line

---

18. Kathy Baldock, *Walking the Bridgeless Canyon* (Reno, NV: Canyonwalker Press. 2014), 5.

up my Christian beliefs with what I was seeing in the witness of these gay Christians? That question kept running through my mind."[19]

Another "traditionalist" Mark Achtemeier writes about the effects on the lives of homosexuals who try to uphold the historic Christian position about homosexuality.

> My observations and experiences were raising a lot of questions about whether traditional church teaching on homosexuality was in accordance with God's will at all. As I became more and more aware of the personal and spiritual devastation that this teaching was causing, I realized that getting to the bottom of these questions was far more than just an intellectual exercise. Lives and souls were very much a stake. I had always assumed that the Bible's teaching on homosexuality was quite clear, but there was no denying the dramatic disconnect between the Bible's predictions about fruits of faithfulness and the actual results I was seeing in the lives of gay people who followed, or tried to follow, this traditional teaching. I began wondering what I had overlooked in my own understanding of the Bible's teaching.[20]

Theologian James V. Brownson had a similar shake–up in his theology when his eighteen year old son informed James and his wife that he was gay. Dr. Brownson states that his prior studies relating to issues of homosexuality "wasn't helpful when it came to the concrete and specific questions I faced with my son. Indeed, the answers that I thought I had found seemed neither helpful nor relevant in the case of my son."[21] A little later he states, "But here is the point I want to make from this personal story: that dramatic shock to my life forced me to reimagine how Scripture speaks about homosexuality. The text had not changed, but my assumptions about what they were self–evidently saying was put to the test."[22]

These three examples (many more could be shown) demonstrate the power and persuasiveness that personal experience can have even with those who are advanced in the faith (or at least should be).

---

19. Ibid., 6.

20. Mark Achtemeier, *The Bible's Yes to Same–Sex Marriage* (Westminster John Knox Press, 2015), 9.

21. Brownson, 11.

22. Ibid., 12–13.

This really shouldn't be a surprise given the experience–centered culture we live in. What happens most of the time is that when people have deep profound experiences, they will use the experiences as measurements of truth and look for a way to bring their theology into line with them. This will help ease any tension that might exist between their theology and the experiences. Jesus said to beware of false prophets (or teachers), which means not just the fruit of their lives, but includes the fruit of the doctrines they teach.

A couple of examples help make this clear. Look at the lives and some of the teachings of Mormons and Jehovah's Witnesses. As friends, neighbors, or community participants, most of them live exemplary lives. They have a strong devotion to family, have a great work ethic, and are quick to volunteer when help in the community is needed. They have a large and active missionary outreach for their church and produce a huge amount of material to spread the teachings of their faith. But much of their doctrine or teaching is contrary to the teachings of the historic Christian church on central doctrinal issues. For example, Mormons teach that God was once a man and dwelt on an "earth" like ours and through exaltation became the God of this earth. They believe that loyal, righteous Mormons can become gods themselves and populate another earth someday. Jehovah's Witnesses believe that Jesus is not God but is the first and greatest creation of God. The say Jesus did not rise in a physical body at his resurrection but rose as a spirit.

The point of this is that "bad fruit" is not just manifest in lives but in teachings and doctrine as well. First John 4:1 says, "Dear friends, do not believe every spirit, but test the spirits to see whether they are from God, because many false prophets have gone out into the world," and 1 Thess. 5:21–22 exhorts us, "Test everything. Hold on to the good. Avoid every kind of evil." Acts 17: 11 reminds us, "Now the Bereans were of more noble character than the Thessalonians, for they received the message with great eagerness and examined the Scriptures every day to see if what Paul said was true." If a church teaches that God accepts loving same–sex sexual relationships, then that teaching cannot be true based on "feeling the Spirit move," but because it is in accord with the whole teaching of Scripture. This brings up the issue of the right and wrong role of feelings and its relationship to doctrine and teaching. Let's illustrate it this way:

THE WRONG ROLE	THE RIGHT ROLE
As a test for truth	Way to express the truth
To determine the truth	To manifest the truth
To inform the truth	To enrich the truth
As a basis for truth	As a byproduct of truth
As a condition of truth	To accompany the truth
To replace the mind	To refresh the soul

One more illustration will help. In the old CRT televisions when the picture was generated, nearly all the information in the picture was in black and white. The color added very little information, but the color made the picture look more like life. In a similar way doctrine gives the black and white information, but the feelings give it warmth and life. Without the feelings it's just black and white information, but without that information it's just meaningless blobs of color.

We should always rejoice in the Lord for His love to us, His kindness, and His blessings. We should also desire the presents of His Spirit to *feel* the power of His love in our lives, but that feeling should never be the basis for changing what His word clearly states, which is that same–sex sexual relationships are wrong in the same way that adultery, fornication, and sex with children or animals are wrong. We should take note that the verses right after Jesus spoke about good and bad fruit in Matthew 7 are verses 21–23: "Not everyone who says to me, 'Lord, Lord,' will enter the kingdom of heaven, but only he who does the will of my Father who is in heaven. Many will say to me on that day, 'Lord, Lord, did we not prophesy in your name, and in your name drive out demons and perform many miracles?' Then I will tell them plainly, 'I never knew you. Away from me, you evildoers!'" Nowhere did Jesus change the moral laws of Scripture, but instead He raised the bar higher than the culture around Him, yet at the same time it is through His Spirit that He empowers us to live that moral life. Jesus demands more than agreement; he demands obedience. John 14:15 tells us what it means when we say we love Christ. "If you love me, you will obey what I command."

Objection 10: Are you not doing exactly what Jesus says you are not supposed to do when in Matt. 7:1–2 he says, "Do not judge, or you too will be judged. For in the same way you judge others, you will be judged, and with the measure you use, it will be measured to you." Are you not passing judgement and condemning fellow believers who name the name of Christ?

Answer: This verse in Matthew is one of the most misquoted and incorrectly applied verses in all of Scripture. Even if you were to do a random "man on the street" survey of those who know virtually nothing about the Bible, most can tell you that "somewhere in the Bible it says don't judge." The use of this "clobber verse" is really meant to shut down discussion and is intended to make the questioner feel guilty about some sin in his life and therefore unqualified to say anything about sinful activity in someone else's life. Is this what Jesus really meant when he said, "Don't judge"? Did he mean we don't have the right to distinguish between right or wrong activity or between moral acts and immoral acts? If Jesus was not saying this (which becomes clear once we know more about him), then what type of judgement was he talking about?

He is referring to hypocritical judgment, the type of judgment that claims inherent moral superiority, the type of person always on the lookout for the "speck in their brother's eye," someone who is quick to judge and slow to forgive, which is just the opposite of what God has done for us, and they kind of judgment that pronounces condemnation rather than lovingly admonishing someone to turn away from sin. Remember the words of Paul in Rom. 3: 23–24, "For all have sinned and fall short of the glory of God, and are justified freely by his grace through the redemption that came by Christ Jesus."

Having said that, it does not mean we cannot speak up when a fellow Christian becomes involved in immorality as in the example of where Paul writes concerning a man who is involved with his father's wife, "Even though I am not physically present, I am with you in spirit. And I have already passed judgement on the one who did this, just as if I were present" (1 Cor. 5:3). Even though Paul was not shy about calling out sin, yet we see his tender instruction to the church: "Brothers, if someone is caught in a sin, you who are spiritual should restore him gently. But watch yourself, or you also may be tempted" (Gal. 6:1).

Jesus gives us the pattern of how we should approach a brother who is in error: "If your brother sins against you, go and show him his fault, just between the two of you. If he listens to you, you have won your brother over. But if he will not listen, take one or two others along, so that 'every matter may be established by the testimony of two or three witnesses.' If he refuses to listen to them, tell it to the church; and if he refuses to listen even to the church, treat him as you would a pagan or a tax collector" (Matt. 18: 15–17). As Eph. 4:15 says, we are to "speak the truth in love . . ." but to say nothing in the face of immorality is *un*loving and *un*caring for those around us. As Christians, we are admonished to distinguish (make judgements) between right and wrong, between moral and immoral behavior, to lovingly call those involved in such behavior to repentance, and restoration but not pronouncing eternal judgement, which is reserved for God alone.

Conclusion

We have looked at multiple verses and the attempts by revisionists to make the Bible say what it clearly does not. Despite all their efforts, the interpretive gymnastics, and the focus on "some possible meaning," the message of Scripture is clear. There is only one God approved way of sexual expression for human beings, and that is one man + one woman bonded together for life. This was God's created intension, and that created intension was marred by sin when human beings decided they would do what they desired.

Something else is going on in this attempt to "reinterpret" the Scriptures that many people dealing with this issue seem to miss. It is the subtle (and sometimes not so subtle) anti–supernaturalism with regard to the writing and writers of Scripture. A clear example is that of D. S. Bailey in whose 1955 book *Homosexuality and the Western Christian Tradition* states that the destruction of Sodom and Gomorrah was caused by an accidental fire in a petroleum rich area that caused a tremendous amount of damage to the city, and as the story was retold over the centuries, it became about divine judgment on the people of that city. With this kind of approach one is tempted to ask if Bailey would interpret Abraham's talk with the Lord in Genesis 18 as a hallucination brought on by being in the hot sun too long.

There is another more subtle anti–supernatural assumption that goes mostly undetected because it seems most reasonable until we consider its implications. It usually is stated like this: "Paul could not have known," or "the biblical writers did not understand as we do. . . ." All of this implies that the writers of Scripture only *believed* they were writing the Word of God. Of course it's true that they wrote to specific people at specific points in history, but that doesn't mean God's intension was for it to stop being relevant to people beyond their immediate time and place even though the author of the text could not see that. If we assume the irrelevance of Scripture because "Paul did not know," then why should we not expect a new book to be added every couple of hundred years by God just to keep up with latest "evolution" of society. Or do we stand with Paul in 2 Tim. 3:16 and17, "All Scripture is breathed out by God and profitable for teaching, for reproof, for correction, and for training in righteousness, that the man of God may be complete, equipped for every good work." Do we agree with Jude 3, "I felt I had to write and urge you to contend for the faith that was once for all entrusted to the saints."

Long–time advocate for reinterpreting Scripture to accommodate homosexuality John J. McNeill, tells us of his approach, "We must, then, approach Scripture with what the feminists call 'a hermeneutic of suspicion'. Our suspicion is that, if there were a gay positive attitude on the part of Jesus and his followers, every effort would be made to bury the evidence."[23] So, according to McNeill, the Scriptures have probably been "scrubbed" of any positive statements about homosexuality. Of course, there is not a shred of evidence for this, so we are back to seeing Elvis in that potato chip . . . again.

The author with whom the re–interpreters have the most difficulty is the Apostle Paul. Jesus they respect, but with Paul the feeling is they can disagree with him much like you would disagree with the local barber or the guy next to you on that flight from New York to L.A. They seem to forget that Paul is the divinely appointed ambassador to the Gentiles (Acts 9:15). As an ambassador Paul represents and speaks for Christ, extending His ministry "to the ends of the earth" (Acts 1:8). We see an example of this type of commissioning from Jesus when he sent out the seventy in Luke 10:16. "He who lis-

---

23. McNeill, 86.

tens to you listens to me; he who rejects you rejects me; but he who rejects me rejects him who sent me." Arguing against Paul is arguing against Christ who sent him, and arguing against Christ is arguing against God. What Paul said, Jesus said.

Attempting to neutralize the Bible's rejection of same–sex sexual practice is to reject God's design for sex and substitute one of our own making. God did not intend for people to think of sex like a buffet table, take some of this or that in order to fill our own sinful desires. God has given two options: (1) monogamous, life–long male / female sex, or (2) celibacy, both of which can honor and serve the Lord. Simply because our culture has decided to cut itself loose from the moorings of God's Word and is adrift on the sea of moral relativity does not obligate God to change the moorings to suit our desires. For the Christian, there is no "tailor shop" where you may go and try on various sexual ethics until you find the one that's comfortable for you. Rather, it is God who, like a sculptor, is transforming us more and more into the image of His Son. As Paul says in Rom. 12:2, "Do not conform any longer to the pattern of this world, but be transformed by the renewing of your mind."

PART 3

Help, Hope, and Healing

10

Help Through Christ's People

One of the memorable statements made by the late great defender of the Christian faith, Walter Martin, was how the defender of orthodoxy could win the argument and still lose the soul. Answering objections, correcting those who use theological gymnastics trying to make Scripture say what it does not say, demonstrating that there is no scientific basis for the "born that way" statement are only necessary steps that help to remove the objects human beings try to hide behind when they seek to deny the truth of how God designed us and His purpose for us.

The church should be a place where the broken (that means all of us) can go to receive the healing and refreshment of our souls as we await the full restoration of our bodies when our Lord returns. Unfortunately for many struggling with homosexuality or same-sex attraction (SSA) too often the response has been less than loving, more condemning, with a fear as though if they should get too close they might catch it like the Ebola virus. Justin Lee in his book *Torn*, quotes author Philip Yancey about a little English girl that prayed, "O God, make the bad people good, and the good people nice."[1]

Part of the reason for the fearful response of many conservative Christians stems from the fact that before the 1960s homosexuality was largely in the shadows and unseen, and even when spoken of, it was just in whispers. After the work of Kinsey and Hooker moved out of the "ivory towers" of specialists and became general knowledge, the old way of quoting a couple of Scripture verses about God's

---

1. Justin Lee, *Torn: Rescuing the Gospel from the Gays-vs.-Christians Debate* (New York: Jericho Books, 2012), 210.

wrath coming down on those who engaged in such practices and then passing them by on the other side of the road, simply did not address the problem.

During the height of the AIDS epidemic, the churches that stood the strongest for Scripture by and large missed an outreach ministry opportunity when tens of thousands of mostly young men were dying of a horrible disease. What the world heard from famous evangelists on TV were things like "this is God's curse on America for accepting homosexual practice" or "these people are now reaping what they have sown." How different might the situation be today if the conservative churches had been out in force to help these dying young men in the same way they are when a natural disaster strikes. One of the difficulties many Christians have with those who have SSA is that once they know they are struggling with this issue, they have difficulty seeing or listening to them through any other lens. One of the reasons for this difficulty is that Christians like most everyone else have accepted the idea of the division of human beings into almost different "species" of "heterosexual," "homosexual," "transsexual," "bisexual" and a whole host of sub–species covering the entire spectrum of possible human sexual activities. This view says that what you feel and experience is how you are defined rather than an objective human nature as created by God and for God in His image.

The idea of sexual orientation undermines the biblical view of human nature by assuming that there is a part of our sexual nature that we cannot control and should not be held accountable for. In her excellent book *Openness Unhindered*, Rosaria Butterfield puts it this way: "Indeed, sexual orientation went from a categorical invention to heralded immortal truth in one hundred years, taking out the concept of being created in God's image and bearing an eternal soul in its wake. It is now a term embraced uncritically by believers and unbelievers alike. Sexual orientation defines selfhood as the sum–total of our fallen human desires. Through it we get no glimpse of how the covenant of grace defends our real identity in Christ, or why, say, biblical marriage is a God–designed creation ordinance and a living reflection of Christ and the church, and not merely a man–made convenience."[2]

_____

2. Rosaria Butterfield, *Openness Unhindered* (Pittsburgh: Crown and Covenant Publications, 2015), 98.

When we look into Scripture, we notice that these modern man–made categories of sexual desire and identity do not exist. For the biblical writers, if someone commits sodomy, it does not matter what their "orientation" is because the act in and of itself violates the created purpose of sexual intercourse. This means that the person committing the sin and the act itself can be distinguished, whereas with the orientation view what a person does is welded to what they are. The old, often dismissed saying that we should "love the sinner but hate the sin" is not difficult to understand when we consider that we do it all the time . . . with ourselves. As Christians we hate the sin we do but love ourselves enough to feed ourselves, clothe ourselves etc.

Christians would be more effective in presenting the hope we have in Christ if they did not accept the "sexual orientation" designation because it lessens the responsibility for the sin the person is involved in. "It's just my orientation" implies a "I'm not responsible" for their thoughts and actions, which is contrary to the gospel message. This also brings with it the idea that there is something equal but just different between opposite–sex and same–sex sexual practice as though these were two viable (perhaps God ordained) options for human sexuality as long as there is love and commitment between the couple. Scripture makes it quite clear that "love and commitment" are not the *basis* for a morally acceptable sexual relationship. If it were acceptable, why then would Paul be upset at the Christians in the church of Corinth when one of their members was living with his father's wife. It seems reasonable to assume that there was love and commitment between this man and woman, but Paul calls the relationship *sexually immoral* (1 Cor. 5:1–5).

All of this is not to deny the reality of feelings but only to deny that feelings are the basis for reality. So often when attempting to minister to those who are seeking help with same–sex attraction, we can get lost in the fog of modern definitions that do not accept the Bible's distinctions that are grounded in creation. Accepting many modern definitions of terms like love, sex, faithfulness, morality, marriage, family, self–identity, tolerance, and diversity would be as productive as trying to drive up an ice covered hill by pressing down hard on the gas pedal. The wheels are spinning fast, but no progress is being made. For example, when Christians reads or hears the statement "love makes a family," they need to ask, really? So this would mean that whatever or whomever one loves could be considered family such as a man and a woman, parents and children, two men or two women, a man with multiple "wives," a woman with multiple "husbands," or perhaps a dog or a cat or a goldfish. In a lecture, Rosaria Butterfield stated that when she was a Marxist, feminist, lesbian they had a saying for how a revolution of thinking could take place: "if you change the language, you change the logic."

Another word that is thrown around today without clear definition is "diversity." Now suppose you were about to go into surgery and the surgeon introduced you to his diverse surgical team. You met Harry the plumber acting as surgical assistant, Mary the waitress as the surgical nurse, and Larry the librarian acting as the anesthesiologists. Most of us would agree that in such a situation a clear definition of "diversity" would be helpful. The point is that in our time words like "love" and "family" are empty of objective meaning and can be filled with whatever subjective feeling the user wishes to pour into them. This means that when the Christian is ministering to someone with unwanted same–sex attraction, he may be using words such that the person listening to them is translating or filling them with meaning that the Christian does not intend.

How then can Christians reach out and minister to help those dealing with same–sex attraction. First, we need to see them as people and not projects. We need to get rid of the idea or implication that what they need is a good heterosexual relationship ("you just need to find the right girl"). That is *FALSE*; what they need is a right relationship with Christ as we all do and then they can begin the long and often difficult journey to having right relationships with members of the same sex.

It is here that the church can have a real impact for Christ with those whom the Holy Spirit is calling away from homosexual practice. We should not be clobbering them with verses they have heard a thousand times before, but impact them by showing the love of Christ in our hearts through genuine interest in *them* the way we should for anyone who came into the church desiring to find out what this "Christian thing" is all about. Many (too many) of those in same–sex sexual relationships tell heart rending stories of rejection and revulsion by church friends and family members who should be the ones that show the compassion and understanding and who seem to have forgotten the words of Paul in 1 Cor. 1:26. "Brothers, consider your calling: not many are wise from a human perspective, not many powerful, not many of noble birth." Paul later remind us in 1 Cor. 6 where after giving a vice list of those who practice evil not inheriting the kingdom of God, reminds them in verse 11, "Some of you were like this; but you were washed, you were sanctified, you were justified in the name of the Lord Jesus Christ and by the Spirit of our God."

One excellent example of how to reach out to those dealing with same–sex attraction is given by Rosaria Butterfield. In her pre–conversion days after she had written an article for the local newspaper attacking the Promise Keepers who were visiting the university where she taught, she received a number of letters from local church goers that assured her she was on the road to hell, but there was one letter that had a different tone to it. This letter came from a pastor named Ken Smith who was the pastor of a local Reformed Presbyterian Church. She replied to his letter, and Ken invited her to dinner with his family. Rosaria recounts what happened. "At my first meal at their home, Ken and Floy omitted two important steps in the rulebook of how Christians should deal with a heathen like me: 1) they did not share the gospel with me, and 2) they did not invite me to church. Because of these omissions to the Christian rulebook as I had come to know it, I felt that when Ken extended his hand to me in friendship, it was safe to close my hand in his."[3]

Christians are to be the representatives of Christ to the world, and as such need to follow His example of speaking the truth in love. This kind of love is not undefined with a plastic meaning that can be stretched and molded to suit our corrupt nature, but love grounded in the nature of our relationship to Christ. As He says in John 14:15, "'If you love Me, you will keep My commandments.'"

Dos and Don'ts

Let's give some dos and don'ts in reaching out to those with unwanted same–sex attraction. DO see those with same–sex attraction as persons made in the image of God for whom Christ died and who

---

3. Ibid., 16.

desires them to come to Him. Don't assume they define terms from the same point of view or world view as you do. Take the time to define your terms clearly so as to minimize the retranslation of terms in their minds so that you are communicating with them and not just preaching at them. Do get to know them as persons, your friends, neighbors, relatives, and co-workers, who may have never had a conversation or encounter with a Christian who was really interested in them. Don't be afraid to relate your own struggles and failings in your walk with Christ to them. Don't accept the word "homophobia" as applying to you. This word is used simply to shut down conversation and is an attempt to shame the Christian with the idea that they only oppose homosexual practice out of fear. Instead, remember what the Scripture says in Rom. 1:16, "For I am not ashamed of the gospel, because it is God's power for salvation to everyone who believes, first to the Jew, and also to the Greek."

The old saying "actions speak louder than words" applies to how Christians should reach out to those seeking help with unwanted same-sex attraction in the church and those neighbors, friends, and relatives who appear content with that attraction. There are several reasons for the confusion on the part of Christians when confronted with friends or neighbors living in same-sex relationships. One is that they don't know what the biblical view of marriage is and why a loving same-sex sexual relationship is wrong other than the fact they don't feel it's personally right for them. They try to compare on the one hand their own opposite sex marriage with all of the love and commitment it has, and on the other hand they hold up the loving committed same-sex "marriage" of their neighbor and focus only on the *similarities* and ask, why can't the love and happiness of this couple be okay with our loving God.

It's interesting to see how often once this question is asked, the Christian asking it will rush out and find some theologian or pastor who will assure them that "all true love is God's love," which will be exactly what Paul warned us about in 2 Tim. 4:3–4.

But what if we change the comparison for a moment and the couple next door is in a loving opposite-sex marriage. They are a warm, friendly, outgoing couple and after establishing a friendship, you discover they are in an "open marriage" and enjoy going out on the weekends to a local sex club and engage in sex with various people and then it's back to work on Monday morning. They even tell you that since they started these "weekend workouts," it has saved their marriage and brought them closer together. Why does the Christian more clearly see the opposite–sex couple as engaging in immorality and yet is confused about the same–sex couple? There are two main reasons: (1) lack of knowledge of the biblical standard and (2) believing that that standard applies to their lives even though it is against societal pressure and acceptance.

The church should be the place where help, real help with unwanted same–sex attraction is met with love and compassion without condemnation. This in no way implies acceptance of the sexual *practices*, but instead points the way out of them to what God desires, which is the freedom for holy living. Help comes not only through our words but through our actions, not by how many Bible verses we have memorized, but by taking the time to find out about them and what their fears and needs are. There is some truth to the bumper sticker that says, "Lord, save me from your followers." Many homosexuals have fears and misunderstandings about the church, some of which are not unjustified and for which the church needs to repent. Christians need to remember that no one is condemned to hell for being homosexual. We know this because no one is in heaven for being heterosexual. The central message of the gospel is not about our sexuality.

It is up to the church to change its attitude, approach, and effort in reaching out to those of us (see Preface) were involved in homosexuality before we can ask them to consider anew what Christ and His church offers in the way of hope and healing. It is to that hope that we turn to now.

11

Hope in Christ
for Those Who Believe Him

A great old hymn puts it this way "My hope is built on nothing less than Jesus' blood and righteousness." For many of those struggling with same–sex attraction, hope is all they have to start with. When you reach the end of your rope, hope is the knot at the end you use to hang on with you might. Hope in Christ and His Word is what the believer hangs on to when all else seems to be saying "give up," "it's pointless," "no one expects this of you," or "God will understand." What is pointless and tragic is that we grieve the Holy Spirit by hanging on to our favorite sin, the one we identify with, the one we are the most comfortable holding on to.

The Scripture is filled with references to our hope in the Lord as just a few examples show. Psalm 71:5, "For you, O Lord, are my hope, my trust, O Lord, from my youth." Psalm 119:81, "My soul longs for your salvation; I hope in your word." Paul tells us in Col. 1:23 to ". . . continue in the faith, stable and steadfast, not shifting from the hope of the gospel you heard, which has been proclaimed in all creation under heaven, and of which I, Paul, became a minister." Further, "suffering produces endurance, and endurance produces hope, and hope does not put us to shame" (Rom. 5:3–4). Lastly, Paul says in Rom, 12:12, "Rejoice in hope, be patient in tribulation, be consistent in prayer." The hope we have as Christians is in Christ and His finished work on the cross. Even when people and programs fail, yet our hope remains in Christ who cannot fail and will never forsake us. Paul in 1 Tim. 1:1 calls Christ Jesus "our hope." Jesus is there waiting like the father of the prodigal son in Luke 15: 11–32, waiting for us to get out of the pig pen and return to the Lord who loves us and desires restoration and relationship with us. Notice Jesus never said that the young man cleaned himself up before returning to his father, so it is with us. Jesus is in the cleaning up "business" and desires for us to let Him do the cleaning if we will repent and let Him do it.

The hope for those involved in same–sex sexual practice is the same hope for all those who trust in Christ even though that hope may be experienced differently from those not involved in that particular sin. We all have the same hope and promise that Jesus gave in John 14:19, "Because I live, you also will live."

12

Healing through God's Spirit

God's desire to bestow healing and restoration on those who repent and return to Him. "'Yet even now,' declares the Lord, 'return to me with all your heart, with fasting, with weeping, and with mourning.' Rend your hearts and not your garments. Return to the Lord your God, for he is gracious and merciful, slow to anger, and abounding in steadfast love, and he relents over disaster'" (Joel 2:12–13). In verse 25 we read this promise: "I will restore to you the years that the swarming locus has eaten. . . ." And Jer. 17:14 declares, "Heal me, O Lord, and I shall be healed; save me, and I shall be saved, for you are my praise."

Healing is different than "cure." A cure is as though nothing had happened, but healing is usually a long process that involves disappointments, discouragement, and failures and too often is the result of our looking back like Lot's wife to the life God has led us away from. When failure does happen, we need to remember the words of the Apostle Paul in Phil. 3:12–14, "Not that I have already obtained this or am already perfect, but I press on to make it my own, because Christ Jesus has made me his own. Brothers, I do not consider that I have made it my own. But one thing I do: forgetting what lies behind and straining forward to what lies ahead. I press on toward the goal for the prize of the upward call of God in Christ Jesus. Healing normally leaves some kind of scar even though functionality has returned. This seems especially true with regard to sexual sin. As Paul says in 1 Cor. 6:18, "Flee from sexual immorality. Every other sin a person commits is outside the body, but the sexually immoral person sins against his own body."

Cure implies a kind of "one shot and you're done," but when it comes to same–sex sexual attraction, we would do better to speak in terms of God continuing to heal rather than someone being cured. By "healed" we do not mean that our sin nature is healed, but that only when we repent can the Holy Spirit begin the restoration of our relationship to Christ. Even when Christ does heal, the scars of sin remain. As Rosaria Butterfield makes clear, "But no matter how many years tick away, I am and will always be Rahab–a woman with a past. So, what does a person like me do with such a past? I have not forgotten. Body memories know my name. Details intrude into my world unpredictably, like when I am kneading the communion bread or homeschooling my children. I take each ancient token to the cross, for prayer, for more repentance, for thanksgiving that God is always right about matters of sin and grace."[1]

Christ through His Holy Spirit breaks the power of SSA, but the memories of that sin will still haunt the mind. The goal of someone whom God is healing of SSA should be to remove from his or her life those things that bring a former life to mind such as, photos, post-cards, and birthday presents–things that remind them of "the good times" while they were walking in "the pleasures of sin" (Heb. 11:25) apart from Christ. Identifying with one's former life as ex–gay, or ex–adulterer or ex–porn addict or whatever former sin caused one to walk away from Christ only weakens one's strength and steadfast-ness in the Lord. Let's illustrate what we are talking about. Suppose you are wearing a suit of chain mail like a knight of the tenth century and you walk in front of a powerful electromagnet. The closer you get to the magnet the stronger the attraction. Likewise, the farther away you are the weaker the attraction becomes. As Christ gives us strength, each step we take away from the magnet lessens its influ-ence on us. None of us asked to be born in a chain mail suit, but that is how our condition has been since Adam. There is no promise that the magnet will be switched off but only that its attraction will become weaker as we walk closer to Christ and allow His Spirit to work in us.

Paul shows us in 1 Cor. 6:11 that Christ permanently changes our identity: "And such were some of you. But you were washed, you were sanctified, you were justified in the name of the Lord Jesus

---

1. Rosaria Butterfield, *Openness Unhindered* (Pittsburgh: Crown and Covenant Publications, 2015), 33.

Christ and by the Spirit of our God." Paul tells us what the result of being washed and sanctified is in 2 Cor. 5:17, "Therefore, if anyone is in Christ, he is a new creation. The old has passed away, behold the new has come." This promise applies to anyone.

This is what Scripture says in James 1:13–15: "Let no one say when he is tempted, 'I am being tempted by God,' for God cannot be tempted with evil, and he himself tempts no one. But each person is tempted when he is lured and enticed by his own desire. Then desire when it has conceived gives birth to sin, and sin when it is fully grown brings forth death."

For most of us who have been involved in same–sex sexual practices the road to healing will be long, difficult, and many times frustrating with steps backward mixed with steps forward. There are two main biggest roadblocks to healing for those with SSA. First is their unwillingness to accept God's Word that such practices are sin and therefore separate them from the loving relationship Christ desires to have with them. Stop believing the oldest lie recorded in Scripture in Gen.3:1, "Did God actually say . . ." by searching out those who will tell them about the most "up to date" understanding of Scripture. This is exactly what Paul warned about in 2 Tim. 4:3–4. "For the time is coming when people will not endure sound teaching, but having itching ears they will accumulate teachers to suit their own passions, and will turn away from listening to the truth and wander off into myths." The second biggest roadblock is the response of well–meaning but uninformed family members, church members, pastors, counselors, those who should be the greatest support but may have never dealt with someone personally who is struggling with same–sex attraction. They may feel uneasy about what to say or how to say it. Knowing how to show acceptance without showing agreement with their behavior is not always easy, but it must be done.

In their excellent book *Space at the Table,* authors Brad Harper, who is an evangelical theologian and professor of theology at Multnomah University in Portland, Oregon, and his gay son Drew Stafford Harper write about the trials and difficulties and rewards of keeping the lines of communication open.

> Whatever you do, don't simply stop talking about the issues.
> But make sure that your conversations with your child about

their sexuality are not about your anger and shame. If they are, then your child will quickly recognize the conflict is really about you and not them. You owe it to yourself, to your child, and to God to express clearly and honestly your disagreement with your child's decision to live out a non–heterosexual sexuality, but then you have to move beyond that. If your child decides to move in a different direction, then the conversation needs to be about how to stay in loving relationship in spite of serious disagreement. This is not the same as just agreeing to disagree and then living the rest of your lives with a rainbow elephant in the room. Not talking about it can be as relationally damaging as waging verbal warfare. – Brad."[2]

For some involved in same–sex sexual practice, the thought that Christians desire to change them into heterosexuals can be a frightening thought. The real goal should always be righteous holy living, letting God fulfill the deepest longings of our hearts and from there seeking God honoring relationships. Most Christians love a happy ending and nothing could be happier for them than to see someone they have been ministering to who is dealing with same–sex attraction entering into a loving opposite–sex marriage. Marriage should not be seen as a "cure" for same–sex attraction but as the end product of God's mercy, many months of prayer, counseling, Bible study, and involvement in church activities.

There is another viable alternative to marriage for those who feel marriage is not right for them . . . celibacy. For many (even many Christians) the idea of being celibate in our sex soaked society is like suggesting we take up waterboarding for fun and relaxation. Yet, for the Christian celibacy is the only God honoring alternative for those not in a marriage relationship. True life–long celibacy is a gift that not many are called to, but those who are called to it should be honored and not disparaged by the church.

Ed Shaw, in his book *Same–Sex Attraction and the Church, the Surprising Plausibility of the Celibate Life,* gives this advice:

How, then, does your church celebrate God's gift of celibacy? My guess is that you'll have a good track record when it comes

---

2. Brad Harper and Drew Harper, *Space at the Table* (Portland, OR: ZEAL Books, 2016), 135.

to promoting marriage (weddings celebrated, numerous sermons on the subject, a course and books recommended from the front) but not much success when it comes to commending singleness. How could you celebrate the single members of your church family? I can think of an example from one church I was a part of: we used a single woman's eightieth birthday as a chance to thank her (and her father God) for all she had given us using her gift of celibacy to build up our church family. I suspect we could have done more to encourage her over the decades, but it was, I hope, better late than never.[3]

One of the aspects of a celibate life and Christian life in general is that of self–sacrifice and self–denial. In fact, Jesus said in Luke 9:23–24, "And he said to all, 'If anyone would come after me, let him deny himself and take up his cross daily and follow me. For whoever would save his life will lose it, but whoever loses his life for my sake will save it.'" Taking up our cross daily involves self–sacrifice and denial and is anything but pain–free.

What is so wrong with same–sex "marriage" anyway? It just seems like the natural progression of two people who are in love who just want to make their commitment official and live their lives in peace and happiness. So why do Christians have such a problem with this?

We have presented a lot of reasons in this book as to why homosexuality or same–sex sexual practices cannot be accepted by those who believe in the Lordship of Christ in their life and believe that the Bible is the final court of appeal for matters of faith and practice. Our culture kneels at the altar of "choice." "Choose whatever feels good to you" is shouted from the rooftops by those who have never understood that there is no better choice than the one God provided for us at creation for our holiness, our happiness, our wellbeing. This does not mean we must reject persons but only their practices as sinful and dishonoring to God. Same–sex sexual practices are a *moral* issue in the same way that abortion or opposite–sex sexual practices outside of marriage are *moral* issues no matter how many of our family, friends, and co–workers engage in it. For those involved in same–sex

---

3. Ed Shaw, *Same–Sex Attraction and the Church* (Downers Grove, IL: Intervarsity Press, 2015), 112.

sexual attraction and practices who desire to follow in obedience to Christ, there is help through Christ's people, hope through belief in Christ's Word, and healing through Christ's Spirit.

One of the most heart troubling and gut wrenching decisions Christian parents could ever go through would be in knowing how to respond to their child's invitation to attend their same–sex "marriage." Here the love and support you desire to show your child smashes head–on into your desire to serve and obey Christ. At this point a question needs to be asked: *what is it they are celebrating?* A wedding is a public celebration of the marriage relationship being entered into by the couple. At some point the person officiating the ceremony will ask "if any knows why these two should not be married, let them speak now or forever hold their peace." The Christian parents will at that point by their silence be giving public approval of a ceremony that mocks God's intention for marriage. While the parent should continue to pray for and love their child and keep the door always open to them, there will nevertheless be a rift between them. The cost of following Christ is made clear in Matt. 10: 35–37, "For I have come to set a man against his father, and a daughter against her mother, and a daughter–in–law against her mother–in–law. And a person's enemies will be those of his own household. Whoever loves father or mother more than me is not worthy of me, and whoever loves son or daughter more than me is not worthy of me."

Marriage is not a human invention, but was designed by God to glorify Him and make possible a level of bonding and closeness between the man and woman that cannot be achieved by any of the beasts God created. Nowhere in Scripture are animals said to become "one flesh." It also made possible for human beings to participate in a finite or limited way the bringing into being another human being made in the image of God and all the responsibilities that flow from that event.

Over the last several decades we have been witness to the gradual decline of the importance and sacredness of marriage and the sacredness of sex as God designed it. In its place is an imitation of marriage that resembles God's intention of marriage about as much as a three–year old's drawing of a tree resembles a living tree.

Our culture has turned marriage into putty to be molded into whatever our sinful heart's desire, and with that we have removed or ignored the limits of what it means to be married. A thing is defined by its limits, and God has made clear in His Word what the limits of marriage are to be, and that limit is one man and one woman for life. No other option for human sexual expression is even hinted at. God specifically makes "a helper fit for him" (Gen. 2:18). Eve bears as much of the image of God as Adam does, yet she compliments or brings completeness to what Adam lacks, and nothing can substitute for the sexual completeness she brings to Adam by God's design.

One of the important aspects of sex between a man and a woman that has not received much attention in our time is its sacredness. Robert Gagnon has pointed out in his writings that the word used in Gen. 2:21 where God takes a "rib" and fashions Eve from it can also be translated "side." This word occurs some 35 times in the Old Testament and in the vast majority of times refers to sacred architecture, such as the side of the temple or the Ark of the Covenant. If this is so, could not human beings who are made in the image and likeness of God be thought of as sacred architecture? This would seem to fit with what Paul says in 1 Cor. 6:19 and 20, "Or do you not know that your body is a temple of the Holy Spirit within you, whom you have from God? You are not your own, for you were bought with a price. So glorify God in your body." Should not the temple of the Holy Spirit be considered sacred architecture?

For the Christian, there is much more to sex than just two bodies and some friction, more than just the "parts fit" biological aspect. There are also theological implications that what we do with our bodies is a form of worship. Paul writes in Rom. 12:1, "I appeal to you therefore, brothers, by the mercies of God, to present your bodies as a living sacrifice, holy and acceptable to God, which is your spiritual worship." A sacrifice to God was sacred, holy, and given as an act of worship. Part of being a "living sacrifice" is to consider our sexuality as sacred and holy. Christians can no more choose how they will express their sexuality than they can choose which god they will worship and still lay claim to being a follower of Christ. This is why for the Christian who honors Christ with his life and not just with his mouth, a "marriage" between members of the same sex is as impossible as a real marriage between someone and his pet goat or a tree. It is as impossible as finding a square circle or a stick with one end.

During the past six decades, we have seen the turning away from natural marriage (God's design) since Kinsey in the 1950s; the introduction of Playboy and the sex for pleasure and non–commitment life–style; the invention of the "pill," which removed the physical consequences of non–married sex and fulfilled Margaret Sanger's dream of women being as "free" from the consequences of sex as men; the cultural influence of Christianity being pushed farther out of public life with the banning of prayer and Bible reading in public schools; the "do your own thing" ideas of the 60s; the passage of "no–fault" divorce laws; the legalization of abortion on demand, which is the last line of defense against unwanted children; the explosion of pornography with its creeping acceptance into movies, TV, magazines, and "romance" books; in the 70s, the illegitimate use of the language of the civil rights movement; in the 80s–and worst of all–the nearly silent acceptance of this by many in the church. To be fair, it was mostly the traditional mainline denominational churches that put up the least resistance. The conservative evangelical churches have continued to speak out about the steady decay of natural marriage in our culture.

All of these events and more served to undermine and weaken marriage as God intended, which created a vacuum into which the organizing homosexual movement stepped in. With its "shock troops" and in–your–face approach, those already confused about sex and marriage mostly backed off. Those like Anita Bryant who stood up and had some success were pie–in–the–face silenced.

What of the future? Now that same–sex "marriage" is legal in the whole country, many evangelical Christians will be thinking that with their goal reached the homosexual community will be satisfied and just go quietly about their lives and leave those who still believe in natural marriage as God designed it alone. It is pure fantasy to believe such a thought. Many of the *leaders* of the various homosexual groups have stated publicly, "Gay marriage is not enough." In *The Daily Beast*, published on June 26, 2015, writer Samantha Allen asked the leaders of several homosexual organizations what was next after the Supreme Court ruling. Here are a couple of their responses. "The leaders of PFLAG National, an organization for families and friends of LGBT people, also contend that homes and schools will prove to be just as critical for LGBT acceptance as courtrooms." "Our education efforts are only increasing, and we find there is an even stronger need for our family and ally voices in rural towns, conservative locations, and in communities where reconciling faith with issues of sexual orientation and gender identity or expression is still an issue."[4]

Another example comes from lesbian activist Masha Gessen, who in a panel discussion titled "Why get married when you can be happy?" at the Sydney Writers Festival in May, 2012, states, "It's a no–brainer that the institution of marriage should not exist." Later she says one of the things that bother her about promoting "gay marriage" is that it involves "lying about what we're going to do with marriage when we get there. . . . Because you know, we lie that the institution of marriage is not going to change and that is a lie. The institution of marriage is going to change and it should change. And again, I don't think it should exist."[5]

Samantha Allen ends her article with this: "The legalization of same–sex marriage today might seem monumental–and it is–but it's only the start of the social and legal reforms LGBT leaders hope to enact in the coming decades. To quote another song that was on the radio when the Supreme Court first took up this question: "we've only just begun."[6]

The greatest weapon in the arsenal of those attacking natural marriage is confusion because when you are confused it becomes difficult to make clear to the inevitable about same–sex "marriage." The Church needs now more than ever to speak with a clear, unified, and loving voice to those involved in same–sex relationships the message of God in Genesis, reaffirmed by our Lord Jesus Christ and the apostle Paul, of forgiveness, help, hope, healing, restoration, and regeneration through repentance. We end with the words of another

4. Samantha Allen, "LGBT Leaders: Marriage Is Not Enough," *The Daily Beast*, June 26, 2015, accessed September 12, 2016, www.the dailybeast.com/lgbt–leaders–gay–marriage–is–not–enough.

5. Masha Gessen, Sydney Writers Festival in Walsh Bay, Sydney, Australia, May 19, 2012.

6. Samantha Allen, "LGBT Leaders: Marriage Is Not Enough," *The Daily Beast*, June 26, 2015, accessed September 12, 2016, www.the dailybeast.com/lgbt–leaders–gay–marriage–is–not–enough.

great old hymn, "Rise up oh men of God the church for you doth wait, her strength unequal to her task, rise up and make her great."

The Significance of the Nashville Statement

We have tried to show in this book the need for the Church to have a clear understanding of God's design for marriage and sexuality. Commit to God's design and verbalizing that understanding is needed more now than at any time in Church history. The attitude and cultural shift that has taken place over the last six decades has made it vital that Christians speak in unity on this bedrock of what Scripture says in matters of marriage and sex.

Just recently, many people from various denominations united in declaring what the Church has always understood on this issue by signing *The Nashville Statement* (see Appendix). "The national coalition says it's their response to an increasingly post–Christian, Western culture that thinks it can change God's design for humans."[7] The *Nashville Statement* is a type of "mere Christianity" document that cuts across denominational lines and whose topic can impact the entire church. The unity displayed by the various signers should not be confused with uniformity nor should cooperation be thought of as the road to assimilation, but this issue of the nature, design, and purpose of sexuality goes to the very heart of the biblical view of what we are as human beings and what God in His love and creation intends for us. Our prayer is that many more will sign *The Nashville Statement* and by doing so declare their stand with the historic Christian Church. Furthermore, *The Nashville Statement* is not a declaration of war, but one of peace, the peace that comes through knowing God's plan and purpose for the blessing and beauty of human sexuality instead of doing as Judges 17:6 says, "Everyone did what was right in his own eyes."

---

7. Holly Meyer, "What Is the Nashville Statement and Why Are People Talking about It?" *The Tennessean*, August 30, 2017, accessed September 20, 2017, http://www.tennessean.com/story/news/religion/2017/08/30/what–nashville–statement–and–why–people–talking–it/616064001/

Appendix
The Nashville Statement[1]

NASHVILLE
STATEMENT
A COALITION FOR BIBLICAL SEXUALITY

"Know that the LORD Himself is God;
It is He who has made us, and not we ourselves..."
–Psalm 100:3

Preamble

Evangelical Christians at the dawn of the twenty–first century find themselves living in a period of historic transition. As Western culture has become increasingly post–Christian, it has embarked upon a massive revision of what it means to be a human being. By and large the spirit of our age no longer discerns or delights in the beauty of God's design for human life. Many deny that God created human beings for his glory, and that his good purposes for us include our personal and physical design as male and female. It is common to think that human identity as male and female is not part of God's beautiful plan, but is, rather, an expression of an individual's autonomous preferences. The pathway to full and lasting joy through God's good design for his creatures is thus replaced by the path of shortsighted alternatives that, sooner or later, ruin human life and dishonor God.

This secular spirit of our age presents a great challenge to the Christian church. Will the church of the Lord Jesus Christ lose her biblical conviction, clarity, and courage, and blend into the spirit of the age? Or will she hold fast to the word of life, draw courage from Jesus, and unashamedly proclaim his way as the way of life? Will

1. The Council on Biblical Manhood and Womanhood, "The Nashville Statement," accessed September 27, 2017. https://cbmw.org/nashville–statement/. Used by permission.

she maintain her clear, counter–cultural witness to a world that seems bent on ruin?

We are persuaded that faithfulness in our generation means declaring once again the true story of the world and of our place in it—particularly as male and female. Christian Scripture teaches that there is but one God who alone is Creator and Lord of all. To him alone, every person owes glad– hearted thanksgiving, heart–felt praise, and total allegiance. This is the path not only of glorifying God, but of knowing ourselves. To forget our Creator is to forget who we are, for he made us for himself. And we cannot know ourselves truly without truly knowing him who made us. We did not make ourselves. We are not our own. Our true identity, as male and female persons, is given by God. It is not only foolish, but hopeless, to try to make ourselves what God did not create us to be.

We believe that God's design for his creation and his way of salvation serve to bring him the greatest glory and bring us the greatest good. God's good plan provides us with the greatest freedom. Jesus said he came that we might have life and have it in overflowing measure. He is for us and not against us. Therefore, in the hope of serving Christ's church and witnessing publicly to the good purposes of God for human sexuality revealed in Christian Scripture, we offer the following affirmations and denials.

Article 1

WE AFFIRM that God has designed marriage to be a covenantal, sexual, procreative, lifelong union of one man and one woman, as husband and wife, and is meant to signify the covenant love between Christ and his bride the church.

WE DENY that God has designed marriage to be a homosexual, polygamous, or polyamorous relationship. We also deny that marriage is a mere human contract rather than a covenant made before God.

Article 2

WE AFFIRM that God's revealed will for all people is chastity outside of marriage and fidelity within marriage.

WE DENY that any affections, desires, or commitments ever justify sexual intercourse before or outside marriage; nor do they justify any form of sexual immorality.

Article 3

WE AFFIRM that God created Adam and Eve, the first human beings, in his own image, equal before God as persons, and distinct as male and female.

WE DENY that the divinely ordained differences between male and female render them unequal in dignity or worth.

Article 4

WE AFFIRM that divinely ordained differences between male and female reflect God's original creation design and are meant for human good and human flourishing.

WE DENY that such differences are a result of the Fall or are a tragedy to be overcome.

Article 5

WE AFFIRM that the differences between male and female reproductive structures are integral to God's design for self–conception as male or female.

WE DENY that physical anomalies or psychological conditions nullify the God–appointed link between biological sex and self–conception as male or female.

Article 6

WE AFFIRM that those born with a physical disorder of sex development are created in the image of God and have dignity and worth equal to all other image–bearers. They are acknowledged by our Lord Jesus in his words about "eunuchs who were born that way from their mother's womb." With all others they are welcome as faithful followers of Jesus Christ and should embrace their biological sex insofar as it may be known.

WE DENY that ambiguities related to a person's biological sex render one incapable of living a fruitful life in joyful obedience to Christ.

Article 7

WE AFFIRM that self–conception as male or female should be defined by God's holy purposes in creation and redemption as revealed in Scripture.

WE DENY that adopting a homosexual or transgender self–conception is consistent with God's holy purposes in creation and redemption.

Article 8

WE AFFIRM that people who experience sexual attraction for the same sex may live a rich and fruitful life pleasing to God through faith in Jesus Christ, as they, like all Christians, walk in purity of life.

WE DENY that sexual attraction for the same sex is part of the natural goodness of God's original creation, or that it puts a person outside the hope of the gospel.

Article 9

WE AFFIRM that sin distorts sexual desires by directing them away from the marriage covenant and toward sexual immorality—

a distortion that includes both heterosexual and homosexual immorality.

WE DENY that an enduring pattern of desire for sexual immorality justifies sexually immoral behavior.

Article 10

WE AFFIRM that it is sinful to approve of homosexual immorality or transgenderism and that such approval constitutes an essential departure from Christian faithfulness and witness.

WE DENY that the approval of homosexual immorality or transgenderism is a matter of moral indifference about which otherwise faithful Christians should agree to disagree.

Article 11

WE AFFIRM our duty to speak the truth in love at all times, including when we speak to or about one another as male or female.

WE DENY any obligation to speak in such ways that dishonor God's design of his image– bearers as male and female.

Article 12

WE AFFIRM that the grace of God in Christ gives both merciful pardon and transforming power, and that this pardon and power enable a follower of Jesus to put to death sinful desires and to walk in a manner worthy of the Lord.

WE DENY that the grace of God in Christ is insufficient to forgive all sexual sins and to give power for holiness to every believer who feels drawn into sexual sin.

Article 13

WE AFFIRM that the grace of God in Christ enables sinners to forsake transgender self– conceptions and by divine forbearance to accept the God–ordained link between one's biological sex and one's self–conception as male or female.

WE DENY that the grace of God in Christ sanctions self–conceptions that are at odds with God's revealed will.

Article 14

WE AFFIRM that Christ Jesus has come into the world to save sinners and that through Christ's death and resurrection forgiveness of sins and eternal life are available to every person who repents of sin and trusts in Christ alone as Savior, Lord, and supreme treasure.

WE DENY that the Lord's arm is too short to save or that any sinner is beyond his reach.

**Scripture
References***

Gen. 1:26–28; 2:15–25; 3:1–24; Ex. 20:14; 20:17; Lev. 18:22; 20:13; Dt. 5:18, 21; 22:5; Jdg. 19:22; 2 Sam. 11:1–12:15; Job 31:1; Ps. 51:1–19; Prov. 5:1–23; 6:20–35; 7:1–27; Isa. 59:1; Mal. 2:14; Matt. 5:27–30; 19:4–6, 8–9, 12; Acts 15:20, 29; Rom. 1:26–27; 1:32; 1 Cor. 6:9–11, 18–20; 7:1–7; 2 Cor. 5:17; Gal. 5:24; Eph. 4:15, 20–24; 5:31–32; Col. 3:5; 1 Thess. 4:3–8; 1 Tim. 1:9–10, 15; 2 Tim. 2:22; Titus 2:11–12; Heb. 13:4; Jas. 1:14–15; 1 Pet. 2:11; Jude 7

* Scripture texts are not a part of the original document but have been added subsequently for reference

Bibliography

Achtemeier, Mark. *The Bible's Yes to Same-Sex Marriage.* Westminster John Knox Press, 2015.

Allen, Doug. "More Heat Than Light: A Critical Assessment of the Same-Sex Parenting Literature, 1995-2013." *Marriage and Family Review* 51, no. 2 (2015): 154-182.

Allen, Douglas W. "Economic Assessment of Same-Sex Marriage Laws." *Harvard Journal of Law & Public Policy*, 29, no.3 (June 22, 2006): 966-971.

_____. "High school graduation rates among children of same-sex households." *Review of Economics of the Household* 11, no. 4 (December 2013): 635-658.

Allen, Samantha. "LGBT Leaders: Gay Marriage Is not Enough." *The Daily Beast.* June 26, 2015. Accessed September 12, 2016. www.thedailybeast.com/lgbt-leaders-gay-marriage-is-not-enough.

Altman, Lawrence K. "New Homosexual Disorder Worries Health Officials." *The New York Times*, May 11, 1982.

Andersson, Gunnar, et al. "The Demographics of Same-sex Marriages in Norway and Sweden." *Demography* 43, no.1 (February 2006): 95.

Bailey, Derrick Sherwin. *Homosexuality and the Western Christian Tradition.* London, England: Longmans, Green and Co., 1955.

Bailey, J. Michael, et al. "Genetic and Environmental Influences on Sexual Orientation and Its Correlates in an Australian Twin Sample." *Journal of Personality and Social Psychology* 78, no.3 (2000): 524-536.

Baldock, Kathy. *Walking the Bridgeless Canyon.* Reno, NV: Canyonwalker Press, 2014.

Bancroft, John. "Alfred C. Kinsey and the Politics of Sex Research." *Annual Review of Sex Research* 15 (2004):16-17.

Bancroft, John, et al. "Male Homosexuality: Nature or Culture?" *Controversies in Sexual*

Medicine 7, no.10 (October, 2010): 3245-3253.

Barrett, C. K. *The Epistle to the Romans.* New York: Harper and Row Publishers, 1957.

Bartchy, S. Scott. "First-Century Slavery and 1 Corinthians 7:21." *Society of Biblical Literature,* Dissertation series, number 11 (1973).

Bayer, Ronald. *Homosexuality and American Psychiatry.* Princeton: Princeton University Press, 1987.

_____. *Private Acts, Social Consequences.* New Brunswick: Rutgers University Press, 1991.

Black, Edwin. *War against the Weak.* New York: Four Walls Eight Windows, 2003.

Blanchard, Ray. "Detecting and Correcting for Family Size Differences in the Study of Sexual Orientation and Fraternal Birth Order." *Archives of Sexual Behavior* 43 (July, 2014): 845–852.

Brown, Taylor N. T., and Jody L. Herman. "Intimate Partner Violence and Sexual Abuse among LGBT People." *The Williams Institute,* UCLA School of Law (November 2015): 2.

Brownson, James V. *Bible, Gender, Sexuality.* Grand Rapids: William B. Eerdmans, 2013.

Bullough,Vern. *Before Stonewall.* New York: Harrington Park Press, 2002.

Butterfield, Rosaria. *Openness Unhindered.* Pittsburgh: Crown and Covenant Publications, 2015.

Byne, William. "Science and Belief: Psychobiological Research on Sexual Orientation."

Journal of Homosexuality 28, no. 3–4 (February 1995): 303–343.

Byne, William, et al. "The Interstitial Nuclei of the Human Anterior Hypothalamus: An Investigation of Variation with Sex, Sexual Orientation, and HIV Status." *Hormones and Behavior* 40, no.2 (September 2001): 86–92.

Carey, Jonathan Sinclair. "D. S. Bailey and 'the Name Forbidden among Christians.'" *Anglican Theological Review* 70, no. 2 (April 1988): 94–115.

Carter, David. *Stonewall.* New York: St. Martin's Press, 2004.

Chesler, Ellen. *Woman of Valor.* New York: Anchor Books, Doubleday, 1992.

Clendinen, Dudley and Adam Nagourney. *Out for Good.* New York: Simon and Schuster, 1999.

Cobin, David M. "A brief look at the Jewish law of manumission." *Chicago–Kent Law Review* 70, no. 3 (April 1995): article 13, 1339.

Corey, Donald Webster. *The Homosexual in America, A Subjective Approach.* New York: Greenberg Publisher, 1951.

Davidson, Richard M. "Homosexuality in the Old Testament." In *Homosexuality, Marriage, and the Church.* Berrien Springs, MI: Andrews University Press, 2012.

De Young, James B. *Homosexuality: Contemporary Claims Examined in the Light of the Bible and Other Ancient Literature and Law.* Grand Rapids: Kregal Publications, 2000.

Diamond, Lisa M. "Female Bisexuality From Adolescence to Adulthood: Results From a 10–Year Longitudinal Study." *Developmental Psychology* 44, no. 1 (January 2008): 5–14.

Diamond, Lisa M., and Clifford J. Rosky. "Scrutinizing Immutability: Research on sexual orientation and U.S. Legal advocacy for sexual minorities." *The Journal of Sex Research* 53, no. 4–5 (2016): 370–371.

Dover, Kenneth. *Greek Homosexuality.* Cambridge: Harvard University Press, 1978.

Drabant, E. M. "Genome Wide Association Study of Sexual Orientation in a Large, Web–based Cohort." Abstract presented at the American Society of Human Genetics Annual Meeting, 2012, 23andMe, Mountain View, CA.

Duarte, Crawford, Stern, Haidt, Jessim, and Tetlock." *Journal of Behavioral and Brain Sciences* 6 (April 2016): 149–166.

Eberstadt, Mary. *How the West Really Lost God*. West Conshohocken, PA: Templeton Press, 2013.

Fergusson, David M., et al. "Is Sexual Orientation Related to Mental Health Problems and Suicidality in Young People?" *Archives of General Psychiatry,* 56, no. 10 (October 1999): 876–880.

Fortson III, S. Donald, and Rollin G. Grams. *Unchanging Witness.* Nashville: B&H Academic, 2016.

Francis, Andrew M. "Family and Sexual Orientation: The Family–Demographic Correlates of Homosexuality in Men and Women." *Journal of Sex Research* 45, no.4 (2008): 371–377.

Friedan, Betty. *The Feminist Mystique.* New York: W. W. Norton and Company, 1963.

Gagnon, Robert. "A Book Not to Be Embraced: A Critical Appraisal of Stacy Johnson's *A Time to Embrace.*" *Scottish Journal of Theology* 62, no. 1 (February 2009): 72.

_____. Homosexuality, Marriage, and the Church, edited by Roy E. Gane, et.al. Berrien Springs: Andrews University Press, 2012.

_____. *The Bible and Homosexual Practice.* Nashville: Abingdon Press, 2001.

_____. "The Scriptural Case for a Male–Female Prerequisite for Sexual Relations: The New Testament Perspective." In *Homosexuality, Marriage and the Church,* edited by Roy E. Gane, et al. Berrien Springs, MI: Andrews University Press, 2012.

Garland, David E. *1 Corinthians.* Grand Rapids: Baker Academic, 2003.

Geisler, Norman. *To Understand the Bible Look for Jesus.* Grand Rapids: Baker Books, 2002.

Gessen, Masha. Sydney Writers Festival in Walsh Bay. Sydney, Australia. May 19, 2012.

Gilman, Steven E., et al. "Risk of Psychiatric Disorders among Individuals Reporting Same- Sex Sexual Partners in the National Comorbidity Survey." *American Journal of Public Health* 96, no.6 (June 2001): 933–939.

Goode, Sarah D. *Paedophiles in Society: Reflecting on Sexuality, Abuse, and Hope.* N.p., UK: Palgrave Macmillian, 2011.

Graglia, F. Carolyn. *Domestic Tranquility: A Brief against Feminism.* Dallas: Spence Publishing Company, 1998.

Great Britain: Committee on Homosexual Offenses and Prostitution. *The Wolfenden Report: Report of the Committee on Homosexual Offenses and Prostitution.* Authorized American ed. New York: Stein and Day Publishers, 1963.

Hamer, Dean, et al. "A Linkage between DNA Markers on the X Chromosome and Male Sexual Orientation." *Science* 261, no. 5119 (July 1993): 321.

Harper, Brad, and Drew Harper. *Space at the Table.* Portland, OR: ZEAL Books, 2016.

Harper, Kyle. *From Shame to Sin: The Christian Transformation of Sexual Morality in Late Antiquity.* Cambridge: Harvard University Press, 2013.

Helminiak, Daniel A. *What the Bible Really Says about Homosexuality.* Tajique, NM: Alamo Press, 2002.

Hemer, Colin J. *The Book of Acts in the Setting of Hellenistic History.* 2nd ed. Warsaw, IN: Eisenbrauns, 2001.

Hitchcock, James. *The Supreme Court and Religion in American Life.* Vol. 2. Princeton: Princeton University Press, 2004.

Hollier, Lauren P., et al. "Adult digit ratio (2D:4D) is not related to umbilical cord androgen or estrogen concentrations, their ratios or net bioactivity." *Early Human Development* 91 (2015): 111–117.

Holloway, April. "Accounts of Roman Infanticide and Sacrifice All Just Myth and Legend?" September 5, 2016. Accessed September 18, 2017. http://www.ancientorigins.net/news history–archaeology/accounts–roman–infanticide–and–sacrifice–all–just–myth–and–legend–006591.

Hooker, Evelyn. "The Adjustment of the Male Overt Homosexual." *Journal of Projective Techniques* 21 (1957): 18–31.

Hooker, M. D. "Adam in Romans 1." *New Testament Studies* 6, no.4 (July 1960): 303.

Horowitz, Daniel. *Betty Friedan and the Making of the Feminist Mystique.* Amherst: University of Massachusetts Press, 2000.

Hubbard, Thomas K. *A Companion to Greek and Roman Sexualities.* Blackwell Publishing, 2014.

Hunter, George William. *A Civic Biology: Presented in Problems.* New York: American Book Company, 1914.

Johnson, Luke Timothy. "Homosexuality and the Church." *Commonweal,* June 11, 2007.

Johnson Jr., S. Lewis. "God Gave Them Up." *Bibliotheca Sacra* 129 (April 1972): 132.

Jones, James H. *Alfred C. Kinsey: A Life.* New York: W.W. Norton & Company, 1997.

_____. *Bad Blood: The Tuskegee Syphilis Experiment.* New York: The Free Press, 1992.

Jones, Stanton L. "Sexual Orientation and Reason: On the Implications of False Beliefs about Homosexuality." (January 2012). Accessed July 12, 2014. http://www.wheaton.edu/CACE/Print–Resources/~/media/Files/Centers–andInstitutes/CACE/articles/Sexual%20Orientation%20and%20 Reason%20 %201–9–20122.pdf.

Kann, Laura, et al. "Sexual Identity, Sex of Sexual Contacts, and Health–Risk Behaviors Among Students in Grades 9–12–Youth Risk Behavior Surveillance, Selected Sites, United States, 2001–2009 Center for Disease Control and Prevention." *Morbidity and Mortality Weekly Report*, June 10, 2011.

Katz–Wise, Sabra L. "Sexual Fluidity and Related Attitudes and Beliefs among Young Adults with a Same–Gender Orientation." *Archives of Sexual Behavior* 44 (July, 2015): 1459–1470.

Kendler, Kenneth S. "Sexual Orientation in a U.S. National Sample of Twin and Non–twin Sibling Pairs." *American Journal of Psychiatry* 157, no. 11 (November 2000): 1843–1846.

Kiefer, Otto. *Sexual Life in Ancient Rome.* New York: Barnes & Noble, 1953.

King, Michael, et al. "A systematic review of mental disorders, suicide and deliberate self harm in lesbian, gay and bisexual people." *BMC Psychiatry* 70, no. 8 (August 18, 2008). Accessed September 23, 2015. https://bmcpsychiatry.biomedcentral.com/articles/10.1186/1471–244X–8–70.

Kinsey, Alfred C. Wardell B. Pomeroy, and Clyde E. Martin. *Sexual Behavior in the Human Male.* Philadelphia: W. B. Saunders Company, 1948.

Landay, Alan. "HIV Patients 'Getting Old before Their Time.'" August 30, 2016. Accessed August 20, 2017, http://www.scidev.net/global/hiv-aids/feature/hiv-patients-old-ageing-disease.html.

Lau, Charles Q. "The stability of same-sex cohabitation, different-sex cohabitation and Marriage." *Journal of Marriage and Family,* 74 (October 2012): 984.

Lee, Justin. *Torn: Rescuing the Gospel from the Gays-vs.-Christians Debate.* New York: Jericho Books, 2012.

Lee, Peter A. et al. "Impact of environment upon Gender Identity and Sexual Orientation: A Lesson for Parents of Children with Intersex or Gender Confusion." *Journal of Pediatric Endocrinology and Metabolism* 18, no. 7 (2005): 625–630.

Licht, Hans. *Sexual Life in Ancient Greece.* New York: Dorset Press, 1993.

Marsden, George M. *The Twilight of the American Enlightenment.* New York: Basic Books, 2014.

McLeod, Hugh. *The Religious Crisis of the 1960s.* Oxford: Oxford University Press, 2007.

McNeill, John J. *Sex as God Intended.* Maple Shade, NJ: Lethe Press, 2008.

Meyer, Holly. "What Is the Nashville Statement and Why Are People Talking about It?" *The Tennessean,* August 30, 201. Accessed September 20, 2017. http://www.tennessean.com/story/news/religion/2017/08/30/what-nashville-statement-and-why-people-talking-it/616064001/

Meyer, Lawrence S., and Paul R. McHugh. "Special Report: Sexuality and Gender." *The New Atlantis: A Journal of Technology and Society,* no. 50 (August 19, 2016): 1–144. Accessed September 12, 2016. www.thenewatlantis.com/docLib/20160819_TNA50SexualityandGender.pdf.

Michaelson, Jay. *God vs. Gay? The Religious Case for Equality.* Boston: Beacon Press, 2011.

Mustanski, Brian S., et al. "A Critical Review of Recent Biological Research on Human Sexual Orientation." *Annual Review of Sex Research* 13 (2002): 89–140.

Nimmons, David. "Sex and the Brain." *Discovery Magazine.* March 1993. Accessed August 19, 2017. http://discovermagazine.com/1994/Mar/sexandthebrain346/.

Pathela, Preeti, et al. "Men who have sex with men have a 140-fold higher risk for newly diagnosed HIV and syphilis compared with heterosexual men in New York City." *Journal of Acquired Immune Deficiency Syndrome* 58, no.4 (December 1, 2011): 408–416.

Patterson, James T. *Eve of Destruction: How 1965 Transformed America.* New York: Basic Books, 2014.

Price, Allen. The University of Texas at Austin. *UT NEWS,* August 29, 2012.

Regnerus, Mark. "How different are the adult children of parents who have same-sex relationships? Findings from the New Family Structures Study." *Social Science Research* 41, no. 4 (July 2012): 752–770.

_____. "Parental same-sex relationships, family instability, and subsequent life outcomes for adult children: Answering critics of the new family structures study with additional analysis." *Social Science Research* 41, no. 6 (November 2012): 1368. Accessed August 18, 2017. www.sciencedirect.com/science/journal/0049089x/41.

_____. "Making Differences Disappear: The Evolution of Science on Same-sex Households." *The Public Discourse*, May 12, 2015. Accessed August 18, 2017. http://www.thepublicdiscourse.com.

_____. "The data on children in same-sex households gets more depressing." The Witherspoon Institute Public Discourse, June 29, 2016. Accessed August 13, 2017. http://www.thepublicdiscourse.com/2016/06/17255/.

Rice, George, et al. "Genetics and Male Sexual Orientation." *Science* 285 (August 1999): 803a.

O'Riordan, Kate. "The Life of the Gay Gene: From Hypothetical Genetic Marker to Social Reality." *Journal of Sex Research* 49, no. 4 (2012): 362–368.

Sanders, A. R., et al. "Genome-wide scan demonstrates significant linkage for male Sexual orientation." *Psychological Medicine* 45 (2015): 1379–1388.

Sandfort, Theo G.M., et al. "Sexual Orientation and Mental and Physical Health Status: Findings from a Dutch Population Survey." *American Journal of Public Health* 96, no. 6 (June, 2006): 1119–1125.

Savin-Williams, Ritch C., et al. "Prevalence and Stability of Sexual Orientation Components during Adolescence and Young Adulthood." *Archives of Sexual Behavior* 36 (June 2007): 385–394.

Sanger, Margaret. *The Pivot of Civilization*. New York: Humanity Books, 2003.

_____. *Women and the New Race*. New York: Truth Publishing Company, 1920.

Schumm, Walter R. "Children of Homosexuals More Apt to be Homosexual? A Reply to Morrison, and Cameron Based on an Examination of Multiple Source Data." *Journal of Biosocial Science* 42, no. 6 (November 2010): 721.

Shaw, Ed. *Same-Sex Attraction and the Church*. Downers Grove, IL: Intervarsity Press, 2015.

Stein, Edward. *The Mismeasure of Desire, the Science, Theory and Ethics of Sexual Orientation*. Oxford: Oxford University Press, 1999).

Sweet, Thersa, and Seth L. Welles. "Associations of Sexual Identity or Same-Sex Behaviors with History of Childhood Sexual Abuse and HIV/STI Risk in the United States." *Journal of Acquired Immune Deficiency Syndrome* 59, no. 4 (April 1, 2012): 400.

Terman, Lewis M. "Kinsey's Sexual Behavior in the Human Male: Some Comments and Criticisms." *Psychological Bulletin* 45, no. 5 (September 1948): 455.

Vines, Matthew. *God and the Gay Christian*. New York: Convergent Books, 2014.

Watts, Steven. *Mr. Playboy, Hugh Hefner and the American Dream*. Hoboken, NJ: John Wiley & Sons, 2008.

Welles, Seth L., et al. "Intimate Partner Violence among Men Having Sex with Men, Women, or Both: Early Life Sexual and Physical Abuse as Antecedents." *Journal of Community Health* 36 (June 2011): 477.

Wenham, G. J. "The Old Testament Attitude to Homosexuality." *The Expository Times* 102, no. 12 (September 1991): 359–363.

Weyr, Thomas. *Reaching for Paradise–The Playboy Vision of America*. New York: New York Times Books, 1978.

Wiik, Kenneth Aarskaug. "Divorce in Norwegian Same-sex Marriages and Registered Partnerships: The Role of Children." *Journal of Marriage and Family* 76 (October 2014): 923.

Williams, Craig A. *Roman Homosexuality*. 2nd ed. Oxford: Oxford University Press, 2010.

Williams, Terrance J., et al. "Finger length ratios and sexual orientation." *Nature* 40 (March 30, 2000): 455–456.

Wold, Donald J. *Out of Order.* Grand Rapids: Baker Books, 1998.

Made in the USA
Columbia, SC
14 May 2020